HOLINESS
IN
ISRAEL

OVERTURES TO BIBLICAL THEOLOGY

The Land
  by Walter Brueggemann

God and the Rhetoric of Sexuality
  by Phyllis Trible

Israel in Exile
  by Ralph W. Klein

The Ten Commandments and Human Rights
  by Walter Harrelson

Texts of Terror
  by Phyllis Trible

The Suffering of God
  by Terence E. Fretheim

New Testament Hospitality
  by John Koenig

Jesus, Liberation, and the Biblical Jubilee
  by Sharon H. Ringe

From Darkness to Light
  by Beverly Roberts Gaventa

The Mighty from Their Thrones
  by J. P. M. Walsh, S.J.

Biblical Perspectives on Aging
  by J. Gordon Harris

The Economy of the Kingdom
  by Halvor Moxnes

Editors

WALTER BRUEGGEMANN, Professor of Old Testament at Columbia Theological Seminary, Decatur, Georgia

JOHN R. DONAHUE, S.J., Professor of New Testament at the Jesuit School of Theology, Berkeley, California

ELIZABETH STRUTHERS MALBON, Associate Professor of Religion, Virginia Polytechnic Institute and State University, Blacksburg, Virginia

CHRISTOPHER R. SEITZ, Assistant Professor of Old Testament, Yale Divinity School, New Haven, Connecticut

HOLINESS IN ISRAEL

JOHN G. GAMMIE

FORTRESS PRESS   Minneapolis

Library of Congress Cataloging-in-Publication Data

Gammie, John G.
　Holiness in Israel.

　(Overtures to biblical theology)
　Includes bibliographical references and indexes.
　1. Holiness—Biblical teaching. 2. Bible O.T.—
Theology. I. Title. II. Series.
BS1199.H6G36　1989　　234'.8　　88–45825
ISBN 0–8006–1549–2

Printed in the United States of America　　1–1549

93　92　91　90　89　1　2　3　4　5　6　7　8　9　10

For
Catherine

Contents

Editor's Foreword

The sequence of books in the Overtures series has developed without design, as manuscripts have been prepared and published. In the face of that fact, the placement of John Gammie's book in the series is worth noting. Recent volumes in the series have attended especially to voices of hurt, marginality, and historical transformation, that is, texts that show the underside of the human enterprise, and God's engagement with that underside. This accent has been evident in the work of Phyllis Trible (*Texts of Terror*, 1984), James L. Crenshaw (*Whirlpool of Torment*, 1984), and Sharon H. Ringe (*Jesus, Liberation, and the Biblical Jubilee*, 1985). Most especially, Terence E. Fretheim (*The Suffering of God*, 1984) has given precise formulation to the vulnerability and availability of God, a theme of enormous importance in recent theological conversation.

Gammie's book takes up, vis-à-vis Fretheim, a countertheme that moves against the emphasis on hurt, marginality, and vulnerability, to explore the majesty, awe, and sovereignty of God. Indeed, Fretheim on "suffering" and Gammie on "holiness" provide a suggestive and foundational dialectic for our continuing theological conversation.

Our awareness of brutality and the marginalizing process in the world evokes, for many, questions and concerns about God's availability for such realities. And if God is available in any way that matters, then it must be through pathos and vulnerability. No doubt our various theological accents are evoked by our situations of faith and interpretation. Our own situation of deep human need has pressed us to the suffering God. Israel's discernment and articulation of God, however, in every circumstance, stays very close to the acknowledgment that the God of Israel is indeed a holy God. Israel's engagement with God dare never presume against the awe, majesty, and sovereignty of God. This dialectic of availability and majesty in God has been articulated in Christian theology in the trinitarian formula. In the texts of ancient Israel, the same dialectic is acknowledged and handled in a variety of other ways. Gammie takes up one side of that troublesome tension.

We may cite three emphases whereby Gammie's book requires our attention. First, his discussion faces carefully and fully the problem of *theological diversity* within the witness of the text. Gammie has no need to engage in reductionism about his theme, but gives each part of the text an honest hearing on its own terms. Not only does he begin with three models of holiness—priestly, prophetic, and sapiential—but he explores the development and mutation of each of these perspectives. Social location, mode of articulation, and historical experience permit and require Israel to speak in many ways about God's holiness. Gammie enters into that rich and daring diversity, but at the same time demonstrates the continuity and persistence of Israel's rendering of God.

Second, Gammie sets his interpretive comments in the midst of an exceedingly *broad base of learning*. He is aware that his insights are nourished and legitimated by much scholarly work that lies outside the field of Old Testament study, and he is aware that his own argument sends runners out in many directions toward allied and parallel discussions. Gammie's scholarship contextualizes Israel's understanding of God in the midst of a variety of intellectual currents. Specifically, Gammie is attentive to anthropological studies showing that the holiness of God is not derived from but is always interfaced with the cohesion and coherence of social community. Israel's discernment of and speech about God are characteristically embedded in concrete social situations. Thus when Israel ponders the boundaries and maintenance of the community, it must think about God's *requirement of purity*. When Israel struggles with the problem of social disproportion, it must struggle with God's *passion for jus-*

tice. The character of God is not merely a projection of social concerns. The character of God receives fresh articulation in the face of such social realities. This book draws on a wide range of critical tools and categories to probe this social embeddedness of theological discourse.

Finally, Gammie's book is important because it is not a study of religious phenomenology. Rather, it is *a theological statement.* After the methodological issues have been faced, one is driven to ask, Who is God? How shall we speak of God? Holiness is not an autonomous theme, but it is a way of discerning who this God is. The God of Israel, as Gammie sees so well, is a God of overwhelmingness and command. The priestly tradition focused on separateness and cleanness bespeaks the ultimacy, mystery, and unapproachability of God. In Israel, however, a sense of wonder in the face of majesty is never undifferentiatedly religious. The prophetic tradition concerns justice and social caring as the substance of God's holiness. There is no way to harmonize or finally adjudicate between these two tendencies in the God of Israel. Prerational majesty and critical social passion belong to God; both are there in a fruitful tension. The stress on cleanness prevents God's holiness from being reduced to moral requirement. Conversely, the urgency of justice precludes holiness from being generic, disinterested religion. This unresolvable tension in the very life of God shapes Israel's faith and evokes Israel as a community of both doxology and commandment, amazement and obedience.

The final chapter of this book on apocalyptic is an appropriate place for bringing together these several crucial theological strands. The powerful practice of hope in Israel waits for the full manifestation of God's utter Godness, a God insistent on God's own way, whose way enhances God's mystery and at the same time cares decisively for the world.

Gammie's careful study represents an important theological resource for our own work. The holiness of God is clearly not simply an antiquarian concern. Our uneasiness with such a theological emphasis is surely reflective of the urgency of that very assertion. God's holiness marked by majesty for God's self and by passion for the justice of the world takes on power and urgency in the face of our own life issues. The holiness of God is urgent in the face of profanation, which empties life of larger passion and dignity. The holiness of God is urgent in the face of pervasive brutality, which trivializes God's purpose and abuses God's world. The holiness of God is urgent in the face of the growing authority of technique, which diminishes mystery that keeps life open. Israel struggles to speak aright about God. Israel knows that right speech about God guards our speech about the world and disciplines our life in the world. God's holiness concerns God's preoccupation with God's own self. That self-concern of God in Israel, however, is never removed from God's concern for the world, which is summoned to a responding holiness. Gammie has provided a rich array of data which draws these ancient claims very close indeed to contemporary issues and possibilities. Readers will be in Gammie's debt for his courage, his care, and his clarity.

Walter Brueggemann
Columbia Theological Seminary

Preface

The basic thesis of this book has been many years in the making and maturing. Fairly early on in my teaching career in Old Testament studies it became apparent to me that for both the priests and the prophets the holiness of God required a cleanness—for the former a cleanness of ritual, for the latter a cleanness of social justice. The question was then raised, Do the wisdom traditions particularly stress the divine holiness? If so, What kind of cleanness do they teach that the holiness of God requires? Prior to raising questions such as these my interest in holiness goes back to a course at Union Theological Seminary on the prophet Isaiah with Professor Samuel Terrien and my introduction therein to Rudolph Otto's classic, *The Idea of the Holy.* And even before that I am aware of how much my quest into holiness in the first place was quickened by the sense of God in Julia Heines, a Dutch-born director of religious education who served in a community church I attended when in high school.

The basic thesis of this volume was first presented to the Presbytery of Eastern Oklahoma in September 1980 and again in a different format to the Graduate Seminary of Phillips University in October 1984; the details of the thesis were worked out, however, in a weekly seminar I was invited to teach at the Perkins School of Theology, Southern Methodist University, in the spring of 1986. To each of these institutions and especially the latter and its Associate Dean James Ward and the students in the seminar I stand in debt.

For not stopping short with a broad statement of the thesis but

going on to include the historical and apocalyptic writings I wish
to thank the urging of Max Miller and especially John Hayes at
the Candler School of Theology, Emory University. Reference
and interlibrary loan librarians at the Bridwell Library at Perkins
and the McFarlin Library of the University of Tulsa were unfail-
ingly helpful. Betty Creech kindly assisted through typing. Two
anonymous readers made astute suggestions on the first draft of
this work. The second draft has been read through by my wife,
Catherine, by my colleague, John Carmody, by the series editor,
Walter Brueggemann, and by the Senior Editor of Fortress Press,
John A. Hollar. For the several ways each one has assisted in
improving the volume, I am grateful.

This volume is the richer for dialogue over the years with my
colleagues at the University of Tulsa, the regional and national
Society of Biblical Literature and the Catholic Biblical Association. Finally, friendship with my esteemed teachers Samuel
Terrien and James Barr has been a special encouragement.

The present study constitutes a thematic analysis of holiness in
the Old Testament and select parts of ancient Judaic literature.
At the outset I did not intend to write such a theology of the Old
Testament, but now that this overview has reached completion, I
am aware I have done so. I am also aware that fuller treatment
could have been given to Isaiah of Babylon, Jeremiah, the Book
of the Twelve Prophets, and the Psalms. A fuller study as well
would have sought to deal with the Song of Songs, Ruth, Lamen-
tations, and Esther. In this Overture to Biblical Theology I have
sought to sketch the outlines of the three basic responses of the
priests, prophets, and sages to holiness. In chapters subsequent to
each I sketch the variations of these three basic themes. The
whole invites the reader to reflect on the centrality of the theological understanding of holiness in each of the major portions of
the Old Testament and in some of the so-called deutero-canonical books.

Abbreviations

ATD	Das Alte Testament Deutsch
CBQ	*Catholic Biblical Quarterly*
CBQMS	*Catholic Biblical Quarterly Monograph Series*
FRLANT	*Forschungen zur Religion und Literatur des Alten und Neuen Testaments*
HSM	*Harvard Semitic Monographs*
HUCA	*Hebrew Union College Annual*
JAAR	*Journal of the American Academy of Religion*
JBL	*Journal of Biblical Literature*
JSOT	*Journal of the Study of the Old Testament*
KAT	Kommentar zum Alten Testament, ed. E. Sellin
NEB	New English Bible
NJV	New Jewish Version
OBT	Overtures to Biblical Theology
OTL	Old Testament Library
RSV	Revised Standard Version
SBT	Studies in Biblical Theology
SBLDS	Society of Biblical Literature Dissertation Series
VTSup	Vetus Testamentum Supplements
ZAW	*Zeitschrift für die alttestamentliche Wissenschaft*

Introduction

Divisions between members of different religious communities—often accompanied still by lingering suspicion if not
downright uncharitable attitudes—are a very real part of contemporary social life. I have become aware that there is no single
doctrine of holiness in the Old Testament but rather a diversity—or, more correctly, a unity with a diversity. The holiness of
God requires a cleanness on the part of human beings, but each
of the three major traditions stresses a different kind of cleanness. In the past and present, of course, biblical writers of the
priestly traditions have been viewed as prototypes of Roman
Catholicism and Jewish orthodoxy, whereas the prophetic writings are often tacitly viewed as exemplars of Protestantism and
Reform Judaism. It is perhaps less clear that more conservative
Protestant and Anabaptist churches may be taken to be ante-
typical of the sages, because of a common stress on *individual*
morality. In any event, I show in this volume that the Bible itself
provides a model of how underlying diverse perceptions (that
holiness requires a *different* response) there is also a unity (*cleanness* is the proper counterpart of holiness). Thus it is my hope
that this study will foster tolerance and respect among religious
communities—and in particular among those communities that
look to the Bible as a special source of guidance.

It is my intention, then, to argue the thesis that the holiness of
God in the Old Testament impressed itself on the three major
classes of Israelite religious leaders in a similar yet diverse fash-

1

ion. Simply stated, the thesis runs like this: To the authors of the priestly tradition, the Holy God clearly extended a call to ritual purity, right sacrifices, separation. To the prophets, holiness clearly issued the summons for the purity of *social* justice and equity in human relations. It is less clear whether or not the Hebrew Scriptures teach that any particularly distinctive vocation was issued to the sages and wise. Investigation into the wisdom psalms and the Book of Job yielded the positive answer that for the sapiential traditions as well the holiness of God calls forth cleanness; the particular stress of the wisdom tradition is that holiness requires the cleanness of *individual* morality.

In the pages below inquiry will be made into the theology of holiness and variations thereof among the ancient Israelite priests (chapters 1–2), prophets (chapters 3–4), and sages (chapters 5–6). In chapter 7, I will show how the priestly, prophetic, and sapiential understanding of holiness are interwoven and advanced in the apocalyptic parts of the prophets and in Daniel. Significant intermingling of the prophetic and priestly understanding of holiness will also be observed in chapter 2 (with Ezekiel and his successors) and in chapter 4 (with select psalms and Deuteronomy).

My summary remarks will draw out of the major findings of these soundings into biblical traditions a few clues with respect to the recovery of a sense of holiness in our age of the eclipse of God.

HOW CENTRAL AND HELPFUL IS HOLINESS IN THE OLD TESTAMENT?

Despite the potential of the biblical theology of holiness as a grounding for a model for interreligious understanding, there are serious drawbacks to any inquiry into the theology of holiness in the Old Testament. The first drawback, as Werner Schmidt has averred, is that the holiness of God is not a fundamental, distinctive, or early conception.[1] If correct—if the notion of the holiness is as peripheral as Schmidt argues—then perhaps this book

---

1. Werner H. Schmidt, *The Faith of the Old Testament: A History* (Philadelphia: Westminster Press, 1983), see "The Holy God," 152–56.

should have been reconsidered. Schmidt's judgment, however, overlooks important studies on theology and holiness that cannot be dismissed.[2] As Ernst Sellin put it: "*God is holy*. Herein we touch on that which constitutes the deepest and innermost nature of the God of the Old Testament."[3] The conception of God's holiness occurs in the earliest poetry (Exod. 15:11, 13; 1 Sam. 2:2); it pervades the priestly traditions, the major prophets Ezekiel and Isaiah (on which see chaps. 2 and 3 below) as well as the postexilic, minor prophets, Haggai, Zechariah, and Malachi; and it is far from peripheral in the sapiential traditions (as chaps. 5 and 6 below will demonstrate).

A second drawback to focusing on the holy and the sacred may derive from recent psychological studies that suggest that such focusing constitutes a fixation on a less than fully mature stage of faith. Thus James W. Fowler's *Stages of Faith: The Psychology of Human Development and the Quest for Meaning*[4] posits that persons in stage three of faith development have a fondness for symbols of transcendence, make harsh judgments on actual people or institutions in the light of the ideal, and are fiercely attached to symbols of the sacred; indeed, they resist demythologization "as an assault on the sacred itself."[5] Investigation of the holy then would hardly seem to be a subject to investigate because it elevates a stage of faith characteristic of adolescence rather than maturity.[6] By way of response, no matter what the

---

2. J. Hänel, *Die Religion der Heiligkeit* (Gütersloh: Bertelmans, 1931), passim; Ernst Sellin, *Theologie des Alten Testaments*, 2d ed., (Leipzig: Quelle & Meyer, 1936), 19–23; Th. C. Vriezen, *An Outline of Old Testament Theology*, 2d ed., (Oxford: Basil Blackwell & Mott, 1962; Dutch, 1949), 149–62: "The holiness of God is the central idea of the Old Testament faith in God" (p. 151); Simon J. deVries, *The Achievements of Biblical Religion: A Prolegomenon to Old Testament Theology* (Lanham, Md.: University Press of America, 1983), 43–118: "Yahweh, the God of the Israelites . . . is unique in [his] holiness, transcendently distinctive while intimately near in [his] immanence" (p. 45; brackets added).

3. Sellin, *Theologie des Alten Testaments*, 19.

4. James W. Fowler, *Stages of Faith* (New York: Harper & Row, 1981).

5. Ibid., 155–63.

6. Ibid., chap. 18, "Stage 3. Synthetic-Conventional Faith," 151–73. There is some merit to Fowler's analysis: holiness is a powerful symbol of the divine transcendence and the holiness of God frequently leads those to whom it appears to harsh judgments and the need for separation from people and things felt to be unclean. Holiness unquestionably elicits fierce loyalty of the

stage of faith, the loss of a sense of the divine holiness would constitute an abandonment of the God of Moses, Isaiah, and Job. And further, I find precisely those characteristics of Fowler's more mature stage of faith ("inclusiveness of community," "radical commitment to justice and love," "selfless passion for a transformed world . . . in accordance with an intentionality both divine and transcendent")[7] to be part and parcel of the biblical doctrine of holiness, which has several aspects, not simply one.

A third reason for questioning the advisability of an inquiry into the theology of holiness derives from the inherent nature of the biblical doctrine of holiness itself. Holiness first and foremost points to divine transcendence, exaltedness, and otherness. Thus for those interested in feminist theology, for example, holiness might seem to be a poor point of entry.[8] And even more hazardous are the obviously male-oriented strictures against menstruating women found within the biblical, priestly traditions, for precisely these traditions espouse teachings about purity and holiness that strike our age as most biased and sexist.[9] As Sallie McFague has acknowledged, however, there are limitations also to those theologies that choose to emphasize divine immanence and God as companion and friend.[10]

Hazardous though the endeavor may be, failure to inquire into the doctrine of holiness would constitute serious neglect of a major biblical teaching. As I see it, successive generations have the obligation to think through the teachings of the faith with the

sort that appeals to the adolescent. Such concessions, however, are not of sufficient weight to convince me that the inquiry into the biblical understanding of holiness should be scuttled.

7. Ibid., 201. These are some of the descriptions Fowler gives of his Stage 6: Universalizing Faith.

8. See, e.g., Sallie McFague, *Metaphorical Theology: Models of God in Religious Language* (Philadelphia: Fortress Press, 1982). Her arguments against too-heavy reliance upon parental models of God as serving to foster hierarchy, subordination, and patriarchal authoritarianism (p. 177) might well be turned against the advisability of incautiously pursuing a reappropriation of the biblical doctrine of holiness.

9. For a pointed critique of the unhappy effects that an uncritical reading of the priestly traditions has had in the West, see Samuel Terrien, "The Numinous, The Sacred and the Holy in Scripture," *Biblical Theology Bulletin* 12 (1982): 88–108.

10. McFague, *Metaphorical Theology*, 190–92.

end in view of continuing to tap its sources of vitality and renewal. Precisely because the interpretation of the biblical doctrine of holiness in the past fed a repressive paternalism and sexism, the present inquiry is urgent.

THE STARTING POINT: THE IDEA OF THE HOLY

Paul Tillich once remarked that he considered Rudolph Otto's work *The Idea of the Holy* to be one of the three most important volumes on religion to be published in the first half of the twentieth century.[11] Older and younger readers in religion will readily agree that Otto's work is a classic which continues to enjoy popularity and reward rereading because it continues to afford new discoveries. Otto set for himself the difficult task of analyzing the suprarational and nonethical element in the human experience of the holy. He called that element the numinous (Latin *numen*, for "divinity, power, god"). Otto described five major aspects of the holy or numinous. With intuitive insight he utilized Latin terms (given in parentheses below) to help capture and mnemonically record the ineffability of the holy:

1. awefulness, plenitude of power which evokes a sense of dread and includes the divine wrath (*tremendum*);

2. overpoweringness, plenitude of being, absolute unapproachability (*maiestas*);

3. urgency, vitality, will, force, movement, excitement, activity, energy which for the mystic is experienced as "consuming fire" (*energicum*);[12]

4. being: "wholly other," different, incommensurable, beyond, transcendent, supernatural (*mysterium*); and,

5. compelling, fascination: it may give rise to feelings of intoxication, the rapturous and exaltation (*fascinans*). This element

11. See Rudolph Otto, *The Idea of the Holy*, 9th ed., trans. John W. Harvey (Oxford: Oxford University Press, 1928; German: *Das Heilige*, 1917). The other two were Albert Schweitzer's *Quest of the Historical Jesus* (New York: Macmillan Co., 1968; German 1906); and Karl Barth's *Epistle to the Romans*, 6th ed., trans. E. C. Hoskyns (Oxford: Oxford University Press, 1968; German: 1918).

12. Otto himself did not employ the Latin *energicum*, but his most avid devotee among Old Testament scholars, D. J. Hänel, rightly did; see Hänel, *Die Religion der Heiligkeit*, 7.

may be present already in longing and in moments of solemnity; it is experienced when one gains mystic insight and at conversion.

This synopsis will suffice to remind readers of how useful an analytical tool Otto furnished students of religion. Otto's analysis of the holy will constitute a starting point and constant frame of reference for this volume. His methodology has informed mine to a considerable extent.

In Otto's own examination of the numinous in ancient, medieval, and Chinese art, the Old and New Testaments, Luther, primitive religions, oriental religions, and early Christianity, he does not apply his schema in any heavy-handed fashion, but rather illustrates how demonstrable and defensible the schema is. Otto's analysis of the numinous is heuristic and may serve as a model of how biblical studies may successfully apply the findings of the history of religion and, to a lesser extent, anthropology, to assist it in making discoveries and observations that otherwise might have slipped by unnoticed.[13]

An initial example of the application of Otto's approach may be given by a brief examination of the magnificent theophany at Sinai (Exodus 19). Each one of the elements of the holy is present: (1) *awefulness, dread, and wrath*: "And the whole mountain quaked greatly" (v. 18c, RSV); "God answered him in the thunder" (v. 19b); "Go down and warn the people . . . lest the LORD break out upon them (vv. 21–22); (2) *majesty and unapproach-*

---

13. Other examples in addition to the application of Otto to Exodus 19 examined below come to mind; see, e.g., those at the end of this note. The fruitfulness of the anthropological studies of Douglas and Leach will be explored in chap. 1. Mircea Eliade's marvelously clear work *Patterns in Comparative Religion*, trans. R. Sheed (New York and Cleveland: Meridian Books, 1963; French, 1948) examines numerous hierophanies (lit., "manifestations of the holy") in the sky, at seas and rivers, stones, trees, and mountains. Through a consideration of Eliade the biblical exegete is made aware of points of contact between the men and women of the Bible and humanity in many other times and places. Biblical revelation thus becomes less distant from the experience of human beings in other times and cultures. Interpretation is thus checked and deepened by comparison with manifold other human experiences with the holy. Eliade's discussions of the sacred tree as a symbol of life and a microcosm of the Whole (pp. 265–71) made me more aware of symbolism of fire in the episode of the burning bush (Exodus 3), which I had previously not considered. Similarly, I gained a deeper perspective on the pillar erected by Jacob (Genesis 32) as an *axis mundi* and gateway to heaven from reading Eliade's chapter "Sacred Stones" (pp. 216–38).

ability: "Take heed that you do not go up into the mountain or touch the border of it" (v. 12), "lest they break through to the LORD" (v. 21); "The people cannot come up to Mount Sinai" (v. 23); (3) *energy, vitality, and movement*: "The LORD descended upon it in fire; and the smoke went up like the smoke of a kiln" (v. 18ab); (4) *mystery*: "Lo, I am coming to you in a thick cloud" (v. 9a); (5) *fascination*: "Do not let the priests and people break through to come up to the LORD" (v. 24b).

The usefulness of the schema does not end with a mere noting of the elements, but may be pressed further. Otto has suggested that whereas human sexual drives are *sub*rational, human questing for the holy or numinous has a *supra*rational source.[14] We will examine the relationship between holiness and sexuality in chapter 1. For now, it is enough to note that for the biblical authors of Exodus 19 the encounter with the holy calls for abstention from sexual intercourse (v. 15). In an uncanny fashion, Otto's analysis alerts us to the diverse facets and dimensions of the response of the people of the Bible to the holiness of God.

Otto's schema may be supplemented in two regards. (1) Although he does entertain the notion of "glory" as an aspect of "overpoweringness," *maiestas*, he does not use this term in either his initial descriptive treatment nor in his treatment of the Old Testament. This omission is an oversight, inasmuch as recent studies of Rolf Rendtorff and Moshe Weinfeld have shown that the Hebrew *kābôd* ("glory") frequently represents the divine majesty. Just as wrath (Greek *orgē*) is singled out as belonging to awefulness, *tremendum*, so glory (Greek *doxa*, Hebrew *kābôd*) may be said properly to belong to the element of overpoweringness, *maiestas*.

(2) Nowhere does Otto sufficiently probe the notion that the holy calls for purity, cleanness, and that frequently purity is to be attained by means of separation. Recent anthropological[15] and

---

14. Otto, *Idea of the Holy*: "'The numinous' infuses the rational from above, 'the sexual' presses up from beneath" (p. 47).

15. Mary Douglas, *Purity and Danger: An Analysis of the Concepts of Pollution and Taboo* (London: Ark Paperbacks, 1984; [1966]), see chap. 3, "The Abominations of Leviticus," 41–57; reprinted in *Anthropological Approaches to the Old Testament*, ed. Bernhard Lang, Issues in Religion and Theology 8 (Philadelphia: Fortress Press, 1985), 100–16.

biblical[16] studies on the cultus have shown that purity, cleanness, is indeed a regular counterpart and requirement of holiness. In Exodus 19, for example, Moses is instructed:

> Go to the people and consecrate them (*wĕqiddaštām*) today and tomorrow, and let them wash their garments, and be ready for the third day; for on the third day the LORD will come down upon Mount Sinai in the sight of all the people. And you shall set bounds for the people round about, saying, "Take heed that you do not go up into the mountain or touch the border of it; whoever touches the mountain shall be put to death." (vv. 10–12, RSV)

In this brief passage from the nonpriestly sources of the Yahwist and Elohist one discovers how holiness requires *cleanness* and *separation* (boundaries) and is a danger to those who transgress the prescribed *limit* and approach too closely. Otto amply documented the notion of unapproachability. It has been the task of recent anthropologists to document the rationale underlying purity and danger.

In this study we will focus not so much on the purity laws themselves, but on how each of the three major religious groups responsible for producing the Scripture—priests, prophets, and sages—were united in awareness that the holiness of the very God of Israel called for cleanness. They differed, of course, in their vision and understanding of what cleanness this awesome God required, but at many points they also shared judgments on the prerequisites of purity.

AIM AND METHOD

The aim of the present volume is, then, descriptive and theological; its methodology may be described as primarily literary and historical analysis with a conscious attempt to utilize the findings of historians of religion (notably Rudolph Otto and Mircea Eliade) and of more recent anthropologists (notably Mary Douglas and Edmund Leach). The work of the latter have been especially helpful in pointing the way to fresh insights into the priestly traditions to which we now turn.

16. Jean Soler, "The Dietary Prohibitions of the Hebrews," *New York Review of Books*, June 14, 1979, pp. 24–30. I am indebted to Jerome Neyrey, S.J., of the Weston School of Theology, for this reference.

CHAPTER 1

The Priestly Understanding
of Holiness

*(The Priestly Code
and Holiness Code)*

It is an eternal statute for your generations to make a separation between holiness and the common, between the unclean and the clean.

(Lev. 10:9b–10, au. trans.)

SEPARATION

Holiness demands separation. Just as God at creation separated the day from the night, the waters above the firmament from the waters below, the seas from the dry land, and days of labor from the day of rest, so God blessed the seventh day and "set it apart "(*wayĕqaddēš 'ōtô*: "sanctified it" or "consecrated it" [Gen. 2:3]). By way of anticipation of the Summary of this book, the separated and consecrated time of the sabbath holds the promise of furnishing clues for recovering the biblical as well as the priestly understanding of holiness.

The notion of separation is pervasive in the priestly traditions of the Bible from the Book of Genesis onward. In diet one must be careful to keep apart from blood (Gen. 9:1–7). In war Abram makes a point of affirming that he wishes to refrain from spoils with which Sodom was associated (Gen. 14:21–24). In circumcision the sons of Israel separate themselves to God as a sign of the covenant (Gen. 17:1–14). The rite of separation is taken with the utmost seriousness: "And if any male who is uncircumcised

9

fails to circumcise the flesh of his foreskin, that person shall be cut off from his kin; he has broken My covenant," Gen. 17:14, NJV). At the death of Sarah, Abraham purchases a separate place for her burial (Genesis 23) where he also is later buried (Gen. 25:9). So also in the priestly traditions of the Book of Exodus, a major feature in the celebration of the Passover is the separation of the unleavened bread from the leavened (Exodus 12) and the major feature in the priestly dietary laws of Leviticus rests in the clear distinction between clean and unclean foods and in abstention from the latter (Leviticus 11).

Perhaps the best place to begin to gain some insight into the priestly understanding of holiness is to review what recent anthropology and traditional Jewish exegesis have taught us with respect to the priestly dietary laws.

Mary Douglas in her *Purity and Danger* has convincingly penetrated the logic underlying the pentateuchal food laws promulgated by the priests.[1] Her argument may be summarized as follows:

(1) at creation a threefold classification of elements (air, water, and earth) was established by the process of division and separation;

(2) for each element or area (heavens, waters, and dry land) normative habits and means of locomotion were established to delimit which creatures were "clean" and hence permissible for food:

heavens;—winged creatures with nonpredatory habits

waters—scaly creatures with fins

dry land—fourfooted creatures chewing the cud (provided the hooves were cloven and the animals nonpredatory); and

(3) animals that did not conform to the norm or type of each division were prohibited.

Cleanness thus depends upon the dual principles of: (1) separation, segregation, division, and (2) conformity to the norm established for each class, element, or division. Douglas's explanation is brilliant and persuasive. It is all the more so since, as noted in

---

1. Mary Douglas, *Purity and Danger: An Analysis of the Concepts of Pollution and Taboo* (London: Ark Paperbacks, 1984; [1966]), 100–16.

the Introduction, Jean Soler in France reached similar conclusions. Douglas is less successful in speaking to the issue of why even the creatures pronounced to be "clean" had to be drained of blood. There is clearly a didactic and ethical purpose behind the prohibition of blood: "It is too closely associated with *nepeš,* that is breath and life, to be permitted: 'Every moving thing that lives shall be food for you; and as I gave you green plants, I give you everything. Only you shall not eat flesh with its life (*nepeš*), that is, its blood'" (Gen. 9:3–4, RSV).

That the Hebraic dietary laws contain a theological, ethical, and didactic intention is already apparent in the prohibition of predatory birds and animals. Perhaps the earliest extrabiblical defense of the Hebraic food laws is found in *The Letter of Aristeas* (c. 150 B.C.E.).[2] This letter, or apology, puts forward a stunningly appealing reason for the biblical food laws: (1) that edible creatures must have cloven hooves teaches that humans must be discriminating, that is, they should exercise reason and sound judgment; (2) chewing the cud is a symbol of memory and the importance of recollection; and (3) that predatory animals are prohibited teaches clearly how violence is to be eschewed and nonviolence embraced (*Letter of Aristeas,* par. 136–69).

Christians are apt to overlook both the Hebraic dietary laws and the rationale behind them. It is salutary both for the spirit and interreligious relations to recall that there are neglected elements in the Hebrew Scriptures from which Christians can learn from their Jewish sisters and brothers. Thus Jacob Milgrom, continuing in the line of *The Letter of Aristeas* and the rabbis, has also convincingly demonstrated: (1) so great is the human propensity for violence, there is great wisdom in the biblical and rabbinic teaching that nonviolence should be inculcated daily; (2) that a primary motive behind the biblical dietary laws was to foster separation from idolatry and the customs of idolaters (cf. Lev. 20:6–7, 26); and (3) that by limiting animals permitted to a few, the Jew is thus enjoined to a higher level of life, which may

2. For a recent discussion of the date and Hebraic character of this document, see my "Hellenization of Jewish Wisdom in the Letter of Aristeas," in *Proceedings of the Ninth World Congress of Jewish Studies: Division A — The Period of the Bible* (Jerusalem: World Union of Jewish Studies, 1986), 207–14.

be called "the holy."[3] Milgrom instructively relates the pursuit of the holy to the divine holiness as follows:

> [T]he emulation of God's holiness demands following the ethics associated with his nature. But since the mention of the propensity toward violence associated with his nature occurs with greater frequency and emphasis in the food prohibitions, than in any other commandments, we can only conclude that they are the Torah's personal recommendation as the best way of achieving this higher ethical life.[4]

In lieu of Milgrom's phrasing, that "the emulation of God's holiness demands following the ethics associated with his nature," I propose: *In response to the divine holiness the priests perceived that God required an ethical and ritual purity as well as the ingestion only of foods that the priestly logic of separation and appropriateness would allow them to declare as clean.*

INITIAL REFLECTION ON THE CHALLENGE OF
THE PRIESTLY NOTION OF SEPARATION

The priestly writers of the Bible share with the prophets and sages the notion that God is holy and that holiness lays demands upon humankind. Prophets and sages, however, do not lay nearly as much stress as the priestly writers do on the determination of what constitutes a sacred object, a sacred place, a sacred person, or a sacred time. In discussing the priestly conception of holiness it is especially important to clarify whether one has in mind the holiness of God, of a shrine or place, of an object or thing, of a time or season, of a person or office. We will consider these matters in a moment. Now, we comment further on the distinctively priestly understanding of holiness.

Despite the fact that the priestly conception of holiness as separation nurtures a sense of order and inculcates nonviolence, there is something about it that repels and remains uncongenial to the modern mind nurtured in societies aspiring to democracy.

3. Jacob Milgrom, "The Biblical Diet Laws as an Ethical System: Food and Faith," *Interpretation* 17 (1963):288–301; reprinted in idem, *Studies in Cultic Theology and Terminology*, Studies in Judaism in Late Antiquity 36 (Leiden: E. J. Brill, 1983), 104–18.
4. Milgrom; "The Biblical Diet Laws," 293; also found in idem., *Studies in Cultic Theology*, 110.

Politically, the principle of separation on the face of it would seem to be not only uncongenial but downright subversive. The principle of separation has been used in the United States and elsewhere by opponents of racial integration in the attempt to retard nonwhite advancement in educational, economic, and political spheres. The principle of separation has been espoused by the Republic of South Africa as an ideological weapon with which to maintain control over its nonwhite population. Thus so suspect from a political perspective, should not the biblical principle of separation simply be allowed to rest? Even from a religious perspective the principle of separation would seem on the face of it to be at best an unfruitful field for probing if not outright subversive to egalitarian urges. Thus a half-century ago the declarations of Ernst Sellin that Old Testament theology should avoid any inquiry into priestly-cultic matters[5] would seem to have been an intuitively sound decision which we might continue to follow today.

The potential dangers of a pursuit of the priestly notion of separation may thus readily be granted. If Old Testament theology were merely a tool of political theology, the subject of separation perhaps could be avoided. If the task of Old Testament theology were conceived to be subservient to a predetermined theological stance, for yet another reason the subject might have been avoided. But if the task of Old Testament theology is understood in a less subservient fashion, the subject may well be pursued for its own sake as well as for the potential lessons it holds in store precisely for theistic faith in the modern age. Accordingly, we may proceed to an examination of the principle of separation in the Priestly Code with respect to sacred shrine, times, persons, and acts.

5. Ernst Sellin, *Theologies des Alten Testaments*, 2d ed. (Leipzig: Quelle & Meyer, 1936), 2. Despite the disclaimer, Sellin did devote some space to the subject (pp. 48–49, 109–16). As noted above, Sellin also was one of several Old Testament scholars to give a place of prominence to the divine holiness (pp. 19–23). He did not, however, pursue the distinctively priestly understanding of the holy. The survey of the history of approaches to Old Testament theology by John H. Hayes and Frederick Prusser, *Old Testament Theology: Its History and Development* (Atlanta: John Knox Press, 1985), points to Sellin's programmatic exclusion of the wisdom literature but does not mention his similar downplaying of the cultic and priestly.

THE TABERNACLE—SYMBOL OF THE HOLY GOD
WHO CANNOT BE CONFINED TO ONE PLACE

Recent interpretation of the Bible has stressed the importance of paying close attention to the clues of the text itself. Therefore, it is all the more convincing to study Joseph Blenkinsopp's essay, "The Structure of P," which demonstrates that the erection of the tabernacle constitutes for the priestly writers "the climax of creation."[6] Just as creation commenced on day one of the first month (Gen. 1:1–5) and on the same day in the liturgical year the new world emerged from the flood waters (Gen. 8:13), so on the same day of the year "the sanctuary was set up and dedicated in the wilderness" (Exod. 40:2).[7] That the building of the tabernacle is viewed as the counterpart to the creation of the world itself is virtually confirmed by the language with which P describes the two events.[8]

Creation of the world	*Construction of the tabernacle*
And God saw everything that he had made, and behold, it was very good (Gen. 1:31)	And Moses saw all the work and behold, they had done it (Exod. 39:43)
Thus the heavens and the earth were finished (Gen. 2:1)	Thus all the work of the tabernacle of the tent of the meeting was finished (Exod. 39:32)
On the seventh day God finished his work which he had done (Gen. 2:2)	So Moses finished the work (Exod. 40:33)
So God blessed the seventh day (Gen. 2:3)	And Moses blessed them (Exod. 39:43)
	(RSV)

Instructions for building the tabernacle, the tent of meeting, and ark are given in Exodus 25—31 along with other instructions

6. Joseph Blenkinsopp, "The Structure of P," *CBQ* 38 (1976):286.
7. Ibid., 283.
8. Ibid., 280.

pertaining to ordination, vestments, and altars. Then, in Exodus 35—40, the actual carrying out of the instructions for building the tabernacle is described. Thus liturgical notices, linguistic parallels, and repetition all serve to underline the centrality of the tabernacle.

The sanctity of the tabernacle is borne out by the terms used to describe it. The Hebrew words for "sanctify," "holiness," and "holy" are *qādaš* (piel), *qōdeš*, and *qādôš*. "Sanctuary" (Hebrew *miqdāš*) is a frequent synonym with the priestly writers for the tabernacle (Hebrew *mišqān*: Exod. 25:8; Num. 3:38; 18:1; etc.). The sanctuary of the tent of meeting is called *qōdeš* (lit. "[chamber of] holiness"; RSV: "holy place": Exod. 28:32; Num. 8:19; etc); the cella or adytum of the tent of meeting is called "the holy of holies" (*qōdeš haqqŏdāšîm*, lit. "the most holy [place]": Exod. 26:33, etc.).

Strict lines of separation are in effect. Aaron and his sons, the priests, could enter the holy place of the tent of meeting (Exod. 28:43) wherein was located the altar of incense (Exod. 30:1–10). Before entering Aaron and his sons had to wash hands and feet with water "that they may not die" (Exod. 30:17–21). Aaron alone could enter the most holy place and that only once a year (Leviticus 16). Careful measures were taken to safeguard his life (Lev. 16:2, 13). Going into the holy place and out from it, he had to wash not only his hands and feet but his body, as well as changing from his vestments to sacral linen vestments (Lev. 16:1–4, 23–24). Before entry into the most holy place, he had to fill it with the smoke of the incense so that the cover of the ark would be hidden (Lev. 16:13). Similarly, the Israelites were permitted to enter the courtyard of the tabernacle but were strictly excluded from the holy place where priests alone could enter. Such a careful demarcation of the three respective spheres of holiness is also observed in nonpriestly sources (see esp. Exodus 19).[9] In this passage Moses is exhorted to consecrate (*qiddaštām*) the people and to have them wash their garments (Exod. 19:10), which task he and they carry out (v. 14). Thus we see Moses

---

9. This point is convincingly made by Jacob Milgrom, *Studies in Levitical Terminology 1* (Berkeley and Los Angeles: University of California Press, 1970), 46.

performing a priestly function of sanctifying the people and making them ready (v. 15) to meet God and stand at the foot of the mountain (v. 17). Here something of a democratization has taken place for the passage underlines that in order to approach the divine holiness cleanness is required not only of priests but of laity as well.

Other factors reinforce the difference between the three spheres of holiness or "graded sanctity" of the tabernacle, as Rabbi W. Gunther Plaut calls it.[10] Plaut continues:

> [T] he materials employed are similarly graded. Its most precious components are made of gold, the least sacred, of copper. There are three degrees of workmanship, according to their sacredness: the degrees are called *choshev, rokem,* and *oreg* [probably varieties of weaving and embroidery]. . . . . There were, finally, gradations of color: blue was reserved for the most sacred, then followed purple, and finally crimson.[11]

With the principle of separation so carefully worked out—even color coded—what is the underlying significance of the tabernacle for the priestly theology of holiness? Starting with the most obvious and working down to the less obvious and more speculative, six points may be made.

1. The priestly theology of holiness strongly endorses clear differentiation between priests and laity and in turn favors singling out one individual priest above others to have access to an area designated as the most holy. Insofar as persons wish to look to the Bible for guidance, this will mean that the biblical priestly writings hardly favor an egalitarianism of service or an absolute parity among the ordained.

2. The tabernacle or tent of meeting represents the presence of God in his holiness and glory. This is especially clearly expressed in the following passage:

> For there I will meet with you, and there I will speak with you, and there I will meet with the Israelites, and it shall be sanctified (*wĕniq-daš*) by My Presence (lit. by my glory: *bikbōdî*). I will sanctify

---

10. W. Gunther Plaut and Bernard J. Bamberger, *The Torah: A Modern Commentary* (New York: Union of American Hebrew Congregations, 1981), 600.

11. Ibid., 600–1.

(wĕqiddaštî) the Tent of Meeting and the altar, and I will consecrate ('āqaddēš) Aaron and his sons to serve me as priests. (Exod. 29:42b–44, NJV)

God is the one who sanctifies tent, altar, and priests, Indeed, the former is set apart, made holy not so much by human action but by the presence of the glory of God.

When Moses had finished the work, the cloud covered the Tent of Meeting, and the glory of the LORD filled the Tabernacle. . . . . When the cloud lifted from the Tabernacle the Israelites would set out, on their various journeys; but if the cloud did not lift, they would not set out until such times as it did lift. (Exod. 40:33b–34, 36–37, NJV)

Here again, the closest of relations between the tabernacle and the divine presence is unmistakable, but it is equally clear that the movement of the divine presence was not dependent upon human action and initiative.

3. The tabernacle does not represent the fixed presence of God in a given spot or locale; rather, precisely because it was collapsible, portable, and capable of being erected in different locations, the tabernacle constituted a powerful symbol of the mobility of the divine presence and holiness. It is common for scholars to emphasize that Ezekiel's vision of God by the Chebar River in Babylonia (Ezekiel 1—3) was a portrayal of the theological truth that God is not space-bound to any one or particular place. Equally as clearly the tabernacle symbolizes the same theological truth. Many scholars have been so eager to identify the tabernacle as a type of the temple that they have simply overlooked this palpable feature with respect to the tabernacle: it was completely portable, and all its parts equipped with rings, poles, or bars for carrying (see Exod. 25:12–15, 26–28; 26:26–30). In my judgment, this feature not only goes back to the period prior to the monarchy[12] but it may well reflect a practice of itinerancy among the priests who ministered to the Israelites in exile.[13]

---

12. As argued by Menahem Haran, "The Nature of ''ōhel mô'ēdh' in Pentateuchal Sources," *Journal of Semitic Studies* 5 (1960): 50–65; idem, "The Priestly Image of the Tabernacle," *HUCA* 36 (1965): 191–226; Frank Moore Cross, "The Priestly Tabernacle," in *Old Testament Issues*, ed. Samuel Sandmel (New York: Harper & Row, 1968), 39–67.

13. To my knowledge, this suggestions has nowhere been espoused by a biblical

4. The facts that the instructions for building the tabernacle were received on Mt. Sinai and that the tables of the law (Decalogue) were deposited in the ark which was to be placed in the holy of holies clearly suggest that the tabernacle was to be taken as a reminder of Sinai, the mount of revelation.[14]

5. The fact that the dimensions of the tabernacle (fifty cubits by one hundred cubits) were precisely one-half those of the temple suggests that the tabernacle was also for the Israelites a reminder of the temple and Mt. Zion on which the latter stood.[15] This position has been frequently advocated in recent times.[16]

6. The hiddenness of the holy place and the holy of holies from normal view, the slaughter of sacrificial animals at the altar outside the tent of meeting, the daubing of altars and other sancta (holy things) with blood, the burning of incense in the holy place, and the cloud of smoke, all suggest that the tent of meeting located within the tabernacle was also clearly symbolic of the

scholar but has for a long time now seemed to me to be both a plausible and natural explanation of the priestly reemphasis on the portability of their shrine. In relatively recent times a problem of a scattered flock without a sufficiency of priests was solved by the Canadian-born Francis Kelley, founder of the Church Extension Society, which by 1939 had been responsible for financing over half of the Roman Catholic churches built in this country up to that time. Kelley, a man of extraordinary organizing and forensic abilities— and later monsignor, and bishop of Oklahoma—came up with the idea of making a movable church by converting a railroad car into a sanctuary equipped with altar and the requisite sacred accoutrements. He named the chapel car "St. Peter." See Francis Kelley, *The Bishop Jots it Down* (New York: Harper & Brothers, 1939), 153–62. I suggest that the priestly writers of the Pentateuch solved a similar problem (a scattered people without priests) in a similarly enterprising and imaginative way.

14. For a recent excellent discussion on Mt. Sinai as symbolic of covenant and revelation, see esp. Edward L. Greenstein, "Biblical Law," in *Back to the Sources: Reading the Classic Jewish Tests*, ed. Barry W. Holtz (New York: Summit Books, 1984), 83–103; and Jon D. Levenson, *Sinai and Zion: An Entry Into the Jewish Bible* (Minneapolis: Winston Press, 1985), part 3: "Sinai, The Mountain of the Covenant," 15–86.

15. For a superb discussion see Levenson, *Sinai and Zion*, part 2: "Zion, The Mountain of the Temple," 89–104.

16. See, e.g., J. R. Porter, "Tabernacle," in *Harper's Bible Dictionary*, ed. Paul J. Achtemeier et al. (New York: Harper & Row, 1985), 1013–14. Porter is less cautious than others when he says of the priestly account: "What it presents is a description of the Temple under the guise of a portable sanctuary" (p. 1013). The support of scholarly convention thus allows him to pass far too quickly over the theological significance of the portability of the tabernacle as I have argued above.

Other World, namely, the hidden realm of danger and death. Such a conclusion has been forcefully argued by anthropologist Edmund Leach.[17] The frequent warnings of how the officiant or people might die if they approached unprepared would certainly underline the notion of the inner shrines as places of danger. Leach's suggestion would also help us to explain the tremendous psychological appeal and fascination of the tabernacle and the sacrifices. Every time the priests, and especially the chief officiant, approached the tent of meeting, they were dealing with potential death and danger in the people's behalf.[18]

17. Edmund Leach, *Culture and Communication: The Logic by Which Symbols are Connected* (Cambridge: Cambridge University Press, 1983; first published 1976), chap. 18, "The Logic of Sacrifice," 81–93; reprinted in Bernhard Lang, ed. *Anthropological Approaches to the Old Testament*, Issues in Religion and Theology 8 & Philadelphia: Fortress Press, 1985), 136–50. In this chapter Leach deals explicitly with Exodus 25—30 and Leviticus 1—10, 16. "The central puzzle about sacrifices centres around the metaphor of death" (p. 81). His insights into ordination as a rite of passage are also illuminating. See my discussion below (pp. 27–30).

18. Mapping the sacred on the basis of the biblical passages mentioned in the previous note is carried to a convincing and illuminating refinement in the following diagram, which I have rearranged and slightly adapted from Leach's figure 9 (*Culture & Communication*, 86).

Text Categories	*Cosmological Space Categories*
Outside the camp	Wild Nature
Inside the camp	Tame Nature
[Place of Assembly]	
Court of the Tabernacle	Intermediate Zone A (Relatively secular)
[Middle Ground]	
Altar of Burnt Offerings	Threshold between This
Permanent Fire	World and the Other World
Tent of Meeting (Holy Place)	
East Side	Intermediate Zone B
Table, candlesticks, altar of incense	(Relatively sacred)
Curtain	Final Limit of This World
[Shrine proper]	
Tent of Meeting (Holy of Holies)	The Other World
West Side	
Ark	

It is interesting to note that Jacob Milgrom—correctly, in my judgment—suggests with special reference to Exodus 19 "The blazing summit, the cloud-covered slopes and visible bottom rim correspond to Tabernacle divisions"

HOLY TIMES

THE SABBATH

For the priestly writers the sabbath was a sanctuary in time, a day set apart from the others. Just as form-critical study has enabled us to discern the centrality of the tabernacle in priestly theology of holiness, so it enables us to discern the crucial importance of the sabbath. The principle of separation was operative in both space and time. It is widely recognized that according to the opening chapters of the Book of Genesis the sabbath was set aside and hallowed (*wayĕqaddēš*) by God as a day of rest following the work of creation (Gen. 2:1–3). It is undoubtedly less well known that the priestly writers intimately linked the tabernacle and sabbath. As form critic and biblical theologian Brevard Childs has rightly pointed out in his commentary on Exodus: "The first account of the tabernacle closes with the sabbath command (31:12ff.); the second account of its building begins with the sabbath command (35:1ff.)."[19] Childs concludes: "The connection between the sabbath and the tabernacle is therefore an important one."[20] We may register provisional agreement with Childs's assessment that for the priestly writers both the sabbath and God's meeting with the people in the tabernacle served as "surety of Israel's sanctity" (Exod. 3:13; 29:43).[21] We may, however, press the matter a bit further to see whether or not some additional connections may be discerned.

(1) In Exod. 31:12–17 the priestly authors make explicit references to the example of God's resting on the seventh day (v. 17); similarly, the pattern for the tabernacle was given by God (Exod. 25:9). Thus tabernacle is built and sabbath is kept at God's command.

(2) Just as there is danger attached to approaching the tabernacle without proper preparation, so there is danger attached to

(*Studies in Levitical Terminology, 1: The Encroacher and the Levite; The Term 'Aboda*; University of California Publications, Near Eastern Studies 14 (Berkeley and Los Angeles: University of California Press, 1970), 44–46.

19. Brevard S. Childs, *The Book of Exodus: A Critical, Theological Commentary*, OTL (Philadelphia: Westminster Press, 1974), 541.

20. Ibid.

21. Ibid.

nonobservance of the sabbath, for it is enjoined that the violator of the sabbath should be put to death (Exod. 31:4–15).

(3) In the probably later priestly writing called the Holiness Code, respect for the tabernacle is raised to be on a par with sabbath remembrance: "You shall keep My sabbaths and venerate My sanctuary: I am the LORD" (Lev. 19:30, NJV).

Despite these remarkable connections some differences remain. The tabernacle is sanctified by God's presence and is thus a symbol of the divine holiness (Exod. 29:43); the establishment of the sabbath is of divine origin (Gen. 2:1–3; Exod. 31:17) but the *keeping* of the sabbath will be a *sign* (Hebrew '*ôt*) between God and his people for the generations to come "that you may know that I the LORD am the one who sanctifies you" (Exod. 31:13, au. trans.). The sabbath is thus not in and of itself a "surety of Israel's sanctity" but rather the keeping of it serves as a declaration, a sign of Israel's knowledge of the source of her holiness; the keeping of sabbath is a symbol of Israel's awareness of it.

In the priestly writings God is the one who sanctifies—whether the tabernacle by his presence or the sabbath with his blessing. The authors of the Decalogue seem less cautious in the language they use to describe the relationship between sanctity and the sabbath. Consecration, sanctification, making holy, is evidently held to be something that human beings could do on the sabbath. "Remember the sabbath day to keep it holy (*lĕqaddĕšô*; lit. "to sanctify it": Exod. 20:8); "Observe the sabbath day to keep it holy" (*lĕqaddĕšô*; lit. "to sanctify it,": Deut. 5:12). In the less well-known and less clear-cut Decalogue of Lev. 19:1–18, 29,[22] the priestly writers of the Holiness Code put it: "You shall each revere his mother and his father and keep my sabbaths. I the LORD am your God" (Lev. 19:3, NJV). Sabbath keeping is here linked with parental respect just as later in Leviticus 19 sabbath keeping is linked with veneration of the tabernacle (v. 30).[23] But

22. For a listing of the Decalogue in Leviticus 19, see Bamberger, "Leviticus," in Plaut and Bamberger's *The Torah: A Modern Commentary*, 894. For a fuller discussion and defense, see Julian Morgenstern, "The Decalogue of the Holiness Code," *HUCA* 26 (1955):1–28.

23. In *Creation and the Persistence of Evil* (San Francisco: Harper and Row, 1988), Jon D. Levenson points to the common link of sabbath and building of tabernacle in the ancient Near Eastern and Israelite creation motif of victory

note how the priestly writers demur at using the verb "to sanctify" in the sabbath command where human beings are the actors. To be sure, as noted earlier, the very *qdš*, "sanctify," in the Decalogue undoubtedly carries with it the meaning "set apart, consecrate" or "declare holy." Yet the priests themselves seem deliberately to avoid the more traditional terminology. This would seem to be their silent testimony: God is the sanctifier of time.

The priestly instructions for keeping the sabbath were not elaborate. It is called "holy" to Israel and "holy to the LORD," a day of complete rest (*šabbat šabbātôn*: Exod. 31:14–15). Thus, following the divine example, no work was to be done on it. What the priests expected would transpire on that day is suggested by their observation that after God had rested on the seventh day, "he was refreshed" (*wayyinnāpaš*: Exod. 31:17). In the priestly listing of appropriate sacrifices to be offered throughout the year, it is stipulated that an extra burnt offering was to be presented on the sabbath in addition to the regular ones (*'olat tamîd* offered in the morning and at twilight [Num. 28:3–10]). No self-denial or special humbling is enjoined for the sabbath such as is enjoined, for example, for the Day of Atonement (cf. Lev. 23:27). The priests thus left much room for subsequent generations to expand upon the positive meaning of this day set apart.

HOLY CONVOCATIONS

Not only is the sabbath sacred, but five other times came to be called "holy convocations": the Passover or Festival of Unleavened Bread, the Feast of Weeks, the Day of the Trumpet Blast (Heb. *těrû'â*: later this day is called Rosh HaShanah: Ezek. 40:1), the Day of Atonement, and the Festival of Booths (Leviticus 23; Numbers 23—29). In the earlier legislation (Exod. 23:14–18; 34:18–25) these occasions are not yet designated as "holy convocations." Rather, the first two and last alone are mentioned (under a different name for the second feast) and singled out as

over forces of chaos (pp. 79–99). Levenson thus alerts us to the strong likelihood that the coupling of veneration of sabbath and of tabernacle in Lev. 19:30 may be both ancient and rooted in Near Eastern cosmogony.

times for pilgrimages on foot to the sanctuary (Exod. 23:14, 17; 34:23). The first and last continue to be called festivals (Num. 28:17; 29:12) and also are distinctive in that both begin on the night of the full moon[24] and last seven (Passover) or eight (Booths) days. The orientation of the Passover to the family is apparent in the priestly legislation: leaven is to be removed from homes, blood is to be smeared on the doorposts of houses (Exod. 12:1–20), and the Passover offering is to be eaten in the house (Exod. 12:46). Holy continues to mean separate, for neither foreigner nor uncircumcised slave, neither resident hired hand nor sojourner nor any uncircumcised male was permitted to eat of the Passover offering (Exod. 12:43–49).

Special significance is attached to each of these days in the priestly legislation and these in turn are expanded by the successive generations that observed them. Passover signified deliverance from Egypt (Exod. 12:17); Weeks the harvesting of new grain (Lev. 23:16, 22); the Trumpet Blast perhaps the trumpet blasts at Sinai (Lev. 23:24; cf. Exod. 19:13, 16, 19); the Day of Atonement the need for self-humbling (Lev. 23:27, 29, 32) and the death of Aaron's two sons who died "before the LORD" when they presented an "alien fire" on the incense altar in the holy place (Lev. 10; 16:1); and Booths the humble dwellings of the Israelites after the deliverance from Egypt (Lev. 23:39–43). In the exilic and postexilic era it was stressed (1) that the completion of the temple under Solomon was celebrated by the seven-day festival (of Booths) (1 Kings 8:2, 65–66; 2 Chron. 7:9) and (2) that under Ezra a high point of rejoicing was reached during the eight days of the Feast of Booths when Ezra read from the book of the law of God. The joy of the feast inhering by virtue of the agricultural season thus became enhanced as fresh memories of momentous, historical events became attached to it.[25]

---

24. Because the priestly calendar was lunar and began at the new moon, the fifteenth of the month would mark the night of the full moon.

25. For additional studies and reflections on Israelite holy days, see esp. Roland deVaux, *Ancient Israel: Its Life and Institutions*, trans. John McHugh, (New York: McGraw-Hill, 1961), 483–510; and Bamberger and Plaut, "Leviticus," in *Torah*, 919–26.

RITES OF PASSAGE

In addition to Sabbath and holy convocations the priestly writers also carefully described ceremonies and practices that marked important transitions in the lives of individuals and families. These include ceremonies and practices at birth, puberty, marriage, ordination, and death. Once again it is interesting to observe the great extent to which the principle of separation gives us an important insight into the priestly understanding of holiness.

Birth. The classical study in rites of passage by Arnold van Gennep identifies circumcision as at once a rite of separation and incorporation.[26] The cutting of the foreskin automatically incorporated an individual into a defined group. Because the removal of the foreskin was permanent, the rite symbolized a permanent incorporation and at the same time also a "sign of union" with the deity and membership in "a single community of the faithful."[27] Not all of Israel's neighbors practiced circumcision (e.g., see Genesis 34) and in the Babylonian exile in particular, inasmuch as the Babylonians did not practice circumcision, the rite served to differentiate Israelite males permanently from the Babylonians.[28]

Genesis 17 makes it plain that the usual significance peoples in other cultures attributed to circumcision the Israelites also attributed to it. The rite was commanded by El Shaddai (God Almighty: one of the distinctive designations among the priestly writers) as a "sign of the covenant" (Gen. 17:11). For the newly born, it was to be performed on the eighth day (Gen. 17:12). It is, however, not simply a rite of incorporation for the individual, male Israelite, but a practice laid upon the entire community,

26. Arnold van Gennep, *The Rites of Passage,* trans. Monika B. Vizedom and Gabrielle L. Caffee (Chicago: University of Chicago Press, 1960), 70–73. This edition has an excellent introduction by Solon T. Kimball, who puts the work of van Gennep in historical-intellectual context and points up its relative neglect among anthropological, sociological, and psychological writers on life crises. Kimball might also have added religious writers to his list.

27. Ibid., 72.

28. Claus Westermann, *Genesis: Kapitel 12–36,* Biblischer Kommentar Altes Testament (Neukirchen-Vluyn: Neukirchener Verlag, 1981), 319–20. Among Israel's neighbors who did practice circumcision, Jer. 9:24–25 lists the Egyptians, Edomites, Ammonites, and Moabites.

and for generations to come (Gen. 17:9–10). Ethical exhortation precedes the ritualistic instruction: (1) "Walk as in my presence (au. trans., lit. "walk before me") and (2) "be persons of integrity" (au. trans., lit. "be blameless ones": Gen. 17:1). The use of the plural form makes it apparent that the writer has all of Israel in mind. Thus vocation to moral living was an integral part of the priestly theology of separation: each Israelite was summoned to walk his or her daily life as if in the presence of God and also with a striving for an integrity in act and being.

There is no evidence of a comparable rite of incorporation for Israelite females at birth.[29]

Puberty. There is not extensive evidence in the Old Testament for the existence of a puberty rite of passage from boyhood to manhood, from girlhood to womanhood. Genesis 17 records that Ishmael was circumcised at age thirteen (v. 25). This may have been a notice required by the flow of the priestly narrative inasmuch as Ishmael was older than Isaac; it may, of course, reflect on the other hand Ishmaelite practice. In any event circumcision at puberty was a rite of transition (*rite de marge*) and initiation as well as of separation and incorporation. In Judaism today the comparable puberty rite is the *bar mitzvah* for boys (and in Reform Judaism, the *bas mitzvah* for girls).[30] In early biblical times the closest thing to a rite of transition for girls at puberty

---

29. For Israelite practice with females at puberty, see below. Note also that in Christian apologetics the point may rightfully be made that infant baptism has replaced circumcision as a communal act and sign of the community's affirmation to be faithful to God in covenant and, further, that this rite is *not* exclusively male. John Calvin (*Institutes of the Christian Religion*, 2 vols., Library of Christian Classics, trans. Ford Lewis Battles [Philadelphia: Westminster Press, 1960]) argued that infant baptism was rooted in the practice of the Old Covenant (pp. 1310, 1325–29), but equally vociferously held that women should *not* practice it (pp. 1321–1323)!

30. The widely disseminated document *Baptism, Eucharist and Ministry*, Faith and Order Paper No. 111 (Geneva: World Council of Churches, 1982) fails, in my judgment, in two specific regards with respect to its treatment on baptism: (1) it does not display any tendency of theological thinking to listen to the social sciences (in an attempt to learn from or enter into dialogue with them); (2) it simply bypasses the important link between circumcision and baptism in reformed theology. The potential creative assistance of such an important passage as Genesis 17 (where circumcision is a rite for infants, a rite of transition from boyhood to manhood, and a rite for adults) has thus been ignored.

was the yearly dancing of the daughters of Shiloh (Judg. 21:16–24), but even here the evidence is by no means unambiguous.

Marriage. The marriage ceremony is not a center of focus within the Old Testament even though the preservation of marriage as an institution is clearly raised to a high theological and social level by virtue of the inclusion of the prohibition of adultery among the Ten Commandments (Exod. 20:14; Deut. 5:18). There is no exact equivalent to the commandment on adultery in the Decalogue of the Holiness Code, and even though the prohibition "Do not profane your daughter by making her a harlot, lest the land fall into harlotry and the land become full of wickedness" (Lev. 19:29) comes close, it still does not deliberately address the subject of marriage. The subject is directly addressed in Lev. 20:10 in severe terms: "If a man commits adultery with a married woman, committing adultery with his neighbor's wife, the adulterer and the adulteress shall be put to death" (Lev. 20:10, NJV).

Injunctions of the death penalty are also offered for incest with one's mother or daughter-in-law, male homosexuality, contemporaneous marriage by a man of a mother and daughter, bestiality, and necromancy (Lev. 20:11–16, 27). Leviticus 18:6–18 and 20:17–21 in the Holiness Code also speak directly of marriage—and extend the list of what kinds of relatives could not intermarry. These passages thus carefully delimit those who should remain separate insofar as the marriage (and sexual) relationship is concerned. That there remains a certain idiosyncracy and male bias in these teachings need not be denied by the modern interpreter: marriages between uncles and nieces are not explicitly proscribed, but marriages between aunts and nephews are (Lev. 20:20); sexual relations between father and daughter are not explicitly proscribed but they are between mother and son (Lev. 20:11); the latter offense is not seen simply as an offense against the mother but also against the husband; male homosexuality is proscribed but no mention is made of homosexuality among women. These priestly guidelines are thus clearly deficient and lacking in evenhandedness insofar as modern egalitarianism is concerned. The extent to which they should be followed roughly or at all is a matter of intense debate.

The anthropologist Mary Douglas assists us greatly in understanding this debate when she points out that deep cosmological convictions are invariably reflected in how a group decides to control the bodily openings (orifices).[31] For the priestly writers of the Holiness Code the above-mentioned relationships that carried the death penalty were clearly those on which they placed the severest taboo. For some modern interpreters those proscribed relationships remain taboo, that is, they are not only deemed inappropriate to holiness but feared for the consequences of what would follow if they were endorsed as permissible.

Ordination. In his book *The Nature and Function of Priesthood: A Comparative and Anthropological Study*, E. O. James observed of the priesthood throughout the ancient Near East: "Although the officiants exercise a great variety of functions . . . they have this in common that they belong to a sacred order like priests, set apart from the 'laity' by some form of consecration."[32] The vestments for that sacred order and rites for entering it in ancient Israel are described by the priestly writers in Exodus 28—29 and 39 and in Leviticus 8.[33] Like the other rites treated above, ordination in ancient Israel was a rite of passage, or as

31. See esp. Mary Douglas, *Natural Symbols: Explorations in Cosmology* (New York: Pantheon Books, 1982; first published 1970) esp. chaps. 2, 3, 6, and 10. For another excellent study on cosmologies and ethics, see *Cosmogony and Ethical Order: New Studies in Comparative Ethics*, ed. Robin W. Lovin and Frank E. Reynolds (Chicago: University of Chicago Press, 1985). The introductory and programmatic essay by the editors also alerted me to the unwisdom of dismissing unthinkingly the fears of the creationists with respect to cosmogonies: "Beliefs about the way the world is may relate in many different ways to beliefs about what we ought to do, and each of these requires careful explication" (p. 30). Similarly, the editors awakened in me a renewed desire to understand the human value judgments underlying cosmogonies that I reject and find difficult to accept: "[W]e take the variety of cosmogonic myths, the cosmogonies of philosophers, and even the scientific cosmogonies of Marx, Freud, and the modern-day cosmologists to be meaningful attempts to say what is really there in the human encounter with nature and social reality, what is fundamental in the changing configurations of experience" (p. 31). I am indebted to Jerome Neyrey, S.J., of the Weston School of Theology for calling the aforementioned book to my attention.

32. E. O. James, *The Nature and Function of Priesthood: A Comparative and Anthropological Study* (London: Thames & Hudson, 1955), 277.

33. In preparing the remarks below I benefited from reading chap. 3 ("Leviticus 8") in Frank H. Gorman, Jr., "Priestly Ritual and Creation Theology: The Conceptual Categories of Space, Time, and Status in Lev. 8; 14; 16; Num. 19: 28–29: (Ph.D. diss., Emory University, 1985), 154–220.

Edmund Leach prefers to call it, a rite of marginality (*rite de marge*).[34] It was a long and drawn-out affair which took place precisely at the margin, that is, at the boundary or threshold between the court of the sanctuary and the sanctuary itself. The focal point is the altar of burnt offerings on which were to be offered each day for seven days running: the bull for expiation of the altar of burnt offerings, a ram to be entirely burnt, and another ram ("a ram of ordination"). Of the latter the priests and ordinands alone were permitted to eat the breast when raised as a "wave offering" (Exod. 29:26–28). Ordinarily, the latter two offerings were part of what used to be called "peace offerings." But now scholars suggest the term "sacrifices of well-being" (cf. Lev. 7:28–34).[35] After the remainder of the ram of ordination had been boiled, the priests ate it (Exod. 29:31–34).

The Hebrew word for ordination used in "ram of ordination" (Exod. 29:26–28; Lev. 8:29) and "basket of ordination" (Lev. 8:31) is *hammillu'îm* and means literally "filling"—deriving perhaps from that with which the priests' hands were "filled" (i.e., the bull, two rams, and unleavened cakes) during the seven-day ordination (Exod. 29:1–3).

The words "consecrate" or "sanctify," "holy," and "sacred" are used many times over in the course of the ordination ceremonies. Oil is used to anoint Aaron, his sons, and their sacerdotal vestments so that they might "be holy" (Exod. 29:21, 29). The uneaten residue from the ram of ordination and the bread in the basket are not to be eaten by the laity "for they are holy" (Exod. 29:33). Any residue from the ram of ordination left overnight may not be eaten—even by the priests—"for it is holy" (Exod. 29:34). Blood from the bull offered as a "sin-offering" (*ḥaṭṭā't*) which now Milgrom and others suggest should be translated as "purgation offering,"[36] was anointed on the altar "to consecrate

---

34. Leach, *Culture and Communication*, 77, 81–90. For a thorough discussion of such rites see Victor Turner, *The Forest of Symbols* (Ithaca, N.Y.: Cornell University Press, 1967), chap. 4, "Betwixt and Between: The Liminal Period in *Rites de Passage*," 93–111.

35. See esp. Jacob Milgrom, "Sacrifices and Offerings, OT," in *Interpreter's Dictionary of the Bible, Supplementary Volume*, ed. Keith Crim et al. (Nashville: Abingdon Press, 1976), 763—71.

36. Ibid.

it, and the altar shall become most holy; whatever touches the altar shall become consecrated" (Exod. 29:36–37, NJV). These verses suggest that a periodic purgation of the outer altar thus was accomplished at the time of ordination. The incense altar was similarly "purged" once a year (Exod. 30:10). Jacob Milgrom has even argued that *every* "purgation offering" had a cleansing effect on that part of the sanctuary where the blood was smeared.[37] Milgrom's case has been carefully argued and has won sufficient adherents so that it may not be lightly dismissed. His case for the effect of the "purgation offering" will, therefore, be considered below in the section on holy acts. For now it may be acknowledged that the seven-successive-day offering of the bull and the smearing and dashing of its blood at the time of ordination as a "purgation" or "sin" "offering" did clearly have a purgative effect on the altar of burnt offerings, rendering it "most holy."

The vestments worn by the ordinands are called holy (Exod. 28:2). They are put on at the outset of the ceremony but only after the priests-to-be have washed at the focal point, the entrance to the tent of meeting (Exod. 29:4). Distinction is made between the vestments of the sons of Aaron (priests) and Aaron (the high priest). All the priests wore linen breeches, tunics, sashes, and turbans, but Aaron alone was vested in ephod, breastpiece (*ḥōšen*) suspended by a pure gold chain, and crown (*nēzer*: Exod. 28:6–40; 29:6; 39:2–30; Lev. 8:6–9). One of the special features of Aaron's headgear was a golden "frontlet" (lit. flower, *ṣîṣ* on which was inscribed "Holy (lit. Holiness) [belongs] to the LORD" (Exod. 28:36–37). A brief notice suggests that the frontlet was believed to have a dual effect: (1) of removing guilt (*'āwôn*) from any of the sacred things the Israelites consecrated and (2) of winning favor with God (Exod. 28:38). The breastpiece with twelve different precious stones, on which were inscribed the names of the twelve tribes, was clearly a symbol of the nation (Exod. 28:22–29) and in it were placed the sacred lots called Urim and Thummim used for seeking divine guidance (Exod. 28:30; cf. Deut. 33:8; Ezra 2:63; 1 Samuel 14). The ephod (Exod.

37. Ibid.

28:6–14) has been explained variously as being a loincloth[38] or "kind of pinafore composed of two pieces of linen joined at the shoulder by straps."[39] Another special feature of Aaron's gear was the robe (*mě'îl*) of pure blue, presumably worn over the ephod (Exod. 28:31–35).

The anthropologist Edmund Leach has suggested that we should see three phases in the ordination of Israelite priests: phase 1: washing and investiture at a place physically removed from ordinary people (rite of separation); phase 2: seven days of being in an "abnormal condition" where the initiate is "without status, outside society, outside time" (*rite de marge:* marginal state); phase 3: "the special costume worn during the 'marginal state' is removed and a new normal costume appropriate to the new normal status is put on," sacrifices are repeated, food restrictions are removed (rite of aggregation [or incorporation]).[40] Even though Leach's observations serve to bring out certain features in the Israelite ordination ceremonies that might otherwise have been overlooked, for example, the marginal state of the ordinand during the seven-day ordination and the gala conclusion of the ordination period when the newly ordained priests offer sacrifices and the people are blessed (Leviticus 9), his views need modification in two regards. One, it is not quite correct to say that the ordination transpired at a place "physically removed from ordinary people" inasmuch as Moses was instructed to "assemble the whole community at the entrance to the tent of meeting" (Lev. 8:3). Two, it is not clear that special garments were worn by the priests to mark their new status after the ordination. Special treatment of the hair is required for all Israelite males (Lev. 19:27), for the high priest (Lev. 21:10), and for Nazirites (Numbers 6), but, despite Lev. 21:5, no distinction in normal priestly coiffure is stipulated.[41]

Death. The priestly writers of ancient Israel carefully pre-

---

38. Martin Noth, *Exodus*, trans. J. S. Bowden, OTL (Philadelphia: Westminster Press, 1962), 220–21.

39. Bamberger and Plaut, *Torah*, 618.

40. Leach, *Culture and Communication*, 77–79.

41. For a fine discussion of the priestly office and Levites both before and after the exile, see de Vaux, *Ancient Israel*, chaps. 5–7.

scribed actions appropriate and prohibited in the handling of their dead. Accordingly, a final rite of passage concerns death and burial. Contact with a dead person required a cleansing with water on the third and seventh day after contact in order for a person to become clean (Num. 19:11). The person who failed to cleanse himself would defile the tabernacle and remain in a state of uncleanness (Num. 19:13). This passage is important because it shows that some offenses would defile the sanctuary and that defilement of the sanctuary could be averted by action taken outside the precincts of the sanctuary.

Specific ceremonies were prescribed for cleansing the tent of a deceased person. One who was clean—not necessarily a priest— would sprinkle the tent and its furnishings on the third and seventh day with "waters of lustration" (lit. "impurity": Num. 19:14–19). The one who did the sprinkling in turn became unclean and had to wash his clothes and bathe in water to become clean (Num. 19:19–22).

It was permitted for priests to "defile themselves" (i.e., to be near and presumably even to touch deceased members of their "nearest of kin: mother, father, brother, and virgin sister" (Lev. 21:1–4). The high priest, however, was forbidden to go near even his deceased father or mother: "He shall not go outside the sanctuary and profane the sanctuary of his God, for upon him is the distinction of the anointing oil of his God" (Lev. 21:10–12, NJV).

The strictures against contact with the dead were also extremely severe for the Nazirite: even if father, mother, brother, or sister should die, he was not to touch them, lest he defile himself (Num. 6:6–7). And even if a person should die near him, he had to shave off his hair on the seventh day, and go through an elaborate ceremony of reconsecration on the eighth day (Num. 6:9–12).

It was particularly dangerous for a priest who had become unclean through touching a dead person (or through other means) not to become clean through bathing: he ran the risk of becoming cut off from service before God, and of death (Lev. 22:1–9). Provision was also made for the priest who offered sacrifices (and thus inevitably came in contact with a dead animal).

The purgation offering, for example, was "most holy" and "whoever (or whatever) touches its flesh shall be holy" (Lev. 6:27). If earthenware vessels were used for boiling this offering, they had to be broken thereafter and bronze vessels used had to be scoured (Lev. 6:28).

As we know from the example of the burial of Sarah, the priestly writers thought it important that interment not take place indiscriminately. Rather, a special burial ground and particularly one separated from the Gentiles was required (Genesis 23). "Abraham proceeded both to lament for Sarah and to weep for her" (Gen. 23:2). According to a recent Jewish commentator these words constitute "a description both of sentiment and of set ritual."[42] Thus at death, at birth, and at ordination, the priestly theology of holiness was dominated by the principle of separation and the requirement of specific ceremonial rites to mark the passage from one status to another.

HOLY PERSONS

ISRAELITES IN THE HOLINESS CODE—HOLY NATION

Within the priestly writings a democratizing element eventually won out—not simply Aaron and his sons are called holy, but all of Israel (Lev. 19:2; 20:7, 26). Tracing the bold outlines of this development is of interest. (1) In the older pentateuchal sources utilized by the priestly writers the phrase "holy nation" is found (Exod. 19:6). (2) In the Priestly Code itself the Israelites are rarely called "holy."[43] (3) In the so-called Holiness Code (Leviticus 17—26) the term "holy (ones)" is freely applied as an invitation and challenge to all citizens. The name and theme of the Holiness Code derives from one of the most famous verses of Scripture: "Say to the congregation of the people of Israel: 'Ye shall be holy (ones) for I the LORD your God am holy" (Lev.

42. Bamberger and Plaut, *Torah*, 156.
43. They are, however, so called. Nonetheless, note: (1) Lev. 11:44, 45 plainly belong to a later addition as is evident from the divergency of the phrasing of vv. 43–47 from what precedes; see Martin Noth, *Leviticus*, trans. J. E. Anderson, OTL (Philadelphia: Westminster Press, 1965), 96; (2) the use by Korah of the saying "All the congregation are holy" (Num. 16:3) serves to underline the point made here that the holiness of all Israel was not an assertion that the Aaronides themselves favored.

19:2; cf. 20:7, 26). Although scholars are divided on the subject of whether or not the Holiness Code is younger or older than the bulk of the Priestly Code,[44] for the purposes of the present study it is sufficient to note that there was a divergency within the priestly groups when it came to readiness to apply the terms "holy (ones)" to the nation. The Holiness Code also differs from the rest of the priestly writings in its uses of the phrase "my holy name" with reference to God (Lev. 20:3; 22:2, 32). The latter fact, along with other considerations, has led a recent scholar to conclude that the authors of the Holiness Code belonged to the priestly wing of the Deuteronomistic School.[45]

As with all the priestly writers, the notion of separation is prominent for the authors of Leviticus 17—26 in their theology of holy people: "You shall be holy to me; for I the LORD am holy, and have separated (*wā'abdil*) you from the peoples that you should be mine" (Lev. 20:26, au. trans.). Thus election is a corollary of the priestly doctrine of holy peoplehood.

Whether the authors of the Holiness Code belonged to the Deuteronomistic School or not, as it seems to me they did, the meaning of the divine challenge to be "holy (ones)" for them extends far beyond the idea of "separation" from other peoples to include the deepest kind of ethical and humanitarian concerns: regard for the poor, the deaf, and blind (Lev. 19:9–10, 14); avoidance of hate (v. 17); love of neighbor as self (v. 18); and love of stranger as self (v. 34). The latter commandment to love the stranger is, curiously, often overlooked by Gentile biblical commentators.

---

44. See, e.g., Julian Morgenstern, "The Decalogue of the Holiness Code," *HUCA* 36 (1955):1–27, who argues for a date just prior to the dedication of the rebuilt temple in 516 B.C.E. (p. 18). In contrast, in his recent study on scribal additions to the Pentateuch, Michael Fishbane presupposes the priority of the Holiness Code (*Biblical Interpretation in Ancient Israel* [Oxford: Oxford University Press, 1985], 175–77).

45. See Alfred Cholewiński, S.J., *Heiligkeitsgesetz und Deuteronomium: Eine vergleichende Studie*, Analecta Biblica 66 (Rome: Biblical Institute Press, 1976). Among the many parallels to which Cholewiński calls attention, the following especially may be mentioned: Leviticus 17 // Deuteronomy 12; Leviticus 19 // Deuteronomy 5; Leviticus 23 // Deuteronomy 16; Leviticus 26 // Deuteronomy 28. Note also the frequent common usage of "the LORD your God."

As noted earlier, virtually all the commandments of the Decalogue are to be found in Leviticus 19.[46] Since this is the case, Leviticus 19 should be considered along with Exodus 20 and Deuteronomy when the Decalogue is studied. Not only are proper attitudes and duties toward fellow human beings enumerated in this chapter as the requirements of holiness but also proper duties and attitudes toward God—among which reverence especially is emphasized (vv. 14, 32). For the reasons given above, Leviticus 19 must clearly be ranked as one of the high points of Old Testament ethics, along with Amos 5, Micah 6, Ezekiel 18, and Job 31. Bernard Bamberger rightly expresses consternation in his commentary that Rudolph Otto made no mention whatsoever of this chapter in his book *The Idea of the Holy*.[47] Bamberger was also entirely correct in affirming that the priests see holiness "as aspiration and task to be approached through a disciplined life."[48] It is thus altogether misleading and a caricature of the priestly understanding of holiness to reduce it to a set of rules pertaining to purity such as Trevor Williams has done in his recent and otherwise insightful and provocative book.[49] Bamberger again is on target: "The ethical component of holiness is not for the priestly writers of the Holiness Code a mere 'extra.'"[50] Rather, for them as for Judaism: "Religion and ethics, though not identical, are inseparable."[51]

Aaron and the Aaronides

There is little doubt that for the pentateuchal, priestly writers, the most holy of human beings is Aaron and, next to him, his

---

46. See n. 22 above.

47. Plaut and Bamberger, *Torah*, 890. For his comments Bamberger in turn draws on Burton M. Leiser, "The Sanctity of the Profane: A Pharisaic Critique of Rudolph Otto," *Judaism* (Winter 1971): 87ff.

48. Ibid.

49. Trevor Williams, *Form and Vitality in the World and God* (Oxford: Clarendon Press, 1985). Williams's basic argument that the Bible is like an ancient map of terrain that has changed is on the face of it appealing but rests on the unprovable assumption that the divine reality changes in commensurate ways to physical reality. Further, it does not seem to me that Williams sufficiently distinguishes between reality about God, cultural and social reality, and the reality of human nature.

50. Ibid.

51. Ibid.

sons. Moses, of course, stands in a unique position. He is the inaugurator, the one who ordains,[52] but the honor of serving in sanctuary and in the holy of holies is not Moses' but Aaron's. Indeed, the priestly writers of the Book of Exodus relate how the cloud and glory of God so filled the tent of meeting that Moses was no longer able to enter (Exod. 40:34-35). That prerogative thus remained for Aaron and his sons (Exod. 27:21; 28:40-43; 29:29; Leviticus 18).

There is widespread agreement among scholars that the portrait of Aaron and his sons in Genesis through Numbers reflects the victory of a southern priestly family, the Aaronides (who looked to Aaron as their founder) over all others including the Mushites (who looked to Moses as their founder).[53] That the followers of Aaron were chosen as holiest among rival priesthoods is especially apparent in the story of the rebellion of Korah (Lev. 16:1—17:11). Korah complains against Moses and Aaron for having exalted themselves since "all the congregation is holy, every one of them" (Num. 16:3). Moses responds that God will show "who is his and who is holy" (Num. 16:5), as indeed he does, for the earth swallows, and fire consumes, all two hundred and fifty of the Korahites (Num. 15:27-35). Moses then pronounces the Aaronides holy (Num. 16:37) and instructs Eleazar, Aaron's son, to hammer out a covering for the altar of incense with the very censers used by the rebel priests, to be a warning that no priest who is not a son of Aaron should draw near to burn incense (Num. 15:36-40). When the people complain, God threatens them, and Aaron intervenes with incense to make atonement (Num. 15:41-49). Then the plague is stopped (Num.

52. For a thorough discussion of this point, see Gorman, "Excursus I: Exod. 34:29-35: Moses the Exalted Inaugurator of the Cult," in "Priestly Ritual and Creation Theology, 221-33.

53. For a discussion and defense of the antiquity of the rivalry between Mushites and Aaronides, see Frank M. Cross, "The Priestly Houses of Early Israel," in his *Canaanite Myth and Hebrew Epic* (Cambridge: Harvard University Press, 1973), chap. 8, 195-215. For a most thorough probing of the Aaronides as a shapers of the Pentateuch, see Ellis Rivkin, *The Shaping of Jewish History: A Radical New Interpretation* (New York: Charles Scribner's Sons, 1971), 21-41. For a probing from earlier times to the postexilic era, see Aelred Cody, *A History of Old Testament Priesthood*, Analecta Biblica 35 (Rome: Pontifical Biblical Institute, 1969); and deVaux, *Ancient Israel*, 345-405.

15:50). In a final display of divine favor, of the twelve rods, the rod of Levi, on which was written Aaron's name, alone sprouted of those that had been placed in the tent (Num. 17:1–11). As noted above, Aaron's vestments—the "holy crown" in particular (Exod. 26:6b)—symbolize his special holiness. Both Aaron and his sons are anointed with holy oil (Exod. 30:25–32).

Despite the high standing of Aaron and his sons, their holiness is derivative and must be understood as subservient to the divine holiness. Aaron and his sons are "those who draw near" (to God). Indeed, a synonym for offering, *qorbān*, means literally "that which is brought near." A crucial passage illustrating the decidedly secondary importance of the priestly sanctity and the need for the priests ever to be on guard against becoming overly presumptuous is found in an evidently well-known saying which Moses recalls to Aaron after his two sons Nadab and Abihu had died. The reason for death is that they brought near an "alien fire," that is, fire brought "'from somewhere' but not from the altar fire which was alone legitimate."[54] Then Moses said to Aaron: "This is what the Lord meant when he said: 'Through those near to me I show myself holy (*'eqqādēš*) and before the face of all the people I manifest my glory'" (*'ekkābēd*: Lev. 10:3, au. trans.). The priests may have thought the saying meant that they were the ones who manifested God's holiness, but the circumstances of its recollection by Moses served as a stark reminder that God remained the subject and prime mover. This passage thus shows that even though a group such as the Aaronides may be behind the Priestly Code, the fact remains that the very same group transmitted traditions that were both unmistakably theocentric and thoroughly aware of the possibilities of presumptuous exercise of priestly rites.

First-born and Levites

In the probably premonarchic Covenant Code (Exod. 20:19—23:33)[55] there is found the saying: "The first-born of your sons (*běkôr bānêkā*) you shall give to me" (Exod. 22:28). This concept

54. Noth, *Leviticus*, 85.
55. See, e.g., Shalom M. Paul, *Studies in the Book of the Covenant in the Light of Cuneiform and Biblical Law*, VTSup 18 (Leiden: E. J. Brill, 1970), 102.

has a long development and metamorphosis. It is related to the similar, but less radical, requirement of first fruits (*bikkûrê 'admātĕkā*) at the feasts of harvest (Exod. 23:16, 19). The famous binding of Isaac (Genesis 22) has been interpreted by many to mark the replacement of the sacrifice of children (and in particular the firstborn) by animal sacrifices.[56] For our purposes, one of the most interesting passages in the development of this concept is when it is brought into relationship with the priestly theology of holiness and with the Levites:

> For every first-born among the Israelites, man as well as beast, is Mine. I consecrated them to Myself; at the time I smote every first-born (*kōl bĕkôr*) in the land of Egypt. Now I take the Levites instead of every first-born of the Israelites; and from among the Israelites I formally assign the Levites to Aaron and his sons, to perform the service for the Israelites in the Tent of Meeting and to make expiation for the Israelites, so that no plague may afflict the Israelites for coming too near the sanctuary. (Num. 8:17–19, NJV; cf. Num. 3:13)

This passage is fascinating in that it does not go the way of the earlier pentateuchal sources in Genesis 22 and suggests indirectly that animal sacrifices may be appointed substitutes for the divine claim on the firstborn among human beings. Rather, it explicitly singles out the Levites as the appointed substitutes from among Israel and then promptly makes them subservient to the Aaronides. In the priestly theology of the exilic era the Levites had a holy status of subordination.[57]

HOLY ACTS—OFFERINGS OF FIRE

There were three main reasons for which offerings were brought near to the sanctuary: as means of thanksgiving, communion, and expiation. The "whole burnt-offerings" (*'ōlôt:* Leviticus

56. The list of scholars adhering to this interpretation includes J. G. Frazer, H. Zimmern, A Jeremias, and W. Robertson Smith (so H. Gunkel, *Genesis*, 9th ed. [Göttingen: Vandenhoeck & Ruprecht, 1977], 239); and George W. Coats (*Genesis*, Forms of the Old Testament Literature 1 [Grand Rapids: Wm. B. Eerdmans, 1983], 181). It is rejected in recent times by Gerhard von Rad, *Genesis*, rev. ed., original translation by John H. Marks, OTL (Philadelphia: Westminster Press, 1972), 238–39; and by Walter Brueggemann, *Genesis* Interpretation (Atlanta: John Knox Press, 1982), 186.

57. For further discussion, see n. 53.

1; 22:17–19), "cereal offerings" (*minḥôt:* Leviticus 2), and "offerings of well-being" (KJV, RSV: "peace-offerings": *šĕlāmîm:* Leviticus 3, 7) each served as offerings of thanksgiving or gifts. The latter, the offerings of well-being or shared offerings, also had a communal aspect in that they were eaten in the sacred precincts by worshipers as well as by priests; they were also the offerings used to mark the fulfillment of vows (Lev. 7:11–16). The two chief offerings of expiation were the "sin offerings" or "purgation offerings" (*ḥaṭṭā'ôt:* Leviticus 4; 5:1–13) and "guilt offerings" or "reparation offerings" (*'ăšāmîm:* Leviticus 5). It was the function of the priests to perform these holy acts by placing a part ("cereal offerings," "sin offerings," "offerings of well-being," "reparation offerings") or all ("whole burnt offerings") of the offering on the outer altar to be consumed by fire. Fire, it will be recalled, is a symbol of that urgent, vital, motile aspect of the holy summarized by Otto's designation *energicum*.

A forceful case has been mounted by Jacob Milgrom of Berkeley (1) to translate *ḥaṭṭā't* as "purgation offering" and (2) to hold that "purgation offering" purged the sanctuary and the sancta (holy things) in it.[58] It is sobering to realize that scholarly consensus with respect to the interpretation of Israel's sacrificial cultus is astonishingly unstable. Now, even more than in recent decades, lively debate is apt to continue. In 1905, Bernhard Stade argued (in a similar fashion to Milgrom) that the Hebrew *ḥaṭṭā't* should not be rendered as "sin offering" but rather (in a suggestion that would be quite unsatisfactory to Milgrom) as "atonement offering" or "offering of consecration."[59] Though Milgrom does not cite Stade, he is in agreement with him in affirming that the synonyms of verb *kipper* (usually rendered "atone") are: *ḥiṭṭē'* ("purify") and *ṭihar* ("cleanse": see Lev. 14:51–52 and Ezek. 43:20, 26).[60] On solid, linguistic grounds, then, one may be in-

---

58. See esp. Jacob Milgrom, "Israel's Sanctuary: The Priestly 'Picture of Dorian Gray,'" in *Studies in Cultic Theology and Terminology*, Studies in Judaism in Late Antiquity 36, (Leiden: E. J. Brill, 1983), 75–84; first published in *Revue Biblique* 83 (1976): 390–99.

59. B. Stade, *Biblische Theologie des Alten Testaments 1*, Grundriss der Theologischen Wissenschaften 2/2 (Tübingen; J. C. B. Mohr [Paul Siebeck] 1905), 165.

60. Ibid., 166; Milgrom, *Studies in Cultic Theology*, 76.

clined to accept Milgrom's suggestion that *ḥaṭṭā't* should be translated "purgation offering": the verb *kipper* is found in every passage in which the "sin offering" or "purgation offering" is described (see, e.g., Leviticus 4, 7, 16). If, however, it can be demonstrated that Milgrom is in error with respect to that which is purged, then one may rightly hesitate to accept his terminology lest it be implied that his conclusions are accepted also. Despite my enthusiasm for Milgrom's program of reexamination of priestly terminology and basic agreement with much of it, it seems to me that he has failed to establish (1) that human beings are not purged with the "purgation offerings" and (2) that *every* "purgation offering" purges a portion of the sanctuary or sancta.

What seems to me to be the most defensible position with respect to the *ḥaṭṭā't*—regardless of whether it is rendered as "sin offering" or "purgation offering"—may be stated as follows.

(1) The priestly writers did not teach that any "sin offering" offered through the year, the flesh of which was not to be eaten by the priests, purged the *incense altar* (which was located *in* the holy place), the holy place, and the holy of holies, but rather that these places were purged only once a year with the "sin offering" on the day of atonement (Leviticus 16; see esp. vv. 24, 33).

(2) The priestly writers did not teach that the "sin offerings," part of which were eaten by the priests, purged the *outer altar* of *burnt offerings* (which was located in the courtyard of the tabernacle); rather, they taught that the outer altar was purged *only* during the seven successive days of "sin offerings" *at the time of ordination* (Exodus 29; see esp. vv. 35–37).

(3) The regular "sin offerings" as well as the "sin offerings" on the day of atonement were understood by the priestly writers to purge from their sins or uncleannesses the *person* or *persons* in whose behalf they were presented (see esp. Lev. 4:20, 26, 31, 35; 5:6).

A detailed defense of these conclusions would necessitate a fairly technical linguistic discussion. My basic defense is that Leviticus 16 and Exodus 29 seem to state quite straightforwardly when the inner and outer altars, respectively, were cleansed (namely, respectively, on Yom Kippur and at ordinations). As for item 3, in all of the instances of the primary legislation on the sin offering (Lev. 4:1—5:13), it seems unnecessarily subtle to suggest that the sinner is not the object of purgation because the particle *'al* is used instead of *'et*.[61]

Two final comments may be made on Milgrom's theory.

(1) Even though it is apparent that Milgrom has greatly advanced the study of Israel's sacrificial cultus and has demonstrated the purgative effect of the *ḥaṭṭā't* offering, we have stopped short of accepting his term "purgation offering" for it because evidence is lacking to show that the sanctuary and the sancta were purged, as he claims, by every *ḥaṭṭā't* offering.

(2) Milgrom has made the dramatic and powerful suggestion that the sanctuary was like the portrait of Dorian Gray, that is, as the people sinned, they defiled the sanctuary and threatened to drive out the Lord's presence such as is described by Ezekiel in Ezekiel 1—3, 8—11, and 40—42. Because of this theory of pollution, sacrifices were necessary to purge the altars especially since they, as it were, absorbed the people's sins and became impure. Under Milgrom's view the slate was constantly being wiped clean, so to speak, with every sin offering. Under the view argued above, the sanctuary for the priestly writers was far more a portrait of Dorian Gray than Milgrom's own theory would allow. The sin offerings purged the people from their sins, but only the sin offerings once a year on the Day of Atonement purged the tent of meeting and only the sin offerings at ordina-

---

61. Here, as frequently, *kipper* takes the preposition *'al* instead of *'et* for a very good linguistic reason, namely, to remind the reader that from which the person or thing has been purged, namely, sin or uncleanness. Thus *'al* is frequently followed by *min* (e.g., Lev. 4:26; 5:6) and even when *min* is absent the very use of *'al* carries with it the reminder that there is a purgation *from* something; the particle *'et* would not convey this meaning. See also Lev. 12:8; 14:19.

It may be noted that my conclusions are in agreement with Rolf Rendtorff, *Studien zur Geschichte des Opfers im Alten Israel*, Wissenschaftliche Monographien zum Alten und Neuen Testament 24 (Neukirchen-Vluyn: Neukirchener Verlag, 1967), 245, who sees the purification of the altars and sanctuary as an added function of the *ḥaṭṭā't*, and Baruch A. Levine, *In the Presence of the Lord*, ed. Jacob Neusner, Studies in Judaism in Late Antiquity 5 (Leiden: E.J. Brill, 1974), who holds that one must differentiate between the two different types of *ḥaṭṭā't* (pp. 101–14).

That the time of ordinations was later fixed seems to me likely on the basis of Ezek. 45:19-20, on which see below p. 56.

tion purged the outer altar. Thus we may conclude: *Sanctuary and sancta indeed reflected the state of the people's sinfulness precisely because the uncleannesses that the former accrued were not removed at every* ḥaṭṭā't *offering.*

SUMMARY AND CONCLUSION

Priestly self-aggrandizement? Despite the unquestionably lofty and deeply ethical requirements of holiness in the priestly writings, some scholars have underlined how self-serving the priestly theology of holiness was to the priests as a class.[62] The issue of the real or possible self-centeredness of the biblical authors is not insignificant and may be addressed in the context of another important issue raised above.

The Effect of the Anthropocentrism of the Social Sciences on the Authority of Scripture. It has been argued above that the observations from the phenomenology of religion (Rudolph Otto), the history of religions (Mircea Eliade), and the anthropology of religion (Mary Douglas, Edmund Leach, and Arnold van Gennep) all are an indispensable aid to the student of holiness in the Bible in that they point out aspects of the biblical phenomenon that might otherwise have been bypassed or overlooked. The social sciences and the academic study of religion thus enhance the breadth and depth of biblical scholarship. All of the aforementioned disciplines, however, are people-centered, that is, anthropocentric, in that their main points of inquiry pertain to human beings. Jon D. Levenson has leveled a trenchant attack on the

---

62. See F. J. Leenhardt, *La Notion de Sainteté dans l'Ancien Testament: Étude de la Racine QDhSh* (Paris: Libraire Fischbacher, 1929), 228. Leenhardt argued that the sacerdotal conception in effect was that holiness constituted a priestly privilege. Indeed, the clergy depended:—in Israel as elsewhere—on the "fiction" of a reserved zone into which the people could not penetrate without danger. It also had to depend on the fiction of actions that the priests alone knew and that they alone were capable of performing as required. Thus the clergy sought to develop the notion of separation, isolation, and exclusivity in the idea of holiness. The holy object which was originally the divine object could not be given to all, but only to the specialists. It would constitute a danger for others. In this fashion the holy became a priestly prerogative and the clergy were charged with the administration of holy objects. As in the affair of Korah (Numbers 16), this privilege came to be contested (Leenhardt, *Notion de Sainteté dans l'Ancien Testament*, 228–29).

kind of anthropocentrism found in historical criticism such as that practiced by Julius Wellhausen.[63] By continuously analyzing the Scripture as the product of self-centered people bent on self-legitimation, he argued, scholars can render the Bible a travesty which fails to see in it revelation and which refuses to accept the occasional arbitrariness of the divine sovereign because of its own passion for social egalitarianism. Thus Levenson holds that uncritical support cannot be given to uncritical social analyses.[64]

The stance of appropriation of the biblical tradition with guarded self-criticism is not a new stance but one for which there rests clear, biblical precedent, The priests, as we have seen, had a strong doctrine of sin, and the prophets, to whom we turn in chapter 3, were fearless in pointing out self-centeredness wherever they saw it. Modern-day religionists who look to the Scripture as an inspired source of authority do both the Scriptures and its human authors a serious disservice if they hesitate to touch upon or investigate the topic of self-centeredness among the biblical authors themselves. If that were the only topic investigated, of course, the disservice would be equally plain. In sum, we conclude that a consideration of the social sciences, the history of religion, and religious institutions should not be overlooked on the basis of sound theological, biblical, and academic grounds. Biblical authority will neither be attenuated nor com-

63. Jon D. Levenson, *Theology of the Program of Restoration of Ezekiel 40—48*, ed. Frank Moore Cross, Jr., HSM 10 (Missoula, Mont.: Scholars Press, 1976).

64. Levenson's point is well taken but, in my judgment, requires qualification. I submit that biblical scholarship should seek to avoid not one but two extremes: (1) anthropocentrism and sociological determinism, which exclude the operation of grace and faith in human affairs, and (2) an arbitrary and authoritarian biblicism which ignores the social sciences and other academic studies of religion as if the Almighty did not work at all in and through human motivations and drives. The more satisfactory course for research into religious matters will allow that at times the Almighty may work in concert with specific human self-interests and at other times contrary to them. Levenson is surely right: to read the Bible *solely* as a document of egocentric human beings in search of self-legitimation would constitute a cynical surrender to anthropocentrism. To show little or no interest in evidence of social struggle within and among the authors of Scripture, however, would be equally unfortunate and fall into the trap of a blind and naive fideism. A solid biblical doctrine of sin alone necessitates taking the social sciences and ancillary disciplines seriously but not as absolutes whose presuppositions should remain unexamined.

promised by the aforementioned academic disciplines but only enhanced inasmuch as precisely these disciplines may serve as heady reminders within a context of a self-critical theism that those who approach the Lord are human also and may approach presumptuously and from self-centered motives.[65]

The Priestly Vision. The priestly theology of holiness can be summarized by the twin notions of separation and purity. As the realms of air, water, and dry land were separated and each realm had placed in it various living creatures, so the priestly mentality sought to think through the question of cleanness in accordance with the principle of separation: only those animals were pronounced clean for eating which conformed to appropriate form and means of locomotion in each realm. Thus too, the notion of separation carried over to priestly thinking about holy place (sanctuary), holy times (sabbath, rites of passage, and holy convocations), holy persons (nation, priests, and Levites). Just as there were separate realms at creation, so there were separate realms in the sanctuary which the non-Israelite, the nonpriestly, and those who were not high priests could not enter. The priestly regulation allowed for the ordination only of males, but it should not be overlooked that the priestly vision posited a parity of male and female (Gen. 1:27) that clearly furnishes the foundation for a parity in ordination today.

A restoration of purity and separation from uncleanness is what the sacrificial system—and in particular the so-called "sin offerings"—sought to restore. The priests thus had an extremely high doctrine of sin and posited that sin had a dual effect of

---

65. The religious philosopher Nicolas Berdyaev succinctly expressed an aspect of the problem we have sought to examine in the above section when he observed that "religion tends to objectify itself in the social structure" (*Solitude and Society*, trans. George Reavey [London: Geoffrey Bles, 1947; first printed 1938], 4). He continued by inquiring into the conflict between cognitive discovery and what is demonstrated by religion: "But actually this conflict can take place and put the philosopher in a tragic dilemma, for, as a believer, he may be prepared to accept revelation. We must rather seek the explanation in the complex nature of religion as a social phenomenon, in the fact that Divine Revelation, which is the pure and original essence of religion, becomes adulterated by the immediate reactions of the human community in which it takes place, and by the way which men make use of it to further their own interests. This fact enables us to consider religion from the sociological standpoint" (ibid.).

defiling both sanctuary and people. It was our contention that the ceremonies of the Day of Atonement focused on purging the inner sanctuary and incense altar and that the seven-day-long ceremonies at ordinations focused on purging the outer altar. Underlying the priestly system of holiness was thus a vision of a creator, ordering God, transcendent and majestic in holiness, who required of his people an inner integrity (Gen. 17:1), humanitarian conduct (Leviticus 19), as well as the maintenance of a ritualistic purity. Failures in the first two regards led to personal uncleanness and defilement of the sanctuary. Both had to be dealt with via ritual, but both were deeply rooted in a world view that unflinchingly affirmed that the holiness of God requires a highly ordered and just conduct with one's fellow human beings as well as a scrupulous maintenance of personal purity. How this basic priestly vision of holiness and its requirements was both reaffirmed and modified by a prophet-priest and subsequent priests and historians who appropriated this priestly tradition is the subject to which we turn in the following chapter.

CHAPTER 2

Variations on the Priestly Understanding of Holiness

(Ezekiel, his Successors, and the Chronistic Work of History)

In this chapter attention will be focused on further developments and refinements of the priestly theology of holiness in the prophet-priest, Ezekiel, his successors, and in the Chronistic Work of History. Through an examination of first Ezekiel's utterances on history, the divine name, his visions, and the requirements of holiness we will initiate our survey of the permutations of the priestly understanding of holiness.

EZEKIEL—THEOLOGIAN OF THE HOLINESS OF GOD

Ezekiel evolved his doctrine of holiness with the consciousness, and in the manner, of a theologian. A theologian is one who thinks out the meaning of faith in a logical, consistent, coherent, and systematic fashion. Of all the authors in the Hebrew Bible Ezekiel above all merits this title. In a refrain that occurs in the book no fewer than sixty-three times, Ezekiel sets forth how God acts "so that you (they) may know that I am the LORD." The sovereign God of Ezekiel acts in response to the acts of humans; after human infidelity and immoral deeds, God judges; even though the divine wrath is aroused, God repents and acts mercifully—frequently "for my name's sake." Whatever God does, however, is done not out of an abstract desire to satisfy the demands of his name; he judges, he spares, he punishes, he delivers so that humans may know that he is the Lord in his sovereignty, holiness, mystery, and majesty.

Holiness in History. The pattern of Ezekiel's theology of history is expounded most clearly in chapter 20. The opening part of the chapter (vv. 1–26) comes from the prophet-priest himself; the latter part (vv. 27–44) from his successors.[1] *Phase one*: God promises to deliver Israel if she forsakes idols; Israel disobeys, but God nonetheless delivers her "for my name's sake, that it might not be profaned before the eyes of the nations" (vv. 5–10).[2] *Phase two*: Statutes and laws are given to Israel, and the sabbaths as a sign "so that they might know that I—I the LORD—sanctify them," but Israel rebelled, and neither followed the laws nor kept the sabbaths holy; this evoked God's wrath, but he acted "for my name's sake, that I might not be profaned before the eyes of the nations" and accordingly resolved that he would not bring them into the land that he had given them (!)(vv. 11–17). *Phase three*: To the second generation in the wilderness God reiterated the appeal to Israel not to make themselves unclean with idols, and to keep the sabbaths holy "that you may know that I—I the LORD—am your God," but this generation too rebelled; God once again acted "for my name's sake, that it might not be profaned before the eyes of the nations," and resolved to scatter them among the nations; he gave them bad statutes and laws and made them unclean through the offering of the firstborn (vv. 18–26).

Several observations may be made about this highly creative theology of history. (1) The conduct of Israel in the wilderness is given as the reason why Israel would not enter the land. Ezekiel thus does not count the first settlement as any real settlement at all. The entry into the holy land lies ahead in the future. (2) Ezekiel shows that he—like the authors of Deuteronomy—is a

---

1. In this judgment I follow Gerhard von Rad, *Old Testament Theology*, vol. 2, *The Theology of Israel's Prophetic Traditions*, trans. D. M. G. Stalker (Edinburgh: Oliver & Boyd, 1965), 226. I do not follow von Rad, however, in his analysis of four stages of history. It seems to me plain that only three are described.

2. This translation and the others in this paragraph are taken from Walther Zimmerli, *Ezekiel 1: A Commentary on the Book of the Prophet Ezekiel, Chapters 1–24*, trans. Ronald E. Clements (Philadelphia: Fortress Press, 1979). Where Clements's rendering has "Yahweh," I have used instead "the LORD."

theologian of the divine name. The name is vulnerable; subject to profanation among the nations. (3) This theology of history is suffused with a priestly outlook. The sabbaths were given by God as a sign so that Israel might know who it was who was consecrating her, setting her apart (vv. 12, 20). Yet Israel profaned the Lord's sabbaths (vv. 13, 16, 21, 24). Israel's sins also included idolatry, rebellion, and failure to keep the law (vv. 8, 13, 16, 21, 24). (4) Some of the bad laws in Israel, the prophet-priest said, were instituted at the behest of God, by way of punishment (v. 25).

The Divine Name. Ezekiel's theology of the divine name is developed by himself and his successors. At some point during the exile, when speaking in behalf of God, he took to referring not simply to "my name" or "for my name's sake," but to "my holy name" and "for the sake of my holy name" (Ezek. 36:21, 22)— and this practice was continued either in his own supplements to his own work or in those of his school (Ezek. 20:39; 39:7 [*bis*], 25; 43:7, 8). In the course of this transition, the accent shifts so as to include not only the divine immanence and vulnerability (in the name) but also the divine transcendence (in its holiness).[3] In any event, the term "my holy name" epitomizes the theology not only of Ezekiel but in a sense of the entire Old Testament. For the God of Israel is at once majestic and transcendent, immanent and accessible, vital and personal.

The fullest theological discussion in the Book of Ezekiel on the holiness of God and "my holy name" is to be found in Ezek. 36:16–38. Because vv. 23b–38 are not found in the Greek Codex 967, scholars have been inclined to conclude that these verses, in any event, come from one of Ezekiel's school. In vv. 16–23a, which by wide agreement come from the hand of the prophet, the same pattern of divine action is seen as was noted above in

---

3. For further discussion on the suffering and vulnerability of God, see Terence E. Fretheim's perceptive analyses in *The Suffering of God: An Old Testament Perspective*, OBT (Philadelphia Fortress Press, 1984), *passim*, and with particular reference to Ezekiel, 131–32. For a convincing demonstration that the theology of the Old Testament (Hebrew Bible) is one that accents both the transcendence and immanence of God, see Th. C. Vriezen, *An Outline of Old Testament Theology*, trans. S. Neuijen (Oxford: Basil Blackwell, 1962; first published in Holland, 1949; 2d ed., 1954), 148–98.

chapter 20. Israel's conduct had defiled the holy name of God
and God resolved upon the exile (vv. 16–19). But the very presence of Israel among the nations as exiles caused the nations to
profane the holy name when they mockingly said, "These are the
people of the LORD, and yet they had to go out of his land" (v.
20, RSV). God therefore resolved to act (in deliverance) not for
the sake of Israel, but for the sake of his holy name. "And I will
sanctify my great (*sic*) name which has been profaned among the
nations and which you have profaned in their midst" (Ezek.
36:23a, au. trans.). In the verses that follow the details of the
promise and resolve already stated are filled in: God will gather
Israel from among the nations, cleanse her from all her uncleannesses caused by idolatry, put a new spirit within her, cause her
to walk in his statutes, and take away from her all famine. The
message if redolent with promise and hope, and — true to Ezekiel—cast in priestly terms. Walther Zimmerli has pointed out
that the promises in Ezek. 36:16–38 are comparable in many
respects to those of Jer. 31:31–34.[4]

Visions of Glory/Holiness. In addition to Ezekiel's analyses of
the divine motivations for actions in history, in yet another
regard Ezekiel shows himself to be both theologian and theologian of holiness. Perhaps not Ezekiel himself, but one of his
school has drawn out how much the teaching of the prophet-
priest centered on visions of the glory of the Lord. In Ezek. 43:1–
5 reference is made to Ezekiel's three visions of glory: (1) the
vision of the departure of the glory of God from Jerusalem; (2)
the vision of the arrival of the glory of the Lord in exile in
Babylonia; and (3) the vision of the return of the glory of the Lord
to Jerusalem by the east gate and into the temple. Moshe Greenberg has convincingly demonstrated the importance of these
verses in furnishing the interpreter with an insight into the theology of the prophet and the organization of the book.[5] The depar-

4. Walther Zimmerli, *Ezekiel 2: A Commentary on the Book of the Prophet
Ezekiel 25–48,* trans. James D. Martin (Philadelphia: Fortress Press, 1983),
249. Zimmerli also points out (pp. 245–46) how Deutero-Isaiah also deals with
precisely the same issue of "the justification of Yahweh's new act of mercy
toward Israel" (cf. Isa. 44:26, 28; 49:17; 54:1–3).
5. Moshe Greenberg, "The Vision of Jerusalem in Ezekiel 8–11: A Holistic

ture of the glory of the Lord from Jerusalem is described in chapters 8–11; its arrival in Babylonia in chapters 1–3; and the return of the glory to the holy mountain is described in chapters 40–48. It may be recalled that in the introduction to this book we showed how the glory (*kābôd*) of the Lord belongs precisely to the aspect of holiness that Rudolph Otto designated as *maiestas*, "majesty." Thus the vision that is the basis of the inspiration for Ezekiel's priestly prophecy (chapters 1–3), his vision of the return of God to Jerusalem (expanded by his school in chapters 40–48), and his vision of the initial departure of the divine glory from Jerusalem (chapters 8–11) are visions of holiness.

That holiness is involved in all its fullness is apparent from even a cursory glance at Ezekiel's vision by the river Chebar. In the flashes of lightning, thunder, effortless movement, wheels of the chariots, and storm of chapters 1–3 we see also very clearly the divine *energicum*, "energy." The divine *maiestas* is evident not only in the glory, brightness, and gleaming but in the throne above the firmament on which sat one like a man. The four faces of the living creatures of man, lion, ox, and eagle were reminiscent of the composite beasts of the ancient Near East associated with the protection and power of royalty. The eyes within the wheels, of course, are symbolic of the divine omniscience and thus of that element of *fascinans* and wonder that struck the sages. The whole vision thus described as "the appearance of the glory of the Lord" (Ezek. 1:28) portrays the divine *mysterium* and the *tremendum* that humans invariably feel when in the presence of holiness: "And when I saw it, I fell upon my face" (Ezek. 1:28).

The Requirements of Divine Holiness

Not only was Ezekiel a priestly prophet and theologian of the divine holiness, he was also a pastor and superb moral theologian. His homilies of divine judgment on the unfaithful shepherds (chap. 34) and of divine hope for the exiles who considered

Interpretation," in *The Divine Helmsman*, Essays in Honor of Lou Silberman, ed. James L. Crenshaw and Samuel Sandmel, (New York, Ktav, 1980), 143–64.

themselves as dead as dry bones in a dry valley (chap. 37) certainly rank among the best-known homilies from all of Scripture. Ezekiel spoke with the eye of a pastor to the needs of those in exile. A similar pastoral concern is reflected in the famous chapter 18 (see also 33:10–20). In this chapter Ezekiel leads the way in challenging and breaking the sense of corporate guilt. By citing examples of a father, son, and grandson, the prophet shows that each individual will be judged by God not on the basis of the good deeds or sins of the previous generation, but on the basis of its own doings. To the exiles, the message was thus plain: the sins of the fathers (for which a judgment has already fallen) do not continue to fall upon the present generation. The choice is open for you to choose—whether the pathway leads to life or death. Thus spoke the pastor. It is less commonly recognized that in vv. 5–9, 10–13, and 14–18. Ezekiel also sets forth the outlines for a moral theology that may justifiably be called a theology of the ethical requirements of holiness.[6]

Ezekiel 18 should be ranked among those passages of the Old Testament that receive special attention in a course on biblical ethics.[7] The fact that Ezekiel may be drawing upon older tradition in his exposition of what is required before one can be declared righteous and thus to enter life (Ezek. 18:9) does not seem to me to detract from the importance of these requirements, but rather to enhance their significance. The commentators point to the similarities between the prohibitions and acts commended in Ezekiel 18 and the prohibitions and acts commended in "the gate liturgies."[8] The similarities suggest that he

6. (1) Of the fourteen or fifteen acts enjoined in Ezek. 18:5–9, etc., a number of them are identical to or similar to those stipulated in Psalm 15 as requisite for the one who would ascend to the holy hill. (2) In the context of the whole book which so stresses the divine holiness, as we have seen above, it is quite legitimate to understand the moral actions enjoined in chap. 18 to be the requirements of holiness.

7. Other passages that I believe should receive special attention are: Leviticus 19, Deuteronomy 5; Psalms 15, 24, 50, 51; Job 31; Jeremiah 10; Amos 5; Sirach 2.

8. Zimmerli, *Ezekiel 1*, 276. On the possible use of Psalms 15 and 24 as Torah Entrance liturgies, see the discussion above at the outset of chapter 3 in this volume.

may be drawing upon the rich tradition of these gate liturgies or Torah Entrance liturgies, as they also have been called. In any event, in the requirements as Ezekiel articulates them, for a man to be a *ṣaddîq*, a just one, he must:

(1) do justice and righteousness;
(2) not eat (in the ceremonies of a foreign god) upon the mountains;
(3) not lift up one's eyes to the idols of the house of Israel;
(4) not approach a neighbor's wife;
(5) not approach a woman in the time of her impurity;
(6) not oppress anyone;
(7) restore to the debtor his pledge;
(8) commit no robbery;
(9) give bread to the hungry;
(10) cover the naked with a garment;
(11) not lend at interest or take any increase;
(12) withhold one's hand from iniquity;
(13) render true judgments between persons;
(14) walk according to the divine ordinances;
(15) keep the statutes so as to act with integrity.[9]

Several comments may be made about this list of the requirements of holiness. (1) Note its similarity to the requirements found in Job 31 (items 3, 4, 9, and 10), in the Decalogue (items 3, 4, and 8; cf. also item 15), in Psalm 15 (items 1, 6, 11, and 15), and in Matt. 25:31–46 (items 9 and 10). (2) There is the typical priestly and Ezekielian admixture of concerns (blood taboo, humanitarianism, fidelity to the Torah, and encouragement of inner integrity). (3) As with the recital of potential offenses to which Job is led when he becomes aware that he is in the presence of holiness (Job 31), so here there is a depth of ethical requirement that pertains not only to outward action but includes also the handling of one's eyes (item 3) and the very manner of one's acting (15). Item 15 reads in full: "He will walk in my statutes and preserve justice by acting truthfully" (*la 'ĕśôt 'ĕmet*: Ezek. 18:9, au. trans.).

---

9. The paraphrasing from Ezek. 18:5–9 is mine.

THE SUCCESSORS OF EZEKIEL

THE GROWTH OF EZEKIEL 40—48

A number of fairly persuasive form-critical studies have appeared since the midcentury mark to demonstrate that the Book of Ezekiel has undergone considerable supplementation.[10] For the sake chiefly of convenience, our discussion on the school or successors of Ezekiel will focus mainly on chapters 40–48. Careful theological study such as is found in the monograph of Jon Levenson on Ezekiel 40–48[11] will seek to take into account the most significant, if not all, of the various redactional layers. To an extent that same attempt to make theological assessments on the basis of literary analysis will be followed here. The following, however, should be kept in mind: quite a few scholars acknowledge that some of the supplementations, at least, may very well have come from the mouth if not the hand of the prophet-priest.[12]

THE OCCASION FOR EZEKIEL 40—48.

At least in part the decision of the exegete of the biblical books must rest not only on literary analysis but also on a glance at the external (sociopolitical, economic, and historical) circumstances of the biblical writers. To an extent, the studies of Gese, Zimmerli, Hossfeld, Fishbane, Talmon, and Levenson, alluded to above, do devote attention to the question: What external cir-

---

10. See esp. Hartmut Gese, *Der Verfassungsentwurf des Ezechiel (Kap. 40–48) traditionsgeschichtlich untersucht* (Tübingen: J. C. B. Mohr [Paul Siebeck], 1957); Zimmerli, *Ezekiel 1*; idem, *Ezekiel 2*; Frank-Lothar Hossfeld, "Untersuchungen zu Komposition und Theologies des Ezechielbuches" (Diss., University of Regensburg, 1976); and Michael Fishbane and S. Talmon, "The Structuring of Biblical Books: Studies in the Book of Ezekiel," *Annual of the Swedish Institute of Theology* 10 (1976):129–53.

11. Jon Douglas Levenson, *Theology of the Program of Restoration of Ezekiel 40–48*, ed. Frank Moore Cross, Jr., HSM 10 (Missoula, Mont.: Scholars Press, 1976).

12. Zimmerli (in *Ezekiel 2*, 462, 547–53) understands the basic vision of Ezekiel 40—48, found in Ezek. 40:1–37, 47–49; 41:1–4, dated, according to the reckoning of the book itself, to ca. 573 B.C.E. Of secondary strata, the most significant for our purposes is the postexilic, Zadokite stratum—celebrated for its championing of the superior place of the sons of Zadok among the descendants of Levi, whereas the Levites in turn are relegated to a secondary and subservient status (Ezek. 44:6–31).

cumstances do the various redactional layers of the book reflect? Levenson makes the point—a good one—that the theology of Ezekiel 40—48 shows not simply an ideal and idealistic interest in the future, but also a very practical one.[13] It is not amiss to ask, When would the assemblage of plans such as are found in Ezekiel 40—48, for example, of the rebuilding of the temple, have been likely to have been put together? Details of the temple measurements are given (Ezekiel 40—42), but there is a relative absence of descriptions of what would be sacrificed. It is urged that the prince should provide offerings and rule justly (Ezek. 45:9–25) but *no* mention of the high priest is to be found in any of the nine chapters! Details are lacking in descriptions of the *sanctum* (holy place) and *sanctum sanctorum* (holy of holies) but details are abundant insofar as the external architectural features such as steps and gates are concerned. All of the above suggest that the *external* occasion and stimulus for the gathering together of Ezekiel 40—48 may well have come from the Persian bureaucracy and governmental pressure to show the need and plan for imperial assistance in rebuilding in the provinces.[14]

If such indeed was the occasion for the final gathering together of the Ezekielian traditions of Ezekiel 40—48, a different light is thrown on two perplexing issues in these chapters: (1) the absence of the use of the term *melek* (king) but use instead of *nāśî'* (prince)[15] and (2) the absence of any reference to the high priest.

---

13. Levenson, *Theology of the Program of Restoration of Ezekiel 40–48*, 45.

14. From the Book of Ezra we gather that even though Cyrus may have issued a decree ordering the rebuilding of the temple in Jerusalem, it was not until the reign of Darius (ca. 522–486 B.C.E.) that activity toward that end began in earnest (Ezra 5—6). Further, we know from the Persian records and the historian Herodotus of Darius's bureaucratic program of gathering together indigenous laws and customs. See, e.g., Herodotus, *The Histories* 3.38, 89, trans. Aubrey de Sélincourt (Harmondsworth: Penguin Books, 1975; first published 1954), 219-20, 242-43; and esp. A. T. Olmstead, *History of the Persian Empire* (Chicago: University of Chicago Press, 1963; first published 1948), 119-34.

The notion of the external occasion for Ezekiel 40—48 going back to the legal activity of Darius the Great and his assemblage of native statements of law was first expressed to me more than a decade ago by S. Dean McBride, Jr.

15. Quite apart from the Persian context, Levenson, *Theology of the Program of Restoration of Ezekiel 40-48*, 44-107, argues that both the title and description of the prince's duties carry sharp criticisms of the conduct of Judah's previous kings.

Perhaps the major impact of the above observations on reflection on the theology of holiness in Ezekiel 40—48 is that then, as now, the articulating of a religious community's aspirations by one of its spokespersons must consciously take into account the effect of that articulation upon the ruling political structure in general and upon concerned governmental officials in particular.

THE THEOLOGY OF HOLINESS IN EZEKIEL 40—48

THEOLOGY OF GLORY

A number of years ago Bengel referred to glory as "holiness uncovered" (*die aufgedeckte Heiligkeit*).[16] In Ezekiel 40—48 the vision of the return of glory to the temple in Jerusalem may be described as holiness unveiled. We have already noted above how glory is a central theme, binding the various parts of the Book of Ezekiel together. In Ezekiel 40—48 there is perhaps not the same intensity, awesomeness, or grandeur to the depictions of glory in comparison with those found in the opening chapters of the book, for the authors are no longer describing the appearance of glory to an individual in exile, but rather the cultic and community requirements for a religious community upon the return of glory to its most sacred mountain (Ezek. 43:1–12). Levenson has shown that we may see in this program of restoration "an attempt to realize the promise of Eden without cancelling the divine singling-out of Zion and David" (cf. Ezek. 40:2) and that "Zion has become the locus of revelation, for it, not Sinai, is now the place of theophany."[17] The numinous aspects of glory noted above for Ezekiel obtain here also. The added dimension is the eschatological to which reference will be made below.

THEOLOGY OF NAME.

Not only glory, but the divine holy name is given a prominence in the theological heart of these chapters (Ezek. 43:1–12). Quite apart from the references to "my holy name" (vv. 7, 8), there is an immanental, accessible, and even anthropomorphic aspect in the

---

16. Cited by Edmond Jacob, *Theology of the Old Testament*, trans. Arthur W. Heathcote and Philip J. Allcock (London: Hodder & Stoughton, 1958), 79–80.
17. Levenson, *Theology of the Program of Restoration of Ezekiel 40–48*, 33, 41.

words the prophet is given to hear from God: "Son of man, this is the place of my throne and the place of the soles of my feet, where I will dwell in the midst of the people of Israel forever" (Ezek. 43:7a). Reference is made to Israel's having "rendered impure" (*ṭm'* piel) God's holy name (vv. 7, 8), whereas earlier in the book the reference is to Israel's having "defiled" (*ḥll*) the holy name (Ezek. 20:39; 36:21, 22). Too much should not be made out of the shift, for as we noted above, there is evidence that each of the three aforementioned verses may well come from one of Ezekiel's successors. Apart from a probable gloss in Amos 2:7, the only other place in the Old Testament where the phrase "defile (*ḥll*) my holy name" is found is in the Holiness Code (Lev. 20:3; 22:2, 32). If conclusions are to be drawn on the basis of these striking similarities, they would move in the direction of establishing a relationship between one of the successors of Ezekiel and the group that produced the Holiness Code.

What defiles or renders impure the holy name is of interest. In Ezek. 43:7–9 it is the "memorials" (so Zimmerli) or "effigies" (NEB alt. reading) of their kings, their harlotry (i.e., idolatry), the too-close proximity of the king's palace to the temple complex, and the abominations they committed, which caused defilement. In the course of Ezekiel 8—10 explicit mention is not made of the "memorials," but mention is made of the abomination of idolatry (Ezek. 8:10). In Ezek. 20:39 the offering of idolatrous gifts defiled the holy name. In Leviticus child sacrifice to Molech (Lev. 20:3) or mishandling the gifts of the people (Lev. 22:2) defiled the holy name. Thus in theological teaching as well as in vocabulary there is a remarkable affinity between the authors of Ezekiel 40—48 and the authors of the Holiness Code.

THEOLOGY OF THE CULTUS

In contrast to the priestly code of the pentateuch, Ezekiel 40—48 contains some surprising omissions: no mention is made of the high priest, the ark, the incense altar (located in the *sanctum*), the details of cultic dress, or the details of the sacrificial acts. Insofar as the cultus is concerned—and matters that pertain to it—the following is an outline of the requirements upon the return of glory to the holy mount:

(1) rebuild the temple along new lines (chaps. 40–42);

(2) remove the "memorials" or "effigies" of kings from the temple (43:7–8);

(3) eliminate the office of high priest (?);

(4) admit no foreigners into the sanctuary (44:6–9);

(5) demote the Levites (44:10–14);

(6) elevate the Zadokites whose conduct has been exemplary (44:15–27);

(7) conduct social reforms (45:9–12);

(8) let the people bring sacrifices for the prince to offer (45:13–17);

(9) cleanse the sanctuary (45:18–20);

(10) keep the Passover (45:21–25);

(11) carefully guard the holiness of the inner temple chambers (44:19; 46:19);

(12) divide the land and apportion it to the tribes, prince, and Zadokites—with the temple in the center (chap. 48).

Several of the ways in which Ezekiel 40—48 complements, supplements, or diverges from what is known from the pentateuchal, priestly legislation may be noted. (1) *Specification of the day for purification of the outer altar (for burnt offerings).* As we observed in chapter one, the priestly code stipulates that the seven-day-long series of offerings at the time of an ordination will render the outer altar "most holy" (Exod. 29:1–37).[18] In Ezekiel, a seven-day purification of the sanctuary which focuses on the outer altar (and is confined to the inner court) is specified to begin on the first day of the first month (Ezek. 45:18–20). This passage in Ezekiel does not specify that this regulation should govern the time of ordinations, but the fact that in both passages a young bull (*par*) is commanded to be offered for seven days running does lend support to this suggestion. It will be recalled that nowhere in the priestly legislation is it stipulated when the seven days of ordination sacrifices should begin. (2) *The changing of vestments.* There is a correspondence in attitude between Ezekiel 40—48 and the priestly traditions with respect to the changing of the priestly vestments upon entry into and leaving

18. See the discussion above on pp. 38–40.

the sacred precincts. For Ezekiel, however, they must be changed upon entry into (and leaving) the inner court (Ezek. 44:17–19), whereas for the priestly traditions the place specified is the *sanctum*, that is, the holy place of the tent of meeting (Leviticus 16). The reason given in Ezekiel appears also to be very much in accord with the Priestly Code: "lest they communicate holiness to the people with their garments" (Ezek. 44:19; cf. Lev. 16:23). (3) *The sanctity of space.* Similarly, there is a correspondence in the differentiation of degrees of sanctity of space. The regulations of Ezekiel 40—48, however, are stricter and harsher. (*a*) Treatment of the foreigner. According to Ezekiel 40—48, no uncircumcised foreigner (*ben nēkār*) is permitted into the sanctuary at all (Ezek. 44:6–9). This regulation is certainly in accord with that of the priestly material in Exodus, where it is also explicitly stated that the uncircumcised foreigner (*ben nēkār*) shall not partake of the Passover—although the circumcised foreigner may (Exod. 12:43–49). (*b*) Treatment of laity. No laity may be permitted into the inner court (cf. Ezek. 44:17–19; 46:20). (*c*) Treatment of Levites. The Levites will be permitted to come into the inner court, but not into the temple itself, nor will they be permitted to serve as priests; rather, they shall serve as gatekeepers and as sacral butchers for the burnt offerings (Ezek. 44:10–14). (4) *Priestly marriage.* In the Ezekielian regulations a priest may marry a widow of a priest (Ezek. 44:22). This may be contrasted with Leviticus 21 where no such allowance is made. (5) *Priestly use of wine.* Wine is expressly proscribed for priests who enter the inner court (Ezek. 44:21). This regulation is comparable to that found in the Priestly Code (Lev. 10:8–9). (6) *Priestly sashes.* In the traditions of Ezekiel 40—48, the priests are forbidden to wear a "girdle" so as to sweat (Ezek. 44:18); thus, belts or sashes would seem to have been proscribed, whereas in the Priestly Code sashes were prescribed (Exod. 28:40).

THEOLOGY AND ETHICS

Just as in the Holiness Code (Leviticus 19) and in the work of Ezekiel himself (Ezekiel 18) there is the highest code of ethics, so there is in Ezekiel 40—48. There is also a close relationship drawn between holiness and morally upright conduct. Idolatries and unfaithfulness (*zĕnût*) defile God's holy name (Ezek. 43:7). The people must keep the Lord's sabbaths holy (Ezek. 44:24). Scales shall be honest; measurements just and accurate; the people are enjoined to put away violence and plunder, to do justice and righteousness and to cease evictions (Ezek. 45:9–12). To be sure, the moral aspect is not spelled out as fully in the Ezekielian program of restoration as it is, for example, in Ezekiel 18, but the items singled out for mention pertain to the social, economic, and cultic conduct. In Ezekiel 40—48, as with the prophet's original prophecy, holiness requires the purity of individual moral conduct and social justice.

HOLINESS AND ESCHATOLOGY

As is well known, the Ezekiel of the program of restoration sees a vision of life-giving, fructifying waters flowing out from the temple mount eastward to the Dead Sea, which in turn will become a fisherman's paradise (Ezek. 47:1–12). Aelred Cody writes in his fine commentary in the series Old Testament Message, "The waters flowing from the mountain of God are waters which bring life to a lifeless region."[19] As Cody suggests, homileticians may see in the temple a type of the church and in the waters a type of baptism that by God's grace will bring healing and new life. Many scholars point out that the revivifying vision of Ezekiel 47 corresponds to Ezekiel's earlier vision of the valley of dead bones that arise to life. Holiness revivifies. Surely there is an incipient challenge here to church and synagogue today. The priestly holiness of the followers of Ezekiel allows for an ordering of life—a reordering that differs from older priestly plans (cf. Ezek. 47:13–23 with Numbers 1—10). It would seem that the Scripture is suggesting that it is given to successive generations of priests to have fresh visions of land and life, of glory and holiness. The details may and do change. The constant is the sanctuary—whether tabernacle or temple. The sanctuary is a central place of holiness because it stands in the midst of the city, the name of which henceforth shall be "The LORD is there" (*Yah-*

---

19. Aelred Cody, *Ezekiel*, Old Testament Message 11 (Wilmington, Del.: Michael Glazier, 1984), 247.

weh šāmmâ)[20] for the Lord's glory, once departed, *has* returned—through the east gate (Ezek. 48:35; 43:5).[21]

This chapter opened with a consideration of holiness in history in the prophet-priest, Ezekiel (chap. 20). In turning now to a third major variation in the priestly theology of holiness we encounter an even more remarkable and much fuller presentation of priestly historical writing.

THE CHRONISTIC WORK OF HISTORY

CRITICAL BACKGROUND

Parallel to the Books of Kings stand the Books of Chronicles. The Books of Chronicles—counted as one in the Hebrew reckoning—constitute the last book of twenty-four in the Hebrew Bible. Preceding Chronicles, which in Hebrew is called *dibrê hayyāmîm* (records of days), is Ezra-Nehemiah—also counted as one book. In English translations Ezra and Nehemiah follow the Books of Chronicles and are frequently held to be the last part of the so-called Chronistic Work of History or Chronicler. According to the influential research of Frank Moore Cross the Chronicler's work was put together in three stages, the last of which is to be dated around 400 B.C.E.[22] The grounds of Cross's argument that the second edition of the Chronicler's work included an earlier version (*Vorlage*) of Ezra 1:1—3:13 has been challenged recently—and successfully in my judgment—by H. G. M. Williamson.[23] Through a comparison of the vocabulary and ideology of

20. This name given to the city in Ezek. 48:35 is reminiscent, of course, of the reference found in the Deuteronomistic prayer of Solomon to the temple as "the place of which thou has said, 'My name shall be there'" (1 Kings 8:29). The double alliteration in the name as given by the Deuteronomists makes it certain that the version in 1 Kings 8:29 would be the one that would impress itself most deeply in the popular imagination (*yihyeh šěmî šām*).

21. I have taken much of the above material on the theology of holiness in Ezekiel 40—48 from a paper I delivered before the Catholic Biblical Association at Georgetown University in August 1986. I have recast the paper entirely but have allowed something of the flavor and overtones of the talk to remain.

22. Frank Moore Cross, "A Reconstruction of the Judean Restoration," *Interpretation* 29 (1975):187–203.

23. H. G. M. Williamson, *Israel in the Books of Chronicles* (Cambridge: Cambridge University Press, 1977).

the Books of Chronicles and the Books of Ezra and Nehemiah, Williamson has shown the likelihood that Chronicles was written and circulated separately from Ezra and Nehemiah.[24] Williamson's views appear to be gaining in scholarly favor.[25] Accordingly, for the purposes of our survey of the views of holiness in the Chronistic Work of History, it would seem to be advisable to be sensitive to differences in the Books of Chronicles as over against Ezra and Nehemiah.

THE THEOLOGY OF HOLINESS IN CHRONICLES, EZRA, AND NEHEMIAH

Taken as a whole, these four books relate a "paradigmatic history" of ancient Israel from the perspective of Judah and Jerusalem.[26] 1 and 2 Chronicles stress David's role as founder of the cultus and Ezra-Nehemiah stress the maintenance of proper social separation for the continuance of worship. Both sets of books stress the maintenance of levitical and priestly activities and responsibilities, the primacy of Judah, the holiness of God, and the manner in which the divine brings to pass retribution with respect to kings and rulers who offend against the cultus and law. A closer look at the latter four themes may serve as a convenient means of unfolding the teaching of these books on holiness.

(1) *Relation of the Levites to Holy Rites and Things.* (a) *Chronicles.* The Levites in the Books of Chronicles enjoy a relatively high position. The demotion favored for the Levites in Ezekiel 40—48 (Ezek. 44:10–14) appears to be a thing of the past. Just what happened historically—based upon a close reading of the

---

24. Ibid. See also H. G. M. Williamson, *1 and 2 Chronicles*, New Century Bible Commentary, ed. Ronald E. Clements and Matthew Black (Grand Rapids: Wm. B. Eerdmans, 1982), 2–23. Williamson dates Chronicles at "some point within the fourth century B.C.E." (*Israel in the Books of Chronicles*, 86) and more specifically, "from about the middle of the fourth century B.C." (*1 and 2 Chronicles*, 16).

25. See, e.g., Rolf Rendtorff, *The Old Testament: An Introduction*, trans. John Bowden (Philadelphia: Fortress Press, 1986; first published in German, 1983), 282–83.

26. The meaning of the term "paradigmatic history" and its contrast with "pragmatic history" will be explored in chap. 4 below.

texts—has been analyzed by Cody[27] to have taken place in the following manner. In the postexilic era the genealogical relation of all priests and Levites to Levi, son of Jacob, was emphasized (see esp. 1 Chronicles 6). Thus the status of Levites was reemphasized and restored in comparison to the crass demotion of Ezekiel 40—48. Cody continues:

> The Levites, then, had their victory of principle: all priests would henceforth be "Levites." But the Zadokites had their victory of strategy: most Levites would no longer be priests. And besides the old gentilitial sense of the word "Levite" a new sense stood: that of a function. The gentilitial sense would be overshadowed by the name of function, and in the restored Jewish community "levite" would mean primarily a cultic functionary of subordinate rank.[28]

The Books of Chronicles furnish the key evidence for this ambiguous development. On the one hand, trusted Levites who served as gatekeepers (RSV) or doorkeepers (NEB) were also given charge of the sacred vessels, furniture, and supplies—checking the former in and out very much as quartermasters (1 Chron. 9:26–29); and concerning perhaps the most sacred of vessels[29] David decreed "that only Levites should carry the Ark of God, since they had been chosen by the Lord to carry it and to serve him for ever" (1 Chron. 15:2, NEB). On the other hand, the position of the Levites—perhaps we should read levites (lower case) following Cody—was even higher, namely as assistants to the priests in the purification of the temple (2 Chron. 29:12–19) or in the flaying of the skins of the sacrificed animals (2 Chron. 29:31–36; 35:10–15). Indeed, in the former passage the Levites are praised for having been "more scrupulous than the priests in hallowing themselves" (2 Chron. 29:34) and work side by side with the priests when the task of preparing the offerings became too onerous for the few priests who there were (2 Chron. 29:32–34). In each of these passages, however, it is apparent that the Levites are decidedly secondary to the priests in status. The same

---

27. Aelred Cody, *A History of Old Testament Priesthood*, Analecta Biblica 35 (Rome: Pontifical Biblical Institute, 1969), 156–74.
28. Ibid., 174.
29. The ark is called "the holy ark" in 2 Chron. 35:3.

is also clear in 1 Chron. 9:17–29 (where the levitical duties as doorkeepers and keepers of rooms are described) but it is clearest of all in 1 Chron. 23:25–32, where it is spelled out for the Levites: "Their duty is to help the sons of Aaron in the service of the house of the Lord" (NEB).[30] In short, in the Books of Chronicles the Levites were not excluded from the inner court as they were in the Zadokite stratum of Ezekiel 40—48. From Leviticus 7 we know that the priests were instructed to fling the blood of the slaughtered offerings at the base of the altar for whole burnt offerings, which was located in the inner court. Thus the Levites could not have been understood to have assisted the priests in the task of flaying the sacrificial animals without having entered the court. The same applies, of course, also to the carrying of the ark. No matter whether 1 Chron. 23:25–32 comes from a priestly glossator or not, the Books of Chronicles testify to priestly persistence in the postexilic era to make sure that the Levites did not overstep their bounds with respect to the holiness attaching to the temple and its cultus. (*b*) *Ezra and Nehemiah*. The same basic view of respected subordinancy seems to obtain in both Ezra and Nehemiah. There is no mention of the ark in either of these books, so the handling of the ark is not at issue. When the temple vessels are handed over after the decree of Cyrus, it is not to the Levites that they are handed but to a priest, Meremoth, son of Uriah, "who had with him Eleazar son of Phinehas, and they had with them the Levites, Jozabad son of Jeshua and Noadiah son of Binnui" (Ezra 8:33, NEB). From Neh. 10:39, however, it would seem that for the author of this book the Levites continued to exercise some supervision of the temple vessels. In some places a near parity would seem to obtain. Thus together the priests and Levites move to rebuild the house of the Lord (Ezra 1:5; 3:8; Neh. 7:39–56). Together they purify themselves at the Passover (Ezra 6:20) and at the dedication of the wall of Jerusalem (Neh. 12:27–30). And in the latter passage the two act in concert to purify the people, the gates, and the wall (v. 30). Nonetheless, as a rule, the role of the Levites as musicians and gatekeepers is emphasized

---

30. Williamson believes that these verses come from a "priestly reviser" who was not responsible for the earlier part of the chapter (*1 and 2 Chronicles*, 161–62.

(see, e.g., Ezra 3:10; Neh. 13:22). In the latter capacity the Levites were especially important in preserving the sanctity of the sabbath: "And I ordered the levites who were to purify themselves, upon entering, to guard the gates so as to keep the sabbath day holy" (Neh. 13:22, au. trans.).

(2) *Holy race.* (*a*) *Chronicles.* In no place in any of the sixty-five chapters of the Books of Chronicles is it suggested that priests, Levites, or Israelites should take caution with respect to marriage outside of the race, tribe, or clan.[31] Thus with respect to the important issue of separation that holiness requires for priestly thinkers, as we saw it, for example, in chapter one, holiness does not seem to require for the authors of Chronicles a separation from other peoples in the matter of marriage. (*b*) *Ezra and Nehemiah.* In the last two works of the Chronistic Work of History, however, the situation is quite different. Ezra finds marriages with Canaanites, Hittites, Perizzites, Jebusites, Ammonites, Moabites, Egyptians, and Amorites quite unacceptable (Ezra 9:1) and relates how Ezra superintended the divorce of the chiefs of the priests, the Levites, and all the Israelites from whatever foreign wives they had taken (Ezra 10). In Nehemiah, the lay reader found the marriage of "some Judeans" with "women from Ashdod, Ammon, and Moab," offensive (Neh. 13:23–27). Quite apart from what these divergencies say on the authorship of Ezra and Nehemiah, it is plain that the concern of the author of Ezra to preserve a "holy race" (Ezra 9:2) applies also—though probably to a lesser extent—to the author of Nehemiah.

(3) *The holiness of God.* (*a*) *Chronicles.* The Books of Chronicles as well as the Books of Ezra and Nehemiah contain blessings and prayers. In the Books of Chronicles alone, however, is reference made to God's "holy name" (1 Chron. 16:35) and to God's "holy dwelling place (*mā'ôn*) in the heavens" (2 Chron. 30:27).[32]

31. Williamson lists a number of passages in Chronicles that record and do not censure such marriages (*Israel in the Books of Chronicles*, 61).

32. In 2 Chron. 36:15 the temple is called simply *mě'ônô* ("his dwelling place"). The distinction thus seems to be made between the heavenly temple of God and the earthly. It may also be observed that in 2 Chron. 30:27 as well as in Deut. 26:15 there is the association between the divine holiness and heaven. James L. Kugel has pressed this observation so that he translates *qōdeš* (lit. "holiness") as "Heaven" in Pss. 77:14; 102:20 (*The Idea of Biblical Poetry:*

The prayer of Solomon uttered at the dedication of the temple (2 Chron. 6:12–42) follows the prayer of 1 Kings 8:22–53, as Williamson says, "remarkably closely."[33] In at least one place, however, the Chronicler shows a greater theocentricity with respect to the divine name than the Deuteronomists. In the second reference to the temple as the dwelling place of the divine name, the Chronicler phrases it: "This place of which thou didst promise (lit. say) to place thy name there" (*lāśûm šimkā šām*: 2 Chron. 6:20, au. trans.).[34] The divine response to the prayer shows a characteristic emphasis of the Chronicler: "When Solomon had finished this prayer, fire came down from heaven and consumed the whole-offering and the sacrifices, while the glory of the LORD filled the house" (2 Chron. 7:1, NEB). There is no counterpart in the version in 1 Kings. Thus the Chronicler shows at once a sense of the numinous and of the divine majesty as well as of the wondrous and thaumaturgical. The successive verses round out this picture.

> The priests were unable to enter the house of the LORD because the glory of the LORD had filled it. All the Israelites were watching as the fire came down with the glory of the LORD on the house, and where they stood on the paved court they bowed low to the ground and worshipped and gave thanks to the LORD because he is good, for his love endures for ever. (2 Chron. 7:2–3, NEB)

Perhaps the best example of the wonder-working power of God in the Chronicler is to be found in the description of the battle between King Jeroboam of Israel and King Abijah of Judah. The latter's armies were accompanied by the priests who sounded their trumpets while the men of Judah raised a shout," and when they did so God put Jeroboam and all Israel to rout before Abijah and Judah . . . . five hundred thousand picked Israelites fell in the battle" (2 Chron. 13:14b–15, 17b). The holiness of God for the Chronicler very much includes the Divine Warrior fighting in behalf of a faithful people. In 2 Chron. 20:21–30, it is reported

Parallelism and Its History [New Haven and London: Yale University Press, 1981], 7, 20).

33. Williamson, *1 and 2 Chronicles*, 217.

34. It seems to me that the NEB misses the theocentricity of the Masoretic text in its rendering of the infinitive *śûm* as a passive: "this place of which thou didst say, '*It shall receive* my name.'"

how Jehoshaphat appoints singers (Levites?) to go before the troops; and the invading Ammonites, Moabites, and men of the hill country of Seir (=Edomites!) were deluded thereby, and defeated. "So the dread of God fell upon the rulers of every country, when they heard that the Lord had fought against the enemies of Israel" (2 Chron. 20:29a). The *ḥerem* of the holy war, however, does not seem to have been in effect, for the Chronicler reports an abundance of booty, with no strictures raised against collecting it (2 Chron. 6:25). Thus in another regard there appears to be a relaxation in the Chronicler of the principles of separation required by holiness.[35] (*b*) *Ezra and Nehemiah.* In marked contrast to the Books of Chronicles, the wondrous and wonder-working aspect of the divine is virtually absent from both Ezra and Nehemiah. God is frequently referred to as the "God of heaven" (e.g., Ezra 1:2, 7:12, 24 (*bis*); Neh. 1:4, 5; 2:5, 20) and in a decree of Artaxerxes even the "God of Jerusalem" (Ezra 7:20). In what is probably an early synagogal prayer in Nehemiah 9, a beautiful statement of a high monotheism is to be found. Seven named Levites said:

> Stand up and bless the LORD your God saying: "From everlasting to everlasting thy glorious name is blessed and exalted above all blessing and praise. Thou alone art the LORD; thou hast made heaven, the highest heaven with all its host, the earth and all that is on it, the seas and all that is in them. Thou preservest all of them, and the host of heaven worships thee. Thou art the LORD, the God who chose Abram and brought him out of Ur of the Chaldees." (Neh. 9:5–7, NEB)

The sense of divine transcendence, on the one hand, and exuberant, human doxology, on the other, are not surpassed anywhere in Scripture. It will be noted that the notion of praise of heavenly hosts, so familiar to contemporary churches in the Doxology, is to be found in this prayer. By and large, however, the focus in Ezra and Nehemiah is not on the transcendence or numinous aspects of the deity, but rather upon the religious accomplishments in Jerusalem of two emissaries of Persian benevolence.

---

35. For a delightful treatment of the thaumaturgical dimensions of Chronicles, see W. F. Stinespring, "Eschatology in Chronicles," *JBL* 80 (1961): 209–19.

(4) *Holiness and Retribution.* (*a*) *Chronicles.* Side by side with the Chronicler's belief that not infrequently in Judah's glorious past under David and his faithful successors did God work protective wonders, the belief is also found that—up until the reign of Josiah, in any event—the justice and mercy of God could be seen to be clearly operative. Especially intriguing are three interrelated features in the Chronicler's doctrine of retribution.

(1) *Punishment during the king's lifetime.* Perhaps the most interesting form of this feature is found in the case of Manasseh, who accrued a considerable number of sacral and other offenses (building altars to the host of heaven in the temple courtyard, sacrificing his sons, soothsaying, divination, and sorcery). God brings the army of the king of the Assyrians to Jerusalem, however, to capture Manasseh and carry him away to Babylon, where the king in humility prays to God and in the end is restored to the throne. "And thus Manasseh learnt that the LORD was God" (2 Chron. 33:1–13).[36] Similar punishments in the flesh are mentioned for the pride of even the righteous king, Hezekiah (2 Chron. 32:22–23) and of the less righteous kings Asa and Joram (2 Chron. 16:1–14; 21:12–20). This leads us to the next important aspect of the Chronicler's theology of retribution.

(2) *The role of burials.* If a king's conduct was "mixed" with respect to sacral matters (e.g., Joash, who led in the repairs of the temple but had stoned to death a priest's son for rebuking king and princes for their idolatry) a burial may be recorded, "but not in the burial-place of the kings" (2 Chron. 24:25). In the Chronicler's scheme, however, if the offending king has suffered physically in some fashion—such as did Asa and Jehoram—he may even have been buried in the city of David but "not in the burial-place of the kings" (2 Chron. 16:14; 21:20). These simple notices suggest that *for the Chronicler there was a measure of justice meted out to a king for his sacral and other offenses in the very manner and place in which the king was buried* (cf. also 2 Chron.

36. This event is not recorded in the Books of Kings and has been the source of considerable scholarly debate. Questions of historicity, of course, are always legitimate. In the paradigmatic history of the Chronicler, however, interpreters are best advised to focus on the incontrovertible: in the eyes of the faith of the author a penitent king could be forgiven.

28:1–4, 22–27). In the Chronicler's scheme of retribution, items (1) and (2) go hand in hand.

(3) *The place of mercy.* The Chronicler records—with obvious favor—a number of incidents where mercy is shown by God and humans. His doctrine of retribution is precise but not rigid. There is room for divine grace and human pardon. Thus in the incident that we may call "The Tale of the Good Samaritans," at the prompting of the prophet Oded and some Ephraimite chiefs, the army of northern Israel is persuaded to clothe (out of their own spoils) and send back to Judah the Judean captives whom they had intended to subject to slavery (2 Chron. 28:9–15).[37]

From the reign of Hezekiah comes perhaps the most striking illustration of the flexibility that the Chronicler demonstrates in his doctrine of retribution for sacral offenses.

> But many in the assembly had not hallowed themselves; therefore the Levites had to kill the passover lamb for every one who was unclean, in order to hallow him to the LORD. For a majority of the people, many from Ephraim, Manasseh, Issachar, and Zebulun, had not kept themselves ritually clean, and therefore kept the Passover irregularly. But Hezekiah prayed for them, saying, "May the good LORD grant pardon to every one who makes a practice of seeking guidance of God, the LORD the God of his fathers, even if he has not observed the rules for the purification of the sanctuary." The LORD heard Hezekiah and healed the people. (2 Chron. 30:17–20, NEB)

In this remarkable passage, we see at once a tempering of the priestly requirements of ritual purity with mercy. The divine mercy is also to be seen in an incident recorded after the wondrous deliverance of Jerusalem through the activity of the angel of the Lord: despite Hezekiah's ingratitude and pride, God relents from sending further punishment upon Judah and Jerusalem once Hezekiah had "humbled himself for the pride of his heart" (2 Chron. 32:24–26, RSV). The Chronicler's doctrine of

---

37. The Israelite army demonstrated mercy apparently because of the persuasive theological reasons proferred by the intercessors: (1) God was punishing Judah (2 Chron. 28:9)—as Oded told them; and (2) "We are guilty enough already" (2 Chron. 28:13c)—as the Ephraimite chiefs reminded them. Mention has already been made of the case of Manasseh, who from his chains prayed to God, "and God accepted his petition and heard his supplication" (2 Chron. 33:13a).

retribution is finely tuned but is not so anthropocentric as to exclude the operation of the divine mercy.

(b) *Ezra and Nehemiah.* In the synagogal prayer recorded in Nehemiah 9, a great emphasis is found on the divine compassion (vv. 21, 27, 28, 31). Ezra's prayer in Ezra 9 similarly displays a sense of gratitude for the divine mercy: following mention of the "shameful humiliation at the hands of foreign kings," he continues, "But now, for a brief moment, the LORD our God has been gracious to us, leaving us some survivors and giving us a foothold in his holy place" (vv. 7c–8a). From the human perspective, Nehemiah displays a practical kindness and compassion for the Levites who had not been getting support out of the tithes (Neh. 13:10). Divine and human favor are, however, hardly leitmotifs in either book. Rather than a willingness to see kindness at work in Samaria (see 2 Chron. 28:9–15) or to record past favors shown to the inhabitants of the north (see 2 Chron. 30:17–20), the Books of Ezra and Nehemiah both show a hardening of attitude with respect to Samaria and what their authors chose to remember about the north (Ezra 4; Neh. 2:10, 19-20; 4:1–9; 6:1–14; 13:28–29).

(c) *Worship and festal celebration as a positive reward in both parts of the Chronistic Work of History.* We should not overlook a positive side to the doctrine of retribution in all four of the books we have been examining. Just as in the Books of Chronicles there is great joy in the pan-Israelite celebrations of the Passover under Hezekiah (2 Chronicles 30) and Josiah (2 Chron. 35:1–19), so in the Book of Ezra there is described the joyful celebration of the Passover (Feast of Unleavened Bread) upon the completion of the rebuilding of the temple (Ezra 6:19–22) and in the Book of Nehemiah there is a joyful celebration of the Feast of Tabernacles during which time Ezra reads from the law (Neh. 8:9–18). The description of these joyful events in both sets of books constitutes one of the significant sutures that binds them together and furnishes justification for thinking in terms of a unified whole. Worship and festal celebration in all four books constitutes an important element in the doctrine of retribution. For worship at the temple and joyful celebration are viewed in both sets of books as signs of, as well as means of, receiving the divine favor (see 1 Chronicles 16; 2 Chronicles 6, 13; Ezra 9:5–15; Nehemiah 9).[38]

SUMMARY

The major traditionists considered in this chapter, who carry forward the priestly traditions (Ezekiel, his successors, and the authors of the Chronistic Work of History), remain in remarkable continuity with the normative priestly understanding of holiness outlined in chapter 1. The holiness of God continued to impress itself on the Israelite priestly tradition as requiring the cleanness of ritual accompanied with appropriate sacrifices, sabbath observance, and the implementation of the principle of separation. Three other specific continuities and developments may be mentioned. (1) The priestly conception of the holy name of God in Ezekiel and his successors becomes a theological center for the understanding of history and the actions of God. (2) There is a remarkable continuity between Ezekiel's articulation of the ethical requirements of holiness and the ethical requirements of holiness found in the Holiness Code and psalms which may have served as "entrance liturgies." (3) In both parts of the Chronistic Work of History there was a marked stress on the joyful celebration of holy days.

In the course of the above chapter we also noted in the Chronistic Work of History the following variations from the normative priestly understanding of holiness: (1) a moderate elevation of the position of the Levites as agents of sacrality;[39] (2) a diverse attitude toward separation from foreign wives; (3) a mixed stress on the wonder-working aspect of the holy God; and (4) a doctrine of retribution emphasizing either the divine compassion or the importance of burial place as a measure of divine favor.

We will now set forth the theology of holiness in the prophets according to the same pattern followed in these opening two chapters. Thus in chapter 3 we will describe the main features in the prophetic doctrine of holiness. In focusing chiefly on Isaiah of

38. In the above treatment I have endeavored to make a fresh reading of the texts.
39. This stands, of course, in contrast to the successors of Ezekiel, who had greatly elevated the status of Zadokite priests to the detriment of Levites.

Jerusalem—with less attention being given to the prophets before and to those who most likely continued in a school of Isaiah—we will outline what may be identified as the normative prophetic response to the holiness of God. And then in chapter 4, we will trace some variations on the normative prophetic response in select traditionists (in this case, Jeremiah, select Psalms, and Deuteronomy) as well as in a major piece of historical writing (in this instance, the Deuteronomistic History).

CHAPTER 3

The Prophetic Understanding of Holiness

(Isaiah of Jerusalem, his Predecessors, and Successors)

PROPHETS AND CULT

The prophets of Israel were heirs of the priesthood and cultus—and not least in their conceptions of holiness.[1] This was so from the beginning on down to the great prophets of the eighth century and to the exile. The prophetic indebtedness to the priesthood and priestly conceptions is exemplified by Samuel. Even though the most famous saying attributed to him has a clear anticultic ring about it ("Behold, to obey is better than sacrifice, and to hearken than the fat of rams," 1 Sam. 15:22b), Samuel, according to tradition, received his first training under priestly tutelage at Shiloh (1 Samuel 1—3). Even when Amos, Isaiah, and Micah are sounding out against the cultus with great forcefulness, the very intensity of their opposition and the fervor of their denunciations betray a depth of influence of the cultus on both their own and the national life (Amos 5:21–24; Isa. 1:12–17; Mic.

---

1. The prophetic inheritance of priestly understanding of holiness was shown already by Helmer Ringgren, *The Prophetical Conception of Holiness*, (Uppsala Universitets Årsskrift 12 (Uppsala: A.-B. Lindquist, 1948): "The prophets obviously accepted the cultic notion of holiness, as it is preserved to us in the ritual laws of the Pentateuch" (p. 18). Esp. in the work of Jacob Milgrom the antiquity of the priestly traditions has been shown. See his "Introduction: On the Dating of P and Related Cultic Issues," *Studies in Cultic Theology and Terminology*, Studies in Judaism in Late Antiquity 36 (Leiden: E.J. Brill, 1983), ix–xiii.

6:11-16). For the prophets the holiness of God did not require the cleanness of ritual first and foremost—but it did require cleanness.

A DIVINE DIMENSION RECOGNIZED BUT PREEMPTED

For reasons that are not altogether unclear many modern approaches to the prophets have undervalued the extent to which a theology of holiness impacted on their thought. This is particularly so with respect to Isaiah of Jerusalem. Yet the holiness of God plays a significant role in the theologies of Isaiah of Jerusalem and his successors. The holiness of God was not a fresh discovery for Isaiah nor for those who followed him. Rather, the prophets and disciples alike inherited by way of priesthood, cult-us—and, only later, prophetic proclamation— the concept of God as a holy and glorious sovereign. This indebtedness may be illustrated by a psalm from outside the Psalter that bears a close relationship to the royal psalms. In 1 Sam. 2:1-10, a thanksgiving psalm, there is an almost uncanny anticipation of the prophetic doctrine of holiness. In the Song of Hannah, which may come from as early as the late tenth or ninth century B.C.E.,[2] key elements emerge that will appear later in the prophetic understanding of the divine: (1) God is praised as holy and powerful and as a refuge (v. 2), (2) who gives power to the weak, progeny to the barren, and life to the poor (vv. 3-8), and (3) who will guard the faithful but fight against their adversaries and empower the human king (vv. 9-10). This song furnishes the poetic structure for the Magnificat in the New Testament (Luke 1:46-55) and has parallels in the Psalter—particularly, as noted, in the so-called Royal Psalms (Psalms 2, 20, 21, 72, 89, 101, 110).

Perhaps a major reason for the relative lack of attention given to the holiness of God as a separate and distinct object for inquiry in recent decades is that it has been preempted by other

2. P. Kyle McCarter, *1 Samuel*, Anchor Bible 8 (Garden City, N.Y.: Doubleday & Co., 1980), 113. Sigmund Mowinckel (*Psalmenstudien*, 6 vols. [Amsterdam: Schippers, 1961; first printed 1921-24], 6: 24, n. 1) chided Gunkel for misunderstanding the original cultic tenor (Bestimmung) of this psalm and others like it. For a fine study tracing the theme of the Song of Hannah through the Old Testament, see J. P. M. Walsh, S.J., *The Mighty from Their Thrones: Power in the Biblical Tradition*, OBT 21 (Philadelphia: Fortress Press, 1987).

biblical motifs and given a secondary or tertiary place within them. An outstanding example of this preemption is the theme of God as the divine warrior, which captured the imagination of post–World War II Western Europe and North America. In Europe one of the most articulate elaborators of this theme was Gerhard von Rad, whose untranslated work on "The Holy War in Ancient Israel" did receive wide circulation in the translation of his *Old Testament Theology*.[3] In North America the theme of the divine warrior was central to one wing of the biblical theology movement.[4] A major theme of many works was that the ancient creeds of Israel bear witness to how the God of Israel accomplished mighty deeds to defend the nation against its foes (von Rad),[5] to deliver the faithful, as at the Exodus (Wright, Anderson, Cross, Freedman, Miller), and does so on holy mountains (Clifford, Levenson). From Cross and Freedman onward it has been a particular interest to point out how early Israelite poetry featuring the divine warrior drew on the poetic models of ancient Canaan (Ugarit).[6] This thrust is also found in the three-volume Anchor Bible commentary on the Psalms by the late Mitchell

---

3. Gerhard von Rad, *Der Heilige Krieg im alten Israel*, Abhandlungen zur Theologie des Alten und Neuen Testaments (Zurich: Zwingli, 1951); and idem, *Old Testament Theology*, 2 vols.; trans. D. M. G. Stalker (Edinburgh: Oliver & Boyd, 1962, 1965).

4. See G. Ernest Wright, *The Old Testament Against Its Environment*, SBT 2 (London: SCM Press, 1950), 20–22; idem, *God Who Acts: Biblical Theology as Recital*, SBT 8 (Chicago: Henry Regnery, 1952), 71; Frank Moore Cross, *Canaanite Myth and Hebrew Epic: Essays in the History of the Religion of Israel* (Cambridge: Harvard University Press, 1973), 91–144; Patrick D. Miller, Jr., *The Divine Warrior in Early Israel*, HSM 3 (Cambridge: Harvard University Press, 1973); Richard J. Clifford, S.J., *The Cosmic Mountain in Canaan and the Old Testament*, HSM 4 (Cambridge: Harvard University Press, 1972); Jon Douglas Levenson, *Theology of the Program of Restoration of Ezekiel 40–48*, HSM 10 Missoula, Mont.: Scholars Press, 1976), 5–53; idem, *Sinai and Zion: An Entry into the Jewish Bible* (Minneapolis: Winston Press, 1985).

5. The dependency of Wright on von Rad's essay, "The Form Critical Problem of the Hexateuch" (first published in German in 1938) is acknowledged by Wright (*God Who Acts*, 70). The essay by von Rad is available in Gerhard von Rad, *The Problem of the Hexateuch and Other Essays*, trans. E. W. Trueman Dickman (Edinburgh: Oliver & Boyd, 1966), 1–78.

6. Frank Moore Cross and David Noel Freedman, *Studies in Ancient Yahwistic Poetry*, SBLDS 21 (Missoula, Mont.: Scholars Press, 1975; reprint of Ph.D. diss., Johns Hopkins University, 1948, 1950).

Dahood.[7] In all of these discussions the holiness of God was acknowledged as present and important but itself seldom became the object of particular or focused inquiry. Parallel to the concentration on divine warrior was the post–World War II focus on covenant, particularly in the works of the late Dennis McCarthy, Klaus Balzer, George Mendenhall, Ronald Clements, and others.[8] A subsidiary theme also of the latter as well as the aforementioned writers is that of the divine suzerain, who is holy and exalted among his holy ones and has shown his covenant loyalty by fighting in Israel's behalf (Exod. 15:1–17; Deuteronomy 32; Psalms 18, 24, 29, 46, 68, 78, 82, 89, 96, 104). The point remains: the holiness of God in recent years has not itself been the object of theological investigation but has usually been so within the framework of other and more dominant theological motifs.

HOLINESS IN ISAIAH AND HIS PREDECESSORS

1. Prophecy emerged in the 700s B.C.E. with stunning force. Martin Buber explains in his classic, *The Prophetic Faith*, "In one generation Israel's faith developed three basic conceptions of the relationship to God."[9] These basic conceptions, according to Buber, were (1) righteousness (*ṣĕdāqâ*) with Amos, (2) lovingkindness (*ḥesed*) with Hosea; and (3) holiness (*qōdeš*) with Isaiah.[10] Even though it has recently been challenged whether or not the phrase "Holy One in your midst" (Hos. 11:9) may properly be called a title, the phrase was probably the source of inspir-

7. Mitchell Dahood, S.J., *Psalms I–III*, 3 vols., Anchor Bible 16–17 (Garden City, N.Y.: Doubleday, 1966–70).
8. Dennis J. McCarthy, *Treaty and Covenant*, Analecta Biblica 21 (Rome: Pontifical Biblical Institute, 1963; 2d ed., 1978); idem, *Old Testament Covenant: A Survey of Current Opinions* (Richmond: John Knox Press, 1972); Klaus Balzer, *Das Bundesformular*, 2d ed., Wissenschaftliche Monographien zum Alten und Neuen Testament 4 (Neukirchen-Vluyn: Neukirchener Verlag, 1964; first published 1960); George E. Mendenhall, *Law and Covenant in Israel and the Ancient Near East* (Pittsburgh: Biblical Colloquium, 1955; first published in *Biblical Archaeology* 17 [1954]:26–46, 50–76); Ronald E. Clements, *Prophecy and Covenant*, SBT 43 (London: SCM Press, 1965); Delbert R. Hillers, *Covenant: The History of a Biblical Idea* (Baltimore: Johns Hopkins University Press, 1969).
9. Martin Buber, *The Prophetic Faith*, trans. C. Witton-Davies (New York: Harper & Brothers, 1960; first published in English in 1948), 129.
10. Ibid.

ation for the name "Holy One of Israel" for God, which occurs
ten times in Isaiah 1—39 (Isa. 1:4; 5:19, 24; 10:20; 12:6; 17:7;
29:19; 30:15; 31:1; 37:23) as well as twelve times in Isaiah 40–66
(Isa. 41:14, 16, 20; 43:3, 14; 45:11; 47:4; 49:7; 54:5; 55:5; 60:9,
14).[11] The passage from Hosea is worth citing because already it
begins to reveal much about the prophetic understanding of holiness:

> I [God] will not execute my fierce anger,
> I will not again destroy Ephraim;
> for I am God and not man ('îš),
> the Holy One in your midst,
> and I will not come to destroy.
>
> (Hos. 11:9)

In this early prophetic usage we see at once that the term "Holy
One in your midst"—whether a title or an adjective—is at one
and the same time a title used by the prophet to differentiate the
divine from the human and in contradistinction to expression of
a consistent divine wrath. Precisely this distinctive usage by
Hosea suggests that he is the source of inspiration for the title
"Holy One of Israel" for Isaiah of Jerusalem because in Hosea the
term "Holy One in your midst" occurs in a passage expressing the
divine anguish in face of the human rejection of God (Hos. 11:1–
9). And not infrequently in Isaiah the term "Holy One of Israel"
is used in passages expressing specifically the divine hurt and
Israel's rejection of God (Isa. 1:4; 5:18–19, 24; 30:8–14; 37:23–
25).[12] Although it is certain that the prophet Amos had an impact
on Isaiah's perceptions of the relative importance of righteous-

11. See also Holy One in Isa. 40:25; 43:15; 49:7. John J. Schmitt ("The God of
Israel and the Holy One," *Hebrew Studies* 24 [1983]:27–31) has conducted
careful, grammatical research on these expressions. Schmitt is uncertain
whether Isaiah has coined the name "Holy One of Israel" and thinks it
originated in the cult rather than being inspired by Hosea (p. 31, n. 3). It does
not seem to me that sufficient evidence is present to decide upon this issue
conclusively because Isaiah drew from both Hosea and the cultus.

12. The occurrence of the title "Holy One of Israel" in Isaianic passages which
relate the hurt of God ("der *verletzten* gottlichen Majestät,: lit. "the wounded
divine majesty") was observed long ago by Anton Fridrichsen, *Hagios-Qadoš*,
(Kristiana: Jacob Dybwad, 1916), 27. More recently, Terence E. Fretheim has
underlined the vulnerability of God in the world where the response can be
one of human derision or incredulity: *The Suffering of God* OBT 14 (Philadelphia: Fortress Press, 1984), 106.

ness and the cultus (cf. Isa. 12:12–17 with Amos 5:21–24; 9:1), the extent to which Amos's perceptions of holiness impacted on Isaiah is less certain. In Amos 4:2 it is related, "The Lord GOD has sworn by his holiness," but there is no such sentiment even approximated in Isaiah. The same is so of the disputed phrase "so that my holy name is profaned" (Amos 2:7),[13] that is, both phraseology and conception of the profanation of the holy divine name are simply absent from Isaiah.

2. Among modern scholars who have sought to examine the theology of Isaiah as a whole, Theodore C. Vriezen and Samuel Terrien have also stressed (along with Martin Buber) the significant role the holiness of God plays in the prophet's thinking.[14] In Vriezen's words: "Just as Isaiah's own life is exposed to the eyes of the Holy One, so he sees his people in their world *sub specie sanctitatis Dei* (from the perspective of the divine holiness).[15] For Vriezen, Isaiah was the first to grasp as absolute the three divine qualities of holiness, glory, and power.[16] Terrien, on the other hand, has affirmed that "[t]he paradox of holiness . . . dominated the thinking . . . of Isaiah of Jerusalem."[17] The paradox is that the transcendent one and "wholly other" should turn toward human beings in self-giving love and that though the Holy God manifests himself to the prophet he is also "the hidden God" (*Deus absconditus*).[18] These insights from Vriezen and Terrien together with Buber's that the concept of holiness is *relational* will both be developed and sharpened below. In order to see how Isaiah's doctrine of holiness fits into his thought overall,

13. For reasons why the phrase is felt to be secondary, see H. W. Wolff, *Amos and Joel*, 2d ed., trans. Waldemar Janzen, S. Dean McBride, Jr., and Charles Muenchow, Hermeneia (Philadelphia: Fortress Press, 1977), 133–34, note p.

14. Theodore C. Vriezen, "Essentials of the Theology of Isaiah," in *Israel's Prophetic Heritage: Essays in Honor of James Muilenburg*, ed. Bernhard W. Anderson and Walter Harrelson (New York: Harper & Row, 1962), 128–46; Samuel Terrien, *The Elusive Presence: Toward a New Biblical Theology* (New York: Harper & Row, 1978), 246–52.

15. Vriezen, "Essentials of the Theology of Isaiah," 146.

16. Ibid., 133.

17. Terrien, *Elusive Presence*, 246. So influential was Hosea on Isaiah that Terrien sees the latter as "a disciple" of the former.

18. Terrien does not spell out that he has two paradoxes in mind, but it is apparent that he does.

it will be helpful to say a further word about the prophet and the book that bears his name.

ISAIAH THE MAN AND THE SHAPING OF PROPHETIC BOOKS

In his magnificent painting of the prophet Isaiah on the ceiling of the Sistine Chapel, Michelangelo has portrayed a sensitive aristocrat, lost in thought and the study of Scripture. The prophet is seated with his right hand crossed over to his left side and fingers inserted in the middle of an unidentified quarto volume which, however, must be understood to be the writings of his predecessors. The prophet's left arm rests on the book and is bent at the elbow with his left hand pointing upward toward his head but perhaps beyond. The prophet's lips are slightly parted, his brow furrowed, and his open eyes gaze downward. The expression on his face, turned away from the book, is at once pained and meditative—as if he were pondering some distressing word concerning his people found within the book he had been reading.[19] Few biblical scholars have communicated the prophetic anguish of Isaiah as forcefully.

Summaries of the prophets and of individual prophets frequently reflect the surveyor and interpreter. Such was the conclusion seventy years ago by the then-young Walter Baumgartner in his inaugural lecture at the University of Marburg on the nineteenth-century conception of prophecy.[20] Increasingly the strange and unusual aspects of the prophets became played down, he observed, and they were portrayed as "wise teachers and pious preachers."[21] Many of the shifts Baumgartner recorded away from the more rationalistic portrayals of the late nineteenth century still obtain today: study of the relation of the canonical prophets with their forebears, study in the light of primitive

19. The interpretation is mine. For another, see Rolf Schott, *Michelangelo*, translated and adapted from the German by Constance McNab (New York: Tudor Publishing Co., 1963), 75–76. In our day, unquestionably the most profound treatment on the prophet as one who empathizes with the divine compassion is Abraham Joshua Heschel, *The Prophets* (New York: Harper & Row, 1962).

20. Walter Baumgartner, "Die Auffassungen des 19. Jahrhunderts vom Israelitischen Prophetismus," in *Zum Alten Testament und Seiner Umwelt: Ausgewahlte Aufsätze* (Leiden: E. J. Brill, 1959), 27–41.

21. Ibid., 34.

peoples elsewhere, facing more squarely the occult aspects of prophecy, study of mythological allusions in the prophets carrying them back to their roots, and clearer understanding of the origin of the prophetic books not so much as the work of individual authors but rather as collections of prophecies over a longer period of time, during which collections had been preserved and finally edited in prophetic circles.[22] Baumgartner's survey serves to remind us that good historical criticism will also take into account the life and times of the historic critics themselves when evaluating their (and our own) work.

One of the most influential surveys of the prophets in recent times is the second volume of Gerhard von Rad's *Old Testament Theology.* As did Michelangelo, von Rad highlighted Isaiah's intelligence: "Not one of the other prophets approaches Isaiah in intellectual vigour or, more particularly, in the magnificent sweep of his ideas."[23] Yet in the concluding paragraph of his survey, this "magnificent sweep of ideas" has narrowed down to two: "As a result of this study, it can be said that the whole of Isaiah's preaching is based on two traditions, the Zion tradition and the tradition about David."[24] This evaluation cannot, in my judgment, be accepted as correct. It is a tribute to the intellectual power and persuasiveness of von Rad himself to have so plumbed the overtones and interrelatedness of the two aforementioned traditions that he could make his claim. His evaluation stands as a tribute to von Rad's own refusal simply to repeat the results of the inquiries of his contemporaries or to state the obvious.[25]

22. Ibid., 37–40. The recent emphases on the development of the Book of Isaiah over a long period of time are many. See esp. Remi Lack, *La Symbolique du Livre d'Isaïe,* Analecta Biblica 59 (Rome: Pontifical Biblical Institute, 1973); J. Vermeylen, *Du prophète Isaïe à l'apocalyptique,* 2 vols. (Paris: J. Gabalda, 1977–78); P. R. Ackroyd, "Isaiah I–XII: Presentation of a Prophet," VTSup 29 (Leiden: E.J. Brill, 1977); John Eaton, "The Origin of the Book of Isaiah," *Vetus Testamentum* 9 (1959):138–57; idem, "The Isaiah Tradition," in *Israel's Prophetic Tradition, Essays in Honour of Peter R. Ackroyd,* ed. Richard Coggins, Anthony Phillips, and Michael Knibb (Cambridge: Cambridge University Press, 1982), 58–76; Joseph Blenkinsopp, *A History of Prophecy in Israel* (Philadelphia: Westminster Press, 1983), 106–18.

23. von Rad, *Old Testament Theology,* 2:147.

24. Ibid., 2:174.

25. See von Rad's introductory discussion in *Old Testament Theology,* 2:147–55. For an excellent survey of much of Isaianic scholarship, including von Rad,

Von Rad's assessment is deficient in three regards: (1) he gives insufficient prominence to Isaiah's doctrine of God and specifically to the holiness of God; (2) in stressing Isaiah's prophecies on Zion he has obscured both its conditional nature and the prophet's universalism; and (3) Isaiah's teaching about the Davidic "anointed one" may best be seen as subsidiary to the theme of divine judgment and justice.

For Isaiah, the rulership of God was not confined to Zion or Israel but was universal and global (Isa. 2:2-4; 6:3; 10:5-15; 11:6-9). Further, for Isaiah the divine demand for justice among people and Davidic king was understood by the prophet to derive from the *divine* king's own passionate commitment to effect just judgments in his own governance (Isa. 5:1-7; 9:2-7 [Hebr., 1-6]). The justice God demands among his people and among other nations is thus not dispassionately required as from an aloof sovereign whose exaltation in holiness removed him from real concern for human affairs. To the contrary, it is precisely failure in the attainment of justice that grieved the Holy One of Israel (Isa. 1:4; 5:18-19, 24; 30:8-14; 37:23-25). Though the title Holy One of Israel suggests an ethnocentricity in Isaiah's proclamation, divine holiness, divine kingship, and divine passion for justice extend to all the earth, which is the divine's "glorious possession" (Isa. 6:3). In this affirmation of God as being sovereign in the double sense of being both holy and just, Isaiah shows himself to be very much in the line of the ancient traditions on which he draws.[26]

see John J. Schmitt, *Isaiah and His Interpreters* (New York/Mahwah, N.J.: Paulist Press, 1986):39-127; for a treasure-trove of bibliographic data on Isaiah, see also John H. Hayes and Stuart A. Irvine, *Isaiah the Eighth Century Prophet: His Times and Preaching* (Nashville: Abingdon Press, 1987).

26. In recent times Martin Buber has suggested that Isaiah's vision-report of "the king," mighty and absolute, constituted a "breakthrough" in Israelite attitude toward divine rulership in that it overcame a reluctance to use outside of the specialized liturgical langauge of the Psalms the title "the king" in relation to God (*Kingship of God*, 3rd ed., trans. Richard Scheimann [New York: Harper & Row, 1967; first German edition, 1932], 38). For Buber the teaching of divine sovereignty (lordship, rulership, or kingship) was not peripheral but was rather of its essence and lifeblood. At the conclusion of his preface to the third edition of *Kingship of God*, Buber summarized his convictions, after engaging in a brief dialogue with Hans-Joachim Kraus, in these words: "It comes down to this: the realization of the all embracing

ISAIAH'S DOCTRINE OF HOLINESS

I find that there are seven main parts to the prophet Isaiah's doctrine of holiness.

1. *Reverence and a sense of the need for cleanness are the most immediate and lasting products of the prophet's encounter with holiness.*

Isaiah's famous vision in the temple of the holy and exalted king evoked in him—concomitantly with reverential fear—a sense of his own and his people's uncleanness. There is an immediacy about Isaiah's utterance on the relationship between the holy and the clean that transcends even that of the priests. To say that human cleanness is the counterpart or appropriate match for the divine holiness would be to put it too abstractly and distantly. Awareness of uncleanness, reverence, fear are the prophet's most immediate responses to holiness—and, as we shall see, what he so deeply experienced, he also taught.

After the seraph's threefold cry of "holy," and the shaking of the foundations and the filling of the nave of the temple with incense smoke, the prophet responds:

> And I said, "Woe is me for I have been silenced because I am a man of unclean lips and I reside in the midst of a people of unclean lips; for my eyes have seen the king, the LORD of hosts." (Isa. 6:5, au. trans.).

The uncleanness of lips that struck the prophet may refer either to his past or anticipated ministry of the word. The presence of the prophet in the temple may have been either at the outset or in the course of his prophetic career. Holiness thus made him aware of a deficiency in his proclamation, of a glibness perhaps, an unworthiness. No longer could he continue to proclaim either in the same way or without a radical reauthentication.

Of the second part of his auditory vision the prophet relates:

> And one of the seraphim flew to me and in his hands was a live coal he had taken with tongs from the altar. And he touched it to my

rulership of God is for Israel her point of beginning and final goal" (my translation of: "Das ist es, warauf es ankommt; Die Verwirklichung der allumfassenden Gottesherrschaft ist das Proton und Eschaton Israels," idem *Königtum Gottes*, 3d ed. [Heibelberg: Lambert Schneider, 1956], lxiv).

mouth and said, "Behold this touches your lips: your guilt departs and your sin has been purged (*tĕkuppār*)." (Isa. 6:6–7, au. trans.)

Iniquity (guilt) and sin are here not handled through sacrifices but by way of a divine emissary's direct intervention. It is possible, of course, that the performance of the sacrifices is assumed and that the prophet—whether actually in the temple, or outside the temple and having a vision as though he were within—is simply not reporting about the usual sacrifices. As we considered in the first chapter, sins of the people were purged by the priest who entered the temple (Lev. 4:13–21) and the people did not enter. Isaiah's vision may thus have been of the particular way in which it had been made known to him that along with the people his lips were unclean and that he had been purged. The vision is neither anticultic nor acultic. For whether or not the prophet was actually situated in the temple when he had it, temple, incense, altar, (incense) smoke, fire on the altar, and the notion of sin purged are hardly cultically neutral.[27]

Why the prophet had a sense of uncleanness of lips—and not of acts or deeds, as elsewhere—may perhaps be explained on the basis of the temple entrance liturgies such as Psalm 15, which we shall have occasion to look at more closely in chapter 5. Four of the ten requirements for entrance into the temple pertain to speech, that is, that which comes forth from the lips (see Ps. 15:2b, 3a, c, 4c). In the undoubtedly later prophetic Psalm 50 we can see the usual emphasis of the temple liturgy on the lips (vv. 16, 19) reinforced by prophetic antisacrificial pronouncements (vv. 8–15).

The prophet embodied the reverence he felt at the inaugural vision of holiness in an oracle delivered perhaps seven or eight years later: "Do not call conspiracy all that this people call conspiracy, and do not fear what they fear, nor be in dread. But the LORD of hosts, him you shall regard as holy; let him be your fear,

---

27. Terrien's assessment ("The prophet's vision transcends the sacerdotal system, for it is God who initiates and fulfils the institutional deed," *Elusive Presence*, 249) may be correct, but rather underplays the extent to which the vision is bounded on all sides by a sacerdotal locus (temple), deeds (maintenance of fire and offering of incense) and thought-world (purging of sin).

and let him be your dread" (Isa. 8:12–13).[28] The prophet proclaims that the reverential fear of God has a freeing effect: potentially threatening political machinations and alliances should not, and will not, become the object of dread if the people would but keep in mind the holiness of God. Isaiah's doctrine of the primacy of faith (see Isa. 7:9; 28:16) is thus closely related to his doctrine of holiness: strength comes from trust in the Holy One of Israel (Isa. 30:15), from relying on his counsel rather than from trusting in alliances with the militarily strong (Isa. 31:1).

That the divine holiness requires cleanness may be observed also in several passages from late in the prophet's career. Though the operation of the cultus may have been implicit, as we have shown above, at the time of the prophet's inauguration, he unmistakably teaches that the cleanness the divine required could not be attained simply through a reliance upon divine grace, but necessitated action also outside of the cultus:

> Bring no more vain offerings;
>   incense is an abomination to me. . . .
> When you spread forth your hands,
>   I will hide my eyes from you;
>   . . . your hands are full of blood.
> Wash yourselves; make yourselves clean;
>   remove the evil of your doings from before my eyes.
>   (Isa. 1:13a, 15–16, RSV)

It is apparent from the context that Isaiah had in mind more than the blood of sacrifices. The priests taught that the cleanness holiness required could be attained through sacrifices; Isaiah also taught that holiness required cleanness, but sacrifices alone were not enough. The prophet's emphasis on cleanness is also seen later in the same passage (Isa. 1:10–20): "Come now, let us reason together, says the LORD: though your sins are like scarlet, they shall be white as snow; though they are red like crimson, they shall become like wool" (Isa. 1:18). From the same period the prophet has revealed in his ears a harsh judgment against

28. Otto Kaiser, *Isaiah 1–12*, OTL (Philadelphia: Westminster Press, 1972), rightly places the oracle of Isa. 8:11–15 at the time of the Syro-Ephraimite War (i.e., ca. 734 B.C.E.). Uzziah's death, the year of his inaugural vision, we set, following Bright, Albright, et. al., at 742 B.C.E.

those who celebrated the departure of Sennacherib with rejoicing rather than entering into mourning as the Lord of hosts had enjoined: "Surely this iniquity will not be purged (*yĕkuppar*) from you till you die, says the LORD of hosts" (Isa. 22:14, au. trans.). Thus throughout his career the prophet clung to the notion that sin defiles but holiness requires cleanness. He is at pains to reveal how cleanness may most appropriately be attained.

2. *Social and legal justice is the primary means by which the cleanness required of holiness can be attained but even this, the prophet taught, was not to be viewed solely as a human accomplishment.*

Isaiah's doctrine of justice and righteousness is intricately intertwined with his doctrines of place, the king, and holiness. Jerusalem was once the place where righteousness dwelt (Isa. 1:21); at some future time it will be called the home of righteousness (Isa. 1:26); indeed, "Zion shall be redeemed by justice, and those in her who repent, by righteousness" (Isa. 1:27). Yahweh's beloved vineyard of Israel, Judah, and Jerusalem comes under the divine judgment because of failure to produce justice and righteousness (Isa. 5:1-7). It is the king's special task to establish justice and righteousness (Isa. 9:7; Heb. 9:6) and to exercise just and righteous judgments both in ruling and in judging cases (Isa. 11:3b-5). The king is enjoined to be particularly mindful of the poor and hungry (Isa. 11:4; 32:5-7), whereas the oppression and exploitation of the defenseless and poor come in for particularly harsh censure (Isa. 1:17; 3:14-15; 10:1-4). Isaiah thus calls for a cessation of oppression (Isa. 1:16-17) and for distributive justice (Isa. 5:22-23).[29] Israel's failure in achieving the latter is primary cause for the pronouncement of the forthcoming divine judgment (cf., e.g., Isa. 5:24-25; 10:1-5; 30:8-17).[30]

29. For an excellent discussion on the various kinds of justice to be found in the prophets according to Aristotelian categories of analysis, see the inaugural address by W. Eugene March, "Justice: The Divine Obsession" (Louisville, Ky.: Louisville Presbyterian Theological Seminary, 1982). For a consideration of yet another type of justice, "purgative," see below under Isaiah's Doctrine of Holiness, item 4. March's notion that the divine work and justice in Isaiah 40—55 is "restorative" (cols. 9–10) appears to me to be a legitimate category that merits further exploration.

30. The last-mentioned passage may be from a successor to Isaiah but the

Justice clearly plays a central role in the theological thinking of the prophet. It is at the same time held up as the appointed means by which the cleanness required of the divine holiness can be achieved by human beings. In terms that echo those of his predecessor Amos, Isaiah utters the Lord's dismay at the sacrificial cultus and his call for justice (Isa. 1:12–17; cf. Amos 5:21–24). The primary difference between the two prophets in these utterances is that Isaiah links justice with cleanness:

> Wash yourselves; make yourselves clean;
>> remove the evil of your doings from before my eyes;
> cease to do evil; learn to do good;
>> seek justice; reprove the oppressor;
> defend the fatherless, uphold the widow's rights.
>   (Isa. 1:16–17, au. trans.)

This prophecy was probably pronounced after Sennacherib's invasion, when the devastation was extensive.[31] The addressees are the rulers and inhabitants of a Jerusalem likened to Sodom and Gomorrah (Isa. 1:8–10). Some hope thus remains for the city if the people act. For Isaiah hope did not rest solely in the people's hands, for the prophet also looked forward to an offspring of David who would rule with righteousness and judge the poor with equity (Isa. 11:4–5). In the above verses the prophet sets forth a two-pronged approach for attaining cleanness: (1) through the performance of acts pleasing in God's sight (Isa. 1:16) and (2) through the law courts: "Seek justice" (*diršû mispāṭ*) may also be translated "require judgment," "pursue legal action" as the rest of v. 17 makes plain: "reprove" (*'aššĕrû*), "defend" (*šipṭû*), and "contend for" (*rîbbû*) are all legal terms. With respect to the first item, the prophet suggests that the city dwellers have repeatedly committed acts they knew to be immoral in the divine sight. Corruption had become habitual, usual. So he advises that they cease their accepted corrupt practices and apply themselves to learning how to act with integrity. Thus spoke the noble, the aristocrat, the frequenter of the royal courts, and one nourished

---

teaching is certainly in accord with that of the master prophet. See Kaiser, *Isaiah 13–29*, 293, who slates this passage to the years 597–587 B.C.E.

31. The passages Isa. 1:2–9, 10–20, 21–28, 29–31 are all most naturally assigned to this period.

in the symbols of priests. The holiness of his royal Lord required a purity that could not be attained painlessly. The washing the prophet declared to be necessary challenged the very privileges of his own class because they were based on oppressive acts and a corrupt legal system.

Raised as he was in nobility, the prophet saw all the more clearly that a major source of the corruption of his own southern city-state of Judah and of northern Israel was the arrogance, haughtiness, pride, and self-exaltation of the ruling classes (Isa. 2:11, 17; 23:9; 28:1, 3; 29:20). Self-satisfaction with their wealth (Isa. 2:7a) led to reliance on armaments (Isa. 2:7b; 31:1) and to idolatry (Isa. 2:8), on the one hand, and to callousness and greed, on the other, to multiply their houses and fields (Isa. 5:8–10) and to "party" late and early (Isa. 5:11–12, 22).[32] This combination of desires nurtured in the upper classes led to legal corruption and oppression of the innocent (Isa. 5:23).

In contrast to self-exaltation, Isaiah promised that humbling would follow (Isa. 5:15; cf. 2:11, 17; 23:9). The self- exalted were not transcendent:

> But the LORD of hosts is exalted in justice (*mišpaṭ*)
> and the Holy God shows himself holy (*niqdaš*) by
>   righteousness.
>
> (Isa. 5:16)

This verse profoundly expresses the Isaianic and prophetic faith. The prophet's reminder that God is exalted ("sits high in judgement," NEB) served as a rebuke to the nobles' self-exaltation. God who alone is transcendent enjoyed exaltation precisely because he is the supreme judge who rules with justice and will bring the arrogant into judgment. At the same time the Holy God "shows himself holy in righteousness." That is, *God manifests the divine holiness by moving human beings to perform righteous acts.* The ultimate source of human righteousness is thus not the human being but rather the supreme and holy ruler who brings justice and righteousness to pass in their midst. Put another way, the Holy God who rules with justice empowers human beings to

---

32. The prophet's teaching thus recalls the triad Wealth, Satiation, and Pride familiar in Greek thought.

accomplish it. Thus the prophet at once encourages his fellow countrymen to assume full responsibility for their actions and at the same time he undercuts the grounds for their boasting in their accomplishments. This is what Buber meant when he taught that the prophetic concept of holiness is relational.[33] God hallows, that is, the divine sanctifies and makes humans fit to continue to stand in the holy presence by leading them to perform social and legal acts of appropriate purity.[34] This relational aspect of Isaiah's doctrine of holiness we may see even more clearly in the next aspect of his teaching to which we turn.

3. *Glory, sovereignty, counsel, and power are not simply abstract correlative qualities or attributes of the divine holiness. Rather, each attribute also points to an aspect of human life which the divine desires to hallow.*

Majesty, kingship, purpose, and strength are for Isaiah corollaries of the divine holiness. Not only in his inaugural vision, but throughout his career, the prophet was given to see each of these divine attributes and the relevance of each to human life.

Glory. The Hebrew word for glory, *kābôd*, is rich in meaning.[35]

33. Buber, *The Prophetic Faith*, 129: "This, that YHVH is present to Israel even with His most sublime and essential characteristic, His holiness, and that Israel is thereby able to receive His influence to follow His footsteps, and to place human activity at the disposal of His activity, in other words, the hallowing of Israel by the whole YHVH (cf. Ex. 31:13), this is the root idea of the divine attribute so dear to Isaiah."

34. The dialectic between the divine and human relationship that I have sought to expound in Isaiah has been ably expressed by Jon Levenson: "The relationship between human endeavor and divine action in the Hebrew Bible is [thus] partly antithetical and partly complementary. It is antithetical in that man cannot assert on his own authority that anything is the will of God. It is complementary in that the will of God is realized, in part, through human action. Man sinning is at odds with God. Man doing what is right is in God's favor. Human righteousness and divine righteousness do not conflict. The conflict comes when man, being man, mistakes his own ideas for divine revelation, or assumes that his own character plays no role in the appropriation of revelation. Human righteousness thus must include constant self-critique, an awareness that human works count ultimately only if they are in line with divine intention and that in some mysterious way it is God himself who creates the motivation to bring them in line" (*Theology of the Program of Restoration of Ezekiel 40—48*), 47.

35. A number of fine and detailed studies have been written on "glory." Still useful are Freiherrn von Gall, *Die Herrlichkeit Gottes* (Giessen: J. Ricker [Alfred Töpelmann], 1900) and Gerhard von Rad's entry under *doxa* in *Kittel's Theological Dictionary of the New Testament*, 10 vols., trans. G. W. Bromiley (Grand Rapids: Wm. B. Eerdmans, 1964; first published in German in 1935),

It carries the connotation of wealth (Gen. 31:1; 1 Kings 3:13; Isa. 10:3), fecundity (Isa. 10:18), fame (Isa. 21:16; Prov. 25:2), possession (Isa. 6:3), honor (Isa. 10:3; Ps. 29:3), worth and value (Prov. 27:3; Isa. 22:24), majesty (Isa. 24:7; 29:4; Ps. 113:4), power (Job 29:20; Isa. 10:16), and status (Isa. 14:18; Ps. 21:5; Heb. 21:6). Isaiah teaches that Israel is valued of God (Isa. 1:9), that true status is not to be found in possessions (Isa. 5:8–10), rather, the one in Jerusalem and Judah who is presently honored (*nikbād*) will find the tables turned on him (Isa. 3:5) precisely because of rebellion against some aspect of the divine glory (Isa. 3:8).[36] True status, nobility, and deserving honor are what the divine wills. Thus he taught,

> A noble man plans noble things
> and he will arise for noble deeds.
> (Isa. 32:8, au. trans.)

Sovereignty. In Isaiah's vision of God, the king above all is One who desires justice and righteousness (Isa. 5:7) and promises to

2:238–42. Edmund Jacob points out that glory has been called "holiness uncovered" (*Old Testament Theology* [New York: Harper & Row, 1958], 80).

Moshe Weinfeld, in an excellent article on *kābôd* in *Theologisches Wörterbuch zum Alten Testament*, 4, Lf. 1/2, ed. G. J. Botterweck, Helmer Ringgren, H.-J. Fabry (Stuttgart: W. Kohlhammer, 1982), cols. 23–40, concludes that *kābôd* has both a *concrete* meaning: "a fiery phenomenon out of which comes forth brilliance and brightness" and an *abstract* meaning: Honor, Worth, Majesty (col. 38). As all etymologists point out, the root of meaning of the Hebrew *kbd* in the pi'el form means literally "to ascribe weight," "to make heavy," hence "to honor" (see Exod. 20:12: "Honor [*kabbed*] thy father and mother." In the introduction to our work above, we suggested in the course of a discussion on Otto's analysis of the holy that *kābôd* may properly be rendered as "majesty." The New Jewish Version frequently translates the Hebrew *kābôd* as "Presence." The reader, of course, should understand "[Majestic] Presence." In a vein similar to Weinfeld, Rolf Rendtorff suggests that *kābôd* be rendered "the humanly discernible portion of the divine activity in which Yahweh in his might is revealed" (my translation, cited by Weinfeld [col. 34] from *Kerygma und Dogma* Beiheft 1; 3d ed., 1965, p. 31). Thus Weinfeld stresses majesty and Rendtorff power. The relationship between the two may be put this way: *majesty* is glory in being (in the philosophical sense of the latter term) and *power* is glory in action or readiness for action.

For an important theological work that gives prominence to the theme of glory, see Hans Urs von Balthasar, *The Glory of the Lord*, 3 vols. (New York/San Francisco: Crossroads/Ignatius, 1982–86).

36. The Hebrew *'ēnê kĕbôdô* might be translated "eyes of his glory"; RSV has "his glorious presence." The notes of *Biblia Hebraica Stuttgartensia* suggest that perhaps the defectively spelled Hebrew word for "eyes" should be deleted.

bequeath these to future human monarchs (Isa. 9:7; Heb. 9:6; 11:3–5) and princes (Isa. 32:1). Thus the divine sovereign seeks the true evidences of royalty (justice and righteousness) and, as we saw in the previous section, the Holy God labors to effect precisely these.

Counsel. Kings may have their counselors; the Lord of hosts is his own counsel. The self-deceptive may with bravado call upon the Holy One of Israel to reveal his counsel (Isa. 5:18–19), and those who rely on armaments may fail to consult the Holy One of Israel (Isa. 31:1), but sound and even wondrous counsel is what Yahweh promises the future righteous ruler (Isa. 11:2; 9:6; Heb. 9:5). God's counsel or plan included, as Johannes Fichtner[37] argued, the preservation of Zion, a converted remnant,[38] and sending a righteous king; it also included God's "strange work" of judgment (Isa. 28:21–22), but above all the divine counsel is summarized in Isaiah's advice to Ahaz to have faith (Isa. 7:9), to both houses of Israel to fear the Lord of hosts and not alliances (Isa. 8:13), and to the fearful Jerusalem to make her foundation stone faith that the ones who pursued justice would not be swept away (Isa. 28:14–18).[39]

Power. The whole earth is the divine possession (Isa. 6:3; cf. Ps. 24:1). Assyria is but as a rod in his hands (Isa. 10:5). The foundations at the temple shook at the sound of his angelic emissaries (Isa. 6:4). "The LORD of hosts is exalted in judgment" (Isa. 5:16, au. trans.). "Behold, the Lord, the LORD of hosts, will lop the boughs with terrifying power; the great in height will be hewn down, and the lofty will be brought low" (Isa. 10:33). The holy power is not, however, something reserved for governance, judgment, or cosmic display: "For thus says the Lord GOD, the Holy

---

37. Johannes Fichtner, "Jahves Plan in der Botschaft des Jesaja," *ZAW* 63 (1951): 16–33.

38. On Isaiah's Doctrine of the Remnant, see below, "The Remnant is Holy," pp. 90–92.

39. In the fine essay by Joseph Jensen, "Yahweh's Plan in Isaiah and in the Rest of the Old Testament," *CBQ* 48 (1986): 443–55, the author focuses on the meaning of '*ṣh* as "plan" but does not press to explore its meaning as "counsel." Not only does Yahweh have in mind a grand scheme (Plan) but also sound counsel (Advice). It is Israel's failure to seek both for which they are rebuked (Isa. 31:1).

One of Israel, 'In returning and rest you shall be saved; in quietness and trust shall be your strength'" (Isa. 30:15).[40]

4. *The holiness of God for Isaiah is not simply punitive or retributive but above all purposive and purgative.*

The prophet taught that some of the divine judgment was sent in punishment or chastisement: "What will you do on the day of punishment, in the storms which will come from afar?" (Isa. 10:3). With anguish the divine asks if he shall not punish (lit. "do to") Jerusalem as he had Samaria because of their respective idolatries (Isa. 10:10–11). Sometimes the punishment sounds as if it is more *retributive*, that is, repayment for a fault or offense. Thus a lack of knowledge (of God and his will) is cited by the prophet as a reason for a forthcoming judgment of exile (Isa. 5:13). Similarly, the proud Assyria vaunts himself like an axe over the axeman and seems to call forth the divine requital (Isa. 10:15–19) as do the proud of Ephraim (Isa. 28:1–4) and of Jerusalem (Isa. 5:15).

Because of the wisdom and counsel of God, Isaiah taught that the judgment he sent was finely tuned: just as human beings used different instruments with which to thresh dill, cummin, and grain, so was God's judgment adjusted—harsh but not such as to crush utterly (Isa. 28:27–29). Whether retributive or punitive or something more, the divine judgment was measured and controlled.

The last cited passage is instructive because it points to a purposiveness in the divine judgment: to harvest, to thresh, to separate the kernel from the chaff. This thought runs throughout the prophet's work. Pruning trees and plants is taken to be a positive action, necessary for full growth (Isa. 5:6), and pruning is what the divine is about in judgment (Isa. 18:5) or burning away the dry grass (Isa. 5:24) or briars and thorns (Isa. 9:18; Heb. 9:17; 10:17). Thus the holiness of judgment is as a consuming fire. The purpose of the judgment, however, is *purgative.* Thus Isaiah

---

40. Walter Brueggemann has developed the notion of divine empowerment in his chapter, "Prophetic Energizing and the Emergence of Amazement," in *The Prophetic Imagination* (Philadelphia: Fortress Press, 1978), 62–79; he does so particularly with respect to Jeremiah and Second Isaiah.

alternates between the three agricultural metaphors of pruning, threshing, and burning and the metallurgical. "Once again I will act against you to refine away your base metal as with potash and purge all your dross" (Isa. 1:25, NEB adapted). In a fourth metaphor taken from the realm of plants and trees Isaiah is especially harsh and on the face of it would seem to have abandoned the notion of purgative judgment for he speaks of the hewing down of trees and of forests (Isa. 6:13; 10:33–34; 11:1; 18:5). But even here the prophet points to what will remain in Israel after the felling (Isa. 6:13; 11:1). That portion of the inaugural vision wherein the prophet's lips are purged with a glowing coal thus constitutes a symbolic summation of his teaching on the inexorable divine judgment: it will be painful, perhaps fiery, but in the last analysis, purifying.[41]

5. *The remnant is holy.*

The fifth part of Isaiah's doctrine of holiness flows from the fourth. After God's awesome judgment on Israel a remnant will remain. This remnant would turn again to God in faith as the prophet's naming of his son makes plain: Shear Yashub, "A Remnant Shall Turn (Again to God)" (Isa. 7:3). It is true, as von Rad has pointed out, that many of the remnant passages in Isaiah 1—39 are from the successors to the prophet.[42] The disciples for the most part deepen the teachings of the prophet. Those who had passed through fire and sword were the residue of the purging process and hence could be called holy in the sense of having been purged and cleansed. That this meaning attaches to "holy" is most apparent from the words of the prophet and disciples.

---

41. For a helpful discussion on the relationship of holiness and grace, see Karl Barth, *Kirkliche Dogmatic* 2/1: *Die Lehre von Gott*, 3d ed. (Zurich: Evangelischer Verlag A.G., Zollikon, 1948), par. 30, 394–413. Barth's dialectical theology is captured well in the following citation: "When we say grace we speak of the forgiveness of sins. When we say holiness, we speak of judgment on sins" (pp. 404–5). "The holiness of God is the unity of his judgment with his grace. God is holy in that his grace is judgment, but his judgment is also grace" (p. 408, au. trans.). In this section we have sought to show that for Isaiah of Jerusalem the notion of purgative judgment furnishes evidence that Barth's more dialectical assessment is quite on target. For acknowledgement that the prophet's thinking itself is more dialectic than is argued in this section, see below, item 6.

42. von Rad, *Old Testament Theology*, 2:165.

And though a tenth remain in it [the land]
it will be burned again,
like a terebinth or an oak whose stump remains
standing when it is felled.
The holy seed is its stump.

(Isa. 6:13)

Thus ends the divine response to Isaiah's inaugural vision after the prophet had asked, How long? that is, how long the people would remain unresponsive to his proclamation. The italicized portion is not in the Septuagint and thus some scholars have conjectured that it was not a part of the original prophetic word. It is in the Isaiah A Scroll from Qumran, however, and is thus not necessarily late. Otto Kaiser has suggested that it was added by the prophet himself.[43]

From a prophecy of mixed beauty transmitted by a successor (Isa. 4:2–6) we read:

> And the one who is left in Zion will be called holy, every one recorded for life in Jerusalem, when the Lord shall have washed away the filth of the daughters of Zion and cleansed the bloodstains of Jerusalem from its midst by a spirit of judgment and by a spirit of burning. (vv. 3–4, RSV adapted)

Though late, this passage, like the former, captures the sense in which the prophet thought of the divine judgment as purgative— as was also demonstrated in the previous section.

Two more passages are of interest in the pursuit of our inquiry into Isaiah's teaching of the remnant as holy.

In a couplet in the Qinah (3 + 2) meter of the dirge, the prophet portrays the women of Zion as the remnant. My own translation of these verses goes:

Your men will fall by the sword
and your strong men in battle.
And her gates will mourn and lament
and she will sit on the ground *cleansed.*

(Isa. 3:25–26)

The italicized word is translated by the RSV as "ravaged," by the NEB "stripped bare." Both are permissible but the usual mean-

43. Kaiser, *Isaiah 1–12*, 84.

ing of the *niph'al* of the verb *nqh* is "to be clean, free";[44] hence my translation. The prophet's choice of words[45] and teaching on the subject of judgment as purgation suggests that my rendition may be closer to the prophet's intended meaning.

Finally, the prophet's words on the future king in Isa. 11:1–9 were uttered in a situation that presupposed an extensive judgment so that only a stump was left. The future king who will ascend from the stump, it is said, will receive a spirit of sixfold enlightenment (wisdom, understanding, counsel, might, knowledge, and fear of the Lord, v. 2). The prophecy concludes: "They shall not hurt or destroy in all my holy mountain; for the earth shall be filled with the knowledge of the LORD as the waters cover the sea" (v. 9). Here the prophet has moved beyond the linkage of the holiness of the remnant and purgative judgment to the notion that holiness for the remnant derives instead from a gift of the spirit of the knowledge of God. Two facets of Isaiah's doctrine of holiness remain to be treated to round it out: its paradoxical character and its vocations.

6. *There is a paradoxical, dialectical, and sometimes dialogical feature in Isaiah's doctrine of holiness not only with respect to manifestation and hiddenness, loftiness and caring, but also with respect to divine versus human initiative and a Zion-parochialism versus universalism.*

The paradoxical aspect of Isaiah's teaching on holiness has been alluded to in the preceding pages. It remains now only to flesh out some of the allusions made above.

Both Tillich and Terrien have called attention to *the paradoxical character of the divine revelation.* Tillich focuses on the axis of revelation and concealment; Terrien on the bearing of this axis on the divine presence.

> The prophet does not describe God Himself in any way. He speaks only of the train which fills the temple, of the angels surrounding

---

44. So Ludwig Koehler and Walter Baumgartner, *Lexicon in Veteris Testamenti Libros* (Leiden: E.J. Brill, 1958), 632.

45. A rich vocabulary was available to the prophet if he had intended to indicate that the women had been "ravaged." Koehler and Baumgartner create a separate meaning to suit this verse, "to be deprived (of the men)": *Lexicon in Veteris Testamenti Libros*, 632.

the Lord's throne, of the shaking of the foundation, and of the smoke filling the house. In this manner he indicates that the revelation of God is at the same time the veiling of God. God can reveal Himself only by remaining veiled.[46]

Tillich's analysis is compelling. The final sentence in the citation, however, stands in need of further explication. Surely the divine can reveal itself with means other than "by remaining veiled." Tillich's statement nonetheless points to both the dimensions of the inexhaustibility and mysteriousness within the divine. The smoke filling the temple was visible, yet like the cloud of smoke (Hebrew *'ab he'ānān*: Exod. 19:9) or the thick darkness (Hebrew *hā'ărāpel*: Exod. 20:21) on Mt. Sinai it also concealed.

Isaiah exercises extreme reserve in his description of the vision: "I saw the Lord seated upon a throne, high and lifted up" (Isa. 6:1). In his biblical theology Terrien discusses its ephemerality:

> The moment before God is swiftly spent, even for a prophet, and it never returns. . . . . For the prophet there is no doubt that the God who hides his face is very much alive. During the eclipse of God, the man of faith formulates a theology of hope; and he is able to wait creatively, for he remembers the power of the prophetic vision. The presence which conceals itself is not absence.[47]

Visibility is not the only indicator of the divine presence.

Another aspect of the paradox of holiness to which Terrien alluded bears investigation, namely, *that the transcendent one and Wholly Other should turn toward human beings in self-giving love.* The one "high and lifted up," far from remaining aloof, enters into continued dialogue with prophet and people—rebuking, proclaiming, exhorting; the divine king exercises judgment and shows compassion (Isa. 1:9). The Holy One of Israel is both hurt and aggrieved at the rejection experienced (Isa. 1:4; 5:18–19, 24; 30:8–14). Holiness for Isaiah is thus far removed from disinterestedness and detachment. Exaltedness does not mean apathy but sympathy born of the deepest caring for humankind and for the victims of oppression (Isa. 5:1–7).

---

46. Paul Tillich, *The Shaking of the Foundations* (New York: Charles Scribner's Sons, 1948), 89.
47. Terrien, *Elusive Presence*, 250–51.

The third paradox of holiness in Isaiah pertains to *divine versus human initiative*. This paradox I have investigated above in items 2 and 3. In a study entitled *Divine Sovereignty and Human Responsibility: Biblical Perspectives in Tension*, D. A. Carson of Trinity Evangelical Divinity School wrestles with this paradox, which he calls "the sovereignty-responsibility tension."[48] Carson steadfastly refuses to explain away the tension by what he calls a "reductionism" which would stress either sovereignty or human initiative. In the sections above I have not sought to examine the paradox of holiness from the perspective of logic, volition, and the mechanics of causation—which appears to be Carson's approach. Rather, I have used the perspective of empowerment and divine enablement or hallowing of humankind for the attainment of the goals held out by the divine sovereign. Carson's solution is on target, but not altogether. Surely he is correct in pointing to the tension between the divine sovereignty and human initiative. Carson is not, however, guided as much by the biblical model as he avers, because he does not sufficiently take into account the dialogical aspect of the biblical proclamation; see, for example, the extremely personal interchange between prophet and divine sovereign (Isaiah 6) and between divine sovereign and Israel, his vineyard (Isaiah 1; 5:1–7).[49] The latter passage expresses the divine disappointment (that Israel had not produced the fruits for which God had hoped) and the middle passage (Isaiah 1) expresses the divine compassion even in the exercise of judgment. In the passages considered in the previous section, judgment is sent by God for a purifying purpose. The biblical focus is never on abstract causality but rather on divine intentionality in response to and in the light of human deeds. This personalistic, dialogic, action, counteraction exchange dominates the prophet's thinking—and this is so even when the metaphors employed by the prophet appear to be more impersonal. See, for example, Isa. 10:15 where the axe vaunts itself or

48. D. A. Carson, *Divine Sovereignty and Human Responsibility: Biblical Perspectives in Tension*, New Foundations Theological Library, ed. Peter Toon and Ralph Morton (Atlanta: John Knox Press, 1981), 1–38, 201–22.
49. Not only in Isaiah but in countless other portions of the Old Testament there is a dialogue between God and persons; e.g. Gen. 12:1–3; 18:22–33; Exodus 3; Amos 7:1–6; Jeremiah 2; Daniel 2; Jonah; etc.

Isa. 29:15–16 where the clay vessel accuses its maker of a lack of understanding.

It would be mistaken to argue, however, that Isaiah's doctrine of holiness is dialogic throughout. Dignity, the evidences of true royalty, counsel, and strength remain in the hands of God and are the Holy One's to give. This portion of Isaiah's doctrine is not so much dialogical as it is relational or bipolar. From the majestic God comes dignity; from the sovereign justice; from the Holy One of Israel counsel, from the powerful strength. Indeed, one of the most profound paradoxes of the book, that "the Holy God shows himself holy in righteousness" (Isa. 5:16b), is not dialogic in the sense of dialogue or action and response; it rather allows for human initiative and an ultimate divine empowerment. The paradox of holiness in Isa. 5:16b is thus dialectic: wherever human beings have been motivated to perform acts of righteousness and justice, therein the Holy One has made manifest holiness.

The fourth paradox of holiness pertains to *place*. God manifests himself in glory and holiness to Isaiah in Zion. Yet that revelation is not provincial in character or restricted in relevance to the temple alone; rather, in Zion Isaiah learns that the fullness of the whole earth is the glory, that is, the possession, of the Lord of hosts (Isa. 6:3). In an extended and moving discussion of the cosmic and ideal significance of Zion in the Hebrew Bible, Jon Levenson develops the notion that "the road up to the Temple is the objective correlative of an inner spiritual development which is crowned by a vision of God in his palace on Mount Zion."[50] Levenson thus expounds the universalistic, symbolic meaning of Zion. The awesome paradox of Isaiah's vision is that the holiness of the divine sovereign transcended the bounds of a single place and included even a word of inexorable judgment on his own beloved city-state. Reflection on the relevance of this paradox for our own day and our own cities and nation is arresting. If encounter with holiness were to include such a judgment on one's own beloved homeland, who could wish for it?

50. Jon D. Levenson, *Sinai and Zion: An Entry into the Jewish Bible* (Minneapolis: Winston Press, 1985). The discussion is found on pp. 89–184; the quotation is from pp. 177–78.

7. *Holiness calls.*

The final facet in Isaiah's doctrine of holiness concerns the vocations of holiness. Encounter with holiness is not an end in itself. Rather, holiness summons, invites, directs, and commands. Several of the vocations of holiness are implied in the facets dealt with above: cleanness (item 1); social and legal justice (item 2); nobility, righteousness, wisdom, and faithfulness (item 3). A few summary words here will therefore suffice.

The prophet's audiences were many, and included the Northern Kingdom (Isaiah 28), King Ahaz of Judah (Isaiah 7—8), King Hezekiah (Isa. 9:2–7 [Hebrew 9:1–6]; 11:1–9), the Southern Kingdom after the fall of Samaria (Isaiah 5), the remnant of the Southern Kingdom in Jerusalem after the devastation of 701 B.C.E. (Isaiah 1), Assyria (Isa. 10:1–19), Philistia (14:28–32), and Egypt (Isaiah 18). The specific vocations of holiness vary according to the audience. The divine holiness calls human beings to wisdom, nobility, and cleanness, to understanding, fidelity, justice/judgment, and righteousness. Understanding is what the people of Judah[51] lacked (Isa. 1:3). A spirit of wisdom and understanding is what will be given to the future king (Isa. 11:2). The city (Jerusalem) was once faithful (Isa. 1:21) and will be called once again "faithful town" (*qiryâ ne'ĕmānâ*: (Isa. 1:26b). Probably a successor to Isaiah echoes the meaning of the name the master prophet gave to his son, A Remnant Shall Repent (*šĕ'ār yāšûb*, Isa. 7:3) when he taught that a remnant would lean on the Holy One of Israel "in truth (*be'ĕmet*, Isa. 10:20). Just as Isaiah summoned Ahaz to have faith (Isa. 7:9), so the future king is one whose loins will be girded with fidelity (*hā'ĕmûnâ*, Isa. 11:5b). When the subtheme is of judgment, frequently the specific vocation is to woe or lamentation (see Isa. 5:8–30; 10:1–4; 14:28–32). The cleanness that holiness requires will be attained for the remnant in the city by the pursuit of justice (Isa. 11:16–17) and once again she will be called "city of righteousness" (*'îr haṣṣedek*, Isa. 1:26b). Holiness calls.

---

51. "Israel" is used in Isa. 1:3b but Judah is clearly intended.

THE THEOLOGY OF HOLINESS IN ISAIAH OF BABYLON AND ISAIAH OF THE RESTORATION

In his textbook on the Old Testament H. Keith Beebe uses the designation Isaiah of Babylon and Isaiah of the Restoration respectively to refer to the authors of Isaiah 40—55 and Isaiah 56—66.[52] The terms are less impersonal and more descriptive than Deutero-Isaiah and Trito-Isaiah and merit wider usage than they have received.

Isaiah of Babylon lived some five generations after the master. Whether or not there was such a thing as an Isaianic School, the former clearly both drew upon the theology of holiness of Isaiah of Jerusalem and creatively developed it. The most obvious point of contact is to be found in the designation for the deity as Holy One (three times: Isa. 40:25; 43:15; 49:7) and Holy One of Israel (nine times: Isa. 41:14, 20; 43:3, 14; 45:11; 47:4; 48:17; 49:7; 54:5).

As for the master, so for the successor: judgment was purgative (cf. Isa. 48:10; 1:25), the city Jerusalem is holy (cf. Isa. 48:2; 52:1; 11:9), cleanness is enjoined (cf. Isa. 52:11–12; 1:16–17), and a restoration of cleanness is envisioned for the city (Isa. 52:1) just as Isaiah of Jerusalem had envisioned a restoration of faithfulness and righteousness (Isa. 1:26). With Isaiah of Babylon there is an increased use of priestly genre, notably the priestly oracle of salvation (Isa. 41:8–16; 43:1–7; 44:1–5; etc.),[53] and the grounds for uncleanness are more priestly in orientation (Isa. 52:1). Whereas in Isaiah of Jerusalem no mention is made of the exodus traditions,[54] in Isaiah of Babylon a new exodus is foreseen (Isa. 51:9–11) and precisely the Holy One of Israel is redeemer (Isa. 41:14; 43:1– 4; 47:4; 48:17; 54:5; cf. 49:7) and savior (Isa. 43:3). In another advancement that Isaiah of Babylon shares with the priestly traditions, the relationship between holiness and crea-

---

52. H. Keith Beebe, *The Old Testament: An Introduction to Its Literary, Historical and Religious Traditions* (Belmont, Calif.: Dickenson Publishing Co., 1970), 241, 352, 364.

53. The classic study on this subject is by Joachim Begrich, "Das priesterliche Heilsorakel," *ZAW* 52 (1934): 81–92.

54. Isa. 10:26 is generally held to be from a successor.

tion is stressed. The Holy One of Israel is Creator (Isa. 41:20) and Maker (Isa. 45:11). The Holy One has created the heavens (Isa. 40:25–26). "I am the LORD, your Holy One, the Creator of Israel, your King" (Isa. 43:15). Thus the holiness of the divine king for this successor to Isaiah of Jerusalem connotes not only justice and righteousness but creation and redemption as well. A final advancement is to be seen in the notion of glory: "And the glory of the LORD shall be revealed and all flesh shall see it together" (Isa. 40:5). For Isaiah of Babylon the Hebrew *kābôd* ("glory") is not used in the sense of "possession" but of "majesty," "rule." The divine glory is not such that it can be shared with another deity (Isa. 42:8; 48:11). Everyone formed and made was created for the divine glory (Isa. 43:7).

The advances in the theology of holiness are even more noticeable in Isaiah of the Restoration. Keeping the sabbath now is given a prominence lacking altogether in his predecessors, Isaiah of Jerusalem and Isaiah of Babylon (Isa. 56:2–3; 58:13; 66:23). The temple has become a self-conscious focus of attention. The author almost nostalgically calls the temple before destruction "our beautiful and holy house" (Isa. 64:11) and looks forward to a rebeautified sanctuary (Isa. 60:13) and a reconstituted worship (Isa. 60:7). There is an intense interiority in this author's piety, which is at once quite priestly and individualist in cast and clearly sets him apart in outlook from his predecessors. Whereas Isaiah of Jerusalem speaks of his and his people's uncleanness (Isa. 6:5) and intimates that there is a connection between Israel's sins and a polluted fabric (Isa. 1:18–20), Isaiah of the Restoration is more explicit in his use of the metaphor of a polluted garment (Isa. 64:6; cf. Leviticus 15). Whereas Isaiah of Jerusalem frequently contrasts those who exalt themselves with the truly exalted One, God (Isa. 2:11; 5:16), he does not do so with the same intense piety as Isaiah of the Restoration: "For thus says the high and lofty One who inhabits eternity, whose name is Holy: 'I dwell in the high and holy place, and also with him who is of a contrite and humble spirit, to revive the spirit of the humble, and to revive the heart of the contrite'" (Isa. 57:15; cf. Ps. 51:19 [Engl. 17]). The core thoughts of exalted holiness and of empowerment are certainly Isaiah's of Jerusalem but the development is distinctive. Similarly, the practice of speaking against an aspect of cultic practice is familiar to us from Isaiah (Isa. 1:11–14); thus the words of Isaiah of the Restoration are very much in the Isaianic tradition: "Fasting like yours this day will not make your voice to be heard on high" (Isa. 58:4b). Likewise the follow-through after the critique is clearly Isaianic, yet distinctive:

> Is not this the fast that I choose:
>   to loose the bonds of wickedness,
>   to undo the thongs of the yoke,
> to let the oppressed go free,
>   and to break every yoke?
> Is it not to share your bread with the hungry,
>   and bring the homeless poor into your house;
> when you see the naked to cover him,
>   and not to hide yourself from your own flesh?
>   (Isa. 58:6–7, RSV)

In his own way, influenced by priestly liturgies,[55] Isaiah of the Restoration expanded on the Isaianic concept that the holiness of God requires above all the cleanness of justice.

Isaiah of the Restoration departs most radically from his predecessors with respect to the place and role of foreigners and aliens in relation to the temple and cultus. For Isaiah of Jerusalem part of the unhappy news of the judgment he proclaimed included the destructive presence of aliens (*zarîm*) in the land (Isa. 1:7). For Isaiah of Babylon part of the good news he proclaimed constituted the announcement that no longer would the uncircumcised and unclean come into Jerusalem the holy city (Isa. 52:1); whereas for Isaiah of the Restoration there takes place what Paul Hanson has rightly called "an astonishing democratization of the formerly exclusive sacerdotal office":[56]

> And the foreigners (*benê hannekar*) who join themselves to the LORD, to minister to him, to love the name of the LORD, and to be his servants, everyone who keeps the sabbath, and does not

---

55. Contemporary scholarship is increasingly emphasizing that Isaiah of Jerusalem as well drew upon the cultus. See below chap. 7, n. 4 for further references.

56. Paul D. Hanson, *The Dawn of Apocalyptic* (Philadelphia: Fortress Press, 1975), 68. Much of this work constitutes an important historical reconstruction on how the author(s) of Isaiah 56—66 represent visionary reconstructionists opposed to the Zadokite reconstructionists of Ezekiel 40—48 (see pp. 32–208).

profane it, and holds fast my covenant—these I will bring to my holy mountain, and make them joyful in my house of prayer; their burnt offerings and their sacrifices will be accepted on my altar; for my house shall be called a house of prayer for all peoples. (Isa. 56:6–7, RSV)

A more marked shift in attitude toward the relationship of foreigners to holiness could hardly be imagined. The shift is not confined to Isaiah 56—66, however, for in one of the most remarkable later additions to the prophecies of Isaiah of Jerusalem, some unknown successor wrote: "In that day Israel will be the third with Egypt and Assyria, a blessing in the midst of the earth, whom the Lord of hosts has blessed, saying 'Blessed be Egypt my people, and Assyria the work of my hands, and Israel my heritage'" (Isa. 19:24–25). Thus the universalism of the theology of holiness already inchoate in Isaiah of Jerusalem (Isa. 6:7) has been remarkably developed by his successors. More than a democratization has taken place, for within the one canonical book we see a movement from xenophobia to xenophilia, from exclusivity to inclusivity.

SUMMARY

In the course of this chapter we have outlined some of the reasons why the clear emphasis on the holiness of God in the prophets has been relatively neglected by twentieth-century biblical theology. Through a close examination of the writings chiefly of Isaiah of Jerusalem we have shown that the basic thesis of this study has been more than confirmed, namely, that in contradistinction to the priests of Israel, the prophets clearly taught that the holiness of God required the cleanness of social justice. Through analysis of seven different aspects of Isaiah's doctrine of holiness we sought to bring refinement to this basic thrust of the prophet's teachings by considering such questions as (1) other byproducts of the prophet's encounter with holiness, (2) the prophet's understanding of the source of social justice, (3) how the glory, sovereignty, counsel, and power of God point up areas of human life that the Holy One of Israel seeks to hallow, (4) the purgative and purposive aspects of the holiness of God, (5) the source of holiness for the remnant, (6) the fourfold paradoxical character of the divine holiness with respect to hiddenness, lofti-ness, divine initiative, and Zion-parochialism, and finally (7) the other aspects of the vocation of holiness along with the vocation to social justice. Certain advancements of this doctrine of holi-ness were traced in Isaiah of Babylon and Isaiah of the Restora-tion.

Having set forth the normative response of the prophets to the divine holiness, we are now prepared to examine the extent to which it is continued, attenuated, or modified in other tradi-tionists who carry forward the thrust of the prophetic teaching (i.e., Jeremiah, select psalms, Deuteronomy, and in the Deuter-onomistic History). In the final chapter of this book we will touch on yet further modifications that the prophetic understanding of holiness receives when it becomes blended with priestly and sapiential traditions in the apocalyptic portions of the prophets and in Daniel. Accordingly, some passages from Isaiah of the Restoration (chaps. 56—66) will also be considered in chapter 7.

CHAPTER 4

Variations and Attenuation of the Prophetic Understanding of Holiness

(Jeremiah, Select Psalms, Deuteronomy, and the Deuteronomistic History)

It is the main thesis of this book that despite a unity of vision of the holiness of God, each of the three major groups of religious functionaries in ancient Israel—priests, prophets, and sages—taught that a different kind of cleanness was required by that holiness. Chapters 1 and 2 explored the proposition that for the priests the cleanness required by holiness is one attained and preserved by separation, ritual expiations, and the maintenance of individual (including sexual) morality. The previous chapter, taking Isaiah of Jerusalem as the fullest prophetic articulation on holiness, set forth the proposition that the prophets emphasized the cleanness of social justice as the most basic requirement of the divine holiness. Taking into account the subtle and several nuances given in Isaiah and his successors to what we have called the normative prophetic response to holiness, we showed how the social justice commended by the prophets sought to emulate that combination of justice and equity that the prophets were given to see was practiced by the divine sovereign. The aim of this chapter is to trace some of the developments, permutations, and attenuation of the prophetic doctrine of holiness in Jeremiah, select Psalms, Deuteronomy, and the Deuteronomistic History.

JEREMIAH

It remains one of the curious aspects of the Hebrew Bible that only two of the three great prophets developed an explicit doctrine of holiness. Jeremiah was of a priestly line (Jer. 1:1) and drew heavily on the traditions of the prophet Hosea, but priestly notions of holiness only enter very slightly into Jeremiah's consciousness and he fails to give any integral or central place to the notion that God is holy. The title "Holy One of Israel" is found twice in passages that relate to Babylon (Jer. 50:29; 51:5) but nowhere else. The prophet Jeremiah or one of his editors speaks of how God had consecrated him (*hiqdaštîkā*) to be a prophet while he was still in his mother's womb (Jer. 1:5) and of how in her youth "Israel was holy (*qōdeš*) to the LORD" (Jer. 2:3), but these notions are neither repeated nor developed. Similarly, the prophet Jeremiah or one of his editors considers the Lord's words to be holy (Jer. 23:9) and that his habitation (*mā'ôn*)— probably the temple—is holy (Jer. 25:30). Twice the prophet or one of his editors refers to the sanctuary (*miqdāš*: Jer. 17:12; 51:51) and once to the future sanctity of the valley of the dead (Jer. 31:40). Jeremiah 17:19–27 contains a little homily on sanctifying the sabbath and Jer. 1:15, which refers to "holy flesh," that is, to sacrifices, is an ironic poem on the "pointlessness of sacrifice" (cf. 6:20; 7:22–23).[1] With these references the *vocabulary* of Jeremiah *on holiness* has virtually been exhausted.[2] The relative paucity of references in Jeremiah to the vocabulary of holiness may serve to indicate the difficulty a researcher will have in pursuing the theology of holiness in the prophet. It nonetheless should be pointed out that there is in Jeremiah a very powerful *implicit* doctrine of holiness: the coming judgment and wrath of God is as awesome as it is inexorable (Jer. 1:11–19; 4:19–26; 15:5–9); the divine is powerful and overpowering (Jer. 10:12–16; 20:7; 25:30–38; 47:2–7), a consuming force (Jer. 5:12–17; 7:30–34; 9:7–9; 10:23–25), mysterious and transcendent (Jer. 18:13–

---

1. The phrase in quotation marks is from Robert P. Carroll, *Jeremiah: A Commentary*, Old Testament Library (Philadelphia: Westminster Press, 1986), 273.

2. The remaining references are Jer. 6:4; 22:7; 51:27, 28, where the verb *qdš* is used in the sense of "prepare."

17; 23:18–20), and the source of a sense of intoxication and fascination (Jer 20:7–12; 25:15–29). As we saw in the previous chapter, in the prophet-priest Ezekiel, in contrast, the teaching of holiness is explicit as well as implicit.

HOLINESS IN THE PSALMS

At the outset of the previous chapter it was also pointed out that the concept of the holiness of God is of considerable antiquity, going back to early monarchic (1 Sam. 2:1–10) or premonarchic times (Exod. 15:1–17). In the collection of psalms that celebrate the kingship of the Lord—Psalms 93—100—the holiness of God is given considerable prominence. A number of years ago Hermann Gunkel suggested that these psalms, which depend on ancient Near Eastern prototypes, are preexilic, but in their present state probably represent a reworking after the experience of the exile and of the influence of Deutero-Isaiah.[3] Evidence of the correctness of Gunkel's conjecture is indeed found in these psalms which combine both priestly and prophetic notions of holiness. Psalm 93:5 reads: "Thy testimonies are very sure;/holiness is fitting for thy house,/O LORD, unto the length of days" (au. trans.). The reference to "testimonies" suggests the high probability that the author lived in a time when the law had reached a position of particular respect, and the verb "is fitting" (*n'h*) is only found elsewhere in this mode in Isaiah of Babylon (Isa. 52:7) and in Canticles (Song of Sol. 1:10). Some of the allusions to holiness bear no clear-cut signs of the postexilic era, for example, "Worship the LORD in holy array; tremble before him all the earth" (Ps. 96:9) and "O sing to the LORD a new song,/for he has done marvelous things!//His right hand and his holy arm / have gotten him victory" (Ps. 98:1), but others may show signs of the exilic or postexilic era: "Rejoice in the LORD, O you righteous,/ and give thanks to his holy name" (Ps. 97:12, RSV; lit. "for the remembrance of his holiness").[4] This psalm

3. Hermann Gunkel, *Einleitung in die Psalmen*, 3d ed. (Göttingen: Vandenhoeck & Ruprecht, 1975), 94–116. The complete work was first published by Gunkel's son-in-law, Joachim Begrich, in 1933, after Gunkel's death.
4. The psalm contains an anti-idolatrous section (vv. 6–9) reminiscent of Isaiah of Babylon. If the RSV rendering were based on the Hebrew *šēm qodšî*

also contains an anti-idolatrous section (vv. 6–9) reminiscent of Isaiah of Babylon (see also Pss. 96:4–5; 97:9).

Of the psalms that celebrate the divine kingship, Psalm 99 especially also celebrates the divine holiness.

> [1] The LORD reigns; let the peoples tremble!
> [3] He sits enthroned upon the cherubim;
>   let the earth quake!
> Let them praise thy great and terrible name!
>   Holy is he!
> [4] Mighty King, lover of justice;
>   thou hast established equity;
> thou hast executed justice
>   and righteousness in Jacob.
> [5] Extol the LORD our God;
>   worship at his footstool!
>   Holy is he!
> [9] Extol the LORD our God,
>   and worship at his holy mountain;
>   for the LORD our God is holy!
>   (Ps. 99:1, 3–5, 9, RSV)

A prophetic thrust is seen throughout these psalms in the emphasis on righteousness and justice of the divine king (Pss. 94:1–2, 24; 96:13; 97:2; 98:9; 99:4) as well as on the divine glory and majesty (Pss. 93:1; 95:3–4; 96:3, 6–8; 97:3, 6).

Another example of an exilic or postexilic modification of a psalm in which prophetic interests feature alongside the holiness of God is Psalm 51. Of all of the psalms from the monarchic period that belong to a category other than the Wisdom Psalms, Psalm 51 above all expresses the depths of the requirements of holiness—a removal of the stain of a rebellious transgression, an inward cleansing from the consequences of moral failure (vv. 1–4; Engl. 1–2). The usual sacrifices of the liturgy are simply not seen to be sufficient to attain cleanness and purification (v. 19; Engl. 17). As is the case later with the Joban poet, the psalmist in

another reason for an exilic or postexilic date would be present. From my research (available in an unpublished paper presented at the 1983 national meeting of the Society of Biblical Literature) I discovered that no one of the occurrences of the expressions "my/thy/his holy name" (cf. Lev. 20:3, 39, 22:2, 32; Ezek. 36:20–22; 39:7, 25; 43:7–8; Amos 2:7; Pss. 33:21; 103:1; 105:3; 106:47; 111:9; 145:21; Isa. 57:15; 1 Chron. 16:10, 35; 29:16) can clearly be assigned a preexilic date.

the presence of holiness becomes aware of the interior integrity that holiness calls forth: "Behold, thou desirest truth (*'emet*) in the hidden parts,/and by stopping me up (*wûběsātūm*), teach me wisdom" (v. 8; Engl. 6). The poet uses the imagery of the stopping up and concealing of wells to express his prayer that through adversity God would instruct him. That holiness requires an interior cleanness is reiterated: "Create for me, O God, a pure mind;/make anew within me a steady spirit" (v. 12; Engl. 10). The presence of holiness does not frighten; rather, the psalmist sees it as the source of his deliverance and ability to attain the nobility to which he feels called:

> Do not send me away from thy presence,
>   nor take from me thy holy spirit.
> Return to me the joy of thy deliverance,
>   and a noble spirit will sustain me.
>   (vv. 13–14; Engl. 11–12, au. trans.)

In the exilic addition to this psalm, the person (priest?) responsible for the addition does not negate any of the above affirmations on the requirements of holiness, but he does place alongside them the petition for the rebuilding of Jerusalem and an affirmation that God will also take delight in the restored offerings on the altar (vv. 20–21; Engl. 18–19). The exilic editor thus attests: holiness requires cultic exteriorization as well as moral interiorization. This teaching, of course, is especially reminiscent of Jeremiah who also taught the need for an *inner* correspondence to *outward* religious symbols (Jer. 4:4).

A THEOLOGY OF THE NUMINOUS PRESENCE:
DEUTERONOMY

The Book of Deuteronomy, like the psalms mentioned in the previous section, is a preexilic work to which exilic and postexilic additions have been made. Like the previously mentioned psalms the Book of Deuteronomy also combines priestly with prophetic concerns even though it calls neither the divine, the divine name, nor the spirit "holy." In its central chapters, however, the authors of this book evolved one of the most complex and impressive theologies of holiness to be found in the Old

Testament. This theology is at once prophetic, priestly and, to an extent, sapiential, as we shall see. The traditions underlying those central chapters, 4–30, are widely recognized to be northern in provenance. With the priestly writers, the northern Deuteronomists taught that holiness required separation. Certain practices of other peoples were forbidden Israel because the nation was holy (Deut. 14:1–2); restrictions on food were laid upon Israel because the nation was holy (Deut. 14:21); because the deity was present in the midst of Israel's camp to protect her from enemies it was required of her to show circumspection with respect to covering the reproductive organs, for the camp was holy (Deut. 23:15; Engl. 14). Prophetic iconoclasm, that is, the breaking down of the altars and images of the inhabitants of the land is also enjoined and conjoined with a teaching reminiscent of the Holiness Code: "For you are a people holy to the LORD your God; the LORD your God has chosen you to be a people for his own possession, out of all the peoples that are on the face of the earth" (Deut. 7:6). Israel's election, holiness, reputation, and distinctiveness among the nations is also bound up with the keeping of the commandments.

> You have declared this day concerning the LORD that he is your God, and that you will walk in his ways, and keep his statutes and his commandments and his ordinances, and will obey his voice; and the LORD has declared this day concerning you that you are a people for his own possession, as he has promised you, and that you are to keep all his commandments, that he will set you high above all nations that he has made, in praise and in fame and in honor, and that you shall be a people holy to the LORD your God, as he has spoken. (Deut. 26:17–19, RSV; cf. 28:9)

Four of the elements in the Deuteronomic theology of holiness are already in evidence in the above-cited passages: presence, keeping of the law, election, and separation. The richness of the doctrine, however, is hardly captured by reference to these four. In order to explicate more fully these basic elements—and the first element in particular—it is necessary to pay attention to the ancillary vocabulary of holiness to which the paradigm of Rudolph Otto has alerted us.

(1) *Through the symbols of fire, voice, smoke, darkness, cloud, and law the Deuteronomic authors depict a powerful theology of the numinous presence of God.* Even though the Deuteronomic authors do not use the term *qādōš* ("holy") of God, they nonetheless describe the presence of an awesome God. "And you came near and stood at the foot of the mountain, while the mountain burned with fire to the heart of heaven, wrapped in darkness, cloud, and gloom. Then the LORD spoke to you out of the midst of the fire; you heard the sound of words, but saw no form; there was only a voice" (Deut. 4:11–12, RSV). Here in brief compass we see expressed the *energicum* aspect of holiness ("fire") and *mysterium* ("darkness, cloud, and gloom" and "voice"). The responsiveness of this holy God and wonder at the divine presence—the *fascinans* aspect—is to be seen in the following: "For what great nation is there that has a god so near to it as the LORD our God is to us, whenever we call upon him? And what great nation is there that has statutes and ordinances so righteous as all this law which I set before you this day?" (Deut. 4:7–8, RSV). The law, *hattôrâ*, is not conceived as a burden but as a gracious indication of the divine presence. As an appropriate response to the numinous presence of God, Israel is instructed to let the people hear the divine words—presumably from the reading of the law—"so that they may learn to fear me all the days that they live on the earth, and that they may teach their children so" (Deut. 4:10). The numinous presence of God in symbol and law requires reverence (*tremendum*) and instruction of offspring.

(2) *The theology of holiness in Deuteronomy has at its core a sense of gratitude that the hidden God (deus absconditus) has graciously consented to reveal the law (lex revelata).* An affirmation of the difference between the divine and humans is made by the authors of Deuteronomy, but also of the divine proximity and imperative in the law: "The secret things belong to the LORD our God; but the things that are revealed belong to us and to our children for ever, that we may do all the words of this law" (Deut. 29:28, RSV; Engl. 29:29). The commandments are neither afar off nor inaccessible, rather, "the word is very near you; it is in your mouth and in your heart, so that you can do it" (Deut. 30:14; cf. Rom. 10:6–9). The chief grounds for gratitude for the

law is that in obedience to it were to be found blessings and life (Deut. 30:15–20).

(3) *In the Deuteronomic theology of election, integral to the theology of holiness, God chooses a place for his name to dwell and Israel as his holy people.* Curiously, the Deuteronomic authors themselves do not use the term "holy name." As von Rad has shown, however, Deuteronomy's is a "name theology."[5] In light of the above, it is submitted that it would be truer to the theology of Deuteronomy to characterize it as a theology of the numinous presence of God, of which election of a place for the divine name to dwell is a part (Deuteronomy 12). In recent times, Samuel Terrien has given a prominence to the theology of the name in his theology of the Old Testament.[6] He challenges von Rad's notion that the divine name in Deuteronomy "verges closely upon an hypostasis."[7] Instead, he argues: "The reality which the word designates implies the cultic congress and the participation of man in the perspective of time. To speak of a place where the name of Yahweh sojourns is to refer to the ceremonial of a congregation at worship."[8] And, further, "The name stood for a religious phenomenon of considerable complexity, which blended divine initiative and human response: the word 'name' appears to have been a device for designating Yahweh's will to create a holy people within the history of mankind and at the same time Israel's acceptance of this election."[9] Terrien's intuition and insight is certainly true to the other aspects of the Deuteronomic theology of holiness alluded to, or explicated, above: to the divine voice Israel is enjoined to hearken (Deut. 4:30; 5:27; 8:20; 28:15a; 30:10a, etc.); to the law and covenant to which she is enjoined to be obedient (Deut. 4:40; 12:28; 28:15b,

---

5. Gerhard von Rad, *Studies in Deuteronomy*, SBT 9 (London: SCM Press, 1953), 37–44.

6. Samuel Terrien, *The Elusive Presence: Toward a New Biblical Theology* (New York: Harper & Row, 1978), 109, 121, 139, 197, 204, 207. Terrien contrasts the theology of the name which focuses upon the hearing of the word with the (largely priestly) theology of glory which focuses upon the seeing of the divine glory.

7. Ibid., 200; the citation is from von Rad, *Studies in Deuteronomy*, 38.

8. Ibid.

9. Ibid.

58–59; 29:8 [Engl. 9]; 30:10b–d, etc.); and, if Israel is obedient, "the LORD will establish you as a people holy to himself, as he has sworn to you" (Deut. 28:9).

Two correlations or correspondences have been highlighted in the above: (1) the correlation between divine act, whether in voice, law, or election of Israel, and the requirement of an obedient response, and (2) the correlation between the two aspects of the divine election—choosing a place for the divine name, and choosing Israel as a holy people. The second correlation follows because of the first. Election lays upon Israel a responsibility. Election of a place for the divine name and of Israel as a holy people requires obedience to the law (Deut. 12:1; 28:9). Both forms of election require a separation.

(4) *The separation required of Israel in the theology of Deuteronomy does not derive from a doctrine that explicitly affirms the holiness of God (as is the case in Israelite priestly traditions), nor does it derive directly from a doctrine that links the divine holiness with righteousness (as is the case in the prophetic traditions), nor does the requirement of separation derive from an overpowering sense of the divine omnipresence (as is frequently the case in the Israelite sapiential traditions); rather, the call for separation is derived from the notion of the oneness of God and of the divine election of a people and of a particular place for worship.* Even though it is apparent that the Deuteronomic authors combine priestly, prophetic, and sapiential interests, the theology of the numinous presence found in the book is distinctive. The authors grounded their call for separation from the peoples and their gods in an explicit monotheism and doctrine of election. The famous Shema calls for the love of God and the instruction of children (Deut. 6:4–9). The responsibility of educating one's children precedes even the call for iconoclasm and separation from the peoples (Deuteronomy 7). Destruction of alternate places of worship is enjoined because God has chosen a particular place for his name to dwell, for offerings, and sacrifices and worship (Deuteronomy 12). To be called to be a holy people is to be called to be a separate people, abiding by the covenant, obeying the laws, pursuing justice, and worshiping God alone.

In older German commentaries on Deuteronomy it was suggested that the theology of the book could be summarized in the phrase: *ein Gott, ein Kult, ein Volk* ("one God, one cultus, one people"). That summary captures an important part of the theology of the book.

In recent times, Paul Hanson has written a moving study, *The People Called: The Growth of Community in the Bible*.[10] Hanson has located three basic and recurring notions underlying the communities described in the long course of biblical history. These notions are righteousness, compassion, and worship. The divine who performs righteous acts requires it of humans; the compassionate God requires the display of a similar compassion; "in worship the dramatic interplay of Yahweh's righteousness and compassion infused the faithful with the qualities empowering them to become a community dedicated to God's justice and peace."[11] Hanson has shown how the Deuteronomic authors, faithful to the earlier Yahwistic notion of community, broadened and deepened it.[12]

(5) *There is a compelling sense of urgency, immediacy, and confidence in the Deuteronomic theology of the numinous presence of God.* Content alone does not tell the full story of the teaching of the Book of Deuteronomy. The authors recall how God was present in the past, is present today, and will be present in the future. The recurring use of the expression "this day" signals this qualitative aspect of the Deuteronomic theology: "And the LORD your God took you and led you from the iron furnace, from Egypt, so that you (plural) might be to him a people with an inheritance as at this day" (Deut. 4:20, au. trans.; cf. 4:37). There is no simple antiquarianism here—a recollection of the past for its own sake—rather, the rhetorical effect of the use of the phrase "as at this day" is to drive home the point that the past deliverance at the Exodus was a sign of the divine election of Israel, which still obtains. Further, the divine presence is not only urgent, it is also *socially* inclusive ("You stand this day all of you before the LORD your God: your heads, your tribes, your elders,

10. Paul D. Hanson, *The People Called: The Growth of Community in the Bible* (San Francisco: Harper & Row, 1986).

11. Ibid., 74.

12. Ibid., 167–76.

and your officers, all the men of Israel, your little ones, your wives, and the sojourner who is in your camp, both he who hews your wood and he who draws your water," Deut. 29:9–10; Engl. 10–11) and *temporally* inclusive ("Nor is it with you only that I make this sworn covenant, but with him who is not here with us this day as well as with him who stands here with us this day before the LORD our God," Deut 29:13–14, RSV; Engl. 14–15). The authors wish to press home to their hearers and readers that the covenant made "this day" applies even to future generations ("with him who is not here with us this day").

It is part of the surpassing genius of this book that in its rhetoric the reader is drawn into the orbit of the events described and commandments uttered. In prophetic address Moses looks to the future and sees that if a future calamity were to come upon Israel, men in the future would explain it on these grounds: "It is because they forsook the covenant of the LORD, the God of their fathers, which he made with them when he brought them out of the land of Egypt, and went and served other gods and worshiped them, gods whom they had not known and whom he had not allotted to them" (Deut. 29:24–25, RSV; Engl. 25–26). The prophecy continues with the mention of the wrath of God and of the divine determination to bring upon Israel "all the curses written in this book; and the LORD uprooted them from their land in anger and fury and great wrath, and cast them into another land, as at this day" (Deut. 29:26–27, RSV; Engl. 27–28). "As at this day"—the author of these lines was obviously living in a time when the exile had become a reality. Because there is not a hint of an indication that the author is thinking in terms of both a northern and a southern exile, it seems to me most likely that chapters 4 and 29–30 of Deuteronomy come from a time before the fall of Jerusalem and the ensuing exile to Babylon. In any event, the author of these chapters writes with a compelling immediacy: even when Israel is driven to a foreign land, if she returns and hearkens to the divine voice with heart and soul, "then the Lord your God will restore your fortunes, and have compassion upon you, and he will gather you again from the peoples where the LORD your God has scattered you" (Deut. 30:1–3, RSV). With some justification, the conservative Israeli

scholar M. H. Segal has argued that Deuteronomy is not "a programme for the reform of an effete and corrupt society almost at
the end of its political life" but rather "a programme of a young
and vigorous people at the beginning of its national existence."[13]
My disagreement with Segal is not the correctness of his observation on the vigor and compelling nature of the language of
Deuteronomy, but with his false inference that words of moral
and spiritual power could not have been uttered in time of calamity.

(6) *Despite the recurrent emphasis in the Book of Deuteronomy
on the importance of obedience to the law, the numinous presence
of God is not grounded in an anthropocentric doctrine of retribution, but rather in the divine compassion and election.* It is
understandable that the "Deuteronomic view of retribution" has
come to be synonymous with a rigorously anthropocentric doctrine of rewards and punishments. The Book of Deuteronomy
does teach that much of the choice of life and death is in the
hands of Israel herself (cf. Deut. 30:15–20). Close examination
reveals, however, that there are several layers of theological attitude toward an anthropocentric retribution.[14] In the last analysis,
human activity is not responsible for Israel's election; rather, it
rests in the divine initiative:

> It was not because you were more in number than any other people
> that the LORD set his love upon you and chose you, for you were
> the fewest of all peoples; but it is because the LORD loves you, and
> is keeping the oath which he swore to your fathers, that the LORD
> has brought you out with a mighty hand and redeemed you from
> the house of bondage, from the hand of Pharaoh king of Egypt.
> (Deut. 7:7–8, RSV)

All suffering was not because of Israel's sin—the way it would be
in a strictly anthropocentric doctrine—but rather,

> He humbled you and let you hunger and fed you with manna,
> which you did not know, nor did your fathers know; that he might
> make you know that man does not live by bread alone, but that man

13. M. H. Segal, *The Pentateuch* (Jerusalem: Magnes Press, 1967), 78.

14. See my essay "The Theology of Retribution in the Book of Deuteronomy,"
CBQ 32 (1970): 1–12.

lives by everything that proceeds out of the mouth of the LORD. (Deut. 8:3, RSV)

Far from being consistently anthropocentric, the authors warn against it:

> Beware lest you say in your heart, 'My power and the might of my hand have gotten me this wealth.' You shall remember the LORD your God, for it is he who gives you power to get wealth; that he may confirm his covenant which he swore to your fathers, as at this day. (Deut. 8:17–18, RSV)

The Book of Deuteronomy continually enjoins obedience to the commandments, statutes, and ordinances by which God has so graciously let his presence be known, but in the final analysis the book does not teach a so-called Deuteronomic view of retribution, that is, one that is rigorously anthropocentric, but rather one that is radically theocentric.

(7) *Although the Deuteronomic authors continued to affirm the numinous presence of God in times of war, they significantly desacralized it—especially with respect to the ancient symbol, the ark.* The presence in Deuteronomy of the ideology of the holy war has been widely recognized since von Rad's studies and needs little reiteration here.[15] There is no question: for the Deuteronomic authors, God will be powerfully present in times of battle:

> Hear O Israel, you draw near this day to battle against your enemies: let not your heart faint; do not fear, or tremble, or be in dread of them; for the LORD your God is he that goes with you, to fight for you against your enemies, to give you the victory. (Deut. 20:3–4)

These words the priest was enjoined to say. In two regards, however, the old ideology of holy war is significantly modified. (1) The ark is no longer given prominence as a symbol of the divine presence in war; rather, it is radically reinterpreted to become the repository for the two tables of the law, and is renamed "the ark of the covenant" (Deut. 10:1–5, 8). Terrien made this point

---

15. von Rad, "Deuteronomy and the Holy War," chap. 4 in *Studies in Deuteronomy*, 45–59; idem, *Der Herilige Krieg im alten Israel*, Abhandlungen zur Theologie des Alten und Neuen Testaments 20 (Zurich: Zwingli, 1951).

several years ago: "The Deuteronomists gave a meaning to the ark that differed dramatically from that of the Holy War tradition."[16] (2) Even though the Deuteronomic authors continue to stress the importance of separation from the deities, the "abominations" of enemies, they make explicit provision for the appropriation of spoils of war—and even of incorporating into Israelite society a spouse from among the vanquished for an Israelite warrior (Deut. 20:10–20; 21:10–14).

TORAH AS SIGN OF PRESENCE AND SOURCE OF GUIDANCE

A few words may now be said by way of summary of the Deuteronomic theology of holiness in numinous presence. The Torah, the ordinances and statutes, are understood to be God's command, uttered by his voice (Deut. 4:9–12). This word is near—in heart and mind—because Israel has not forgotten it, but kept it and taught it (Deut. 30:11–14; 6:6–9). Protestants have had a hard time appropriating the teaching of Deuteronomy. Protestant commentators on Deuteronomy of both evangelical and neoorthodox persuasion have been wont to deliver antinomistic homilies (so, e.g., the late Peter Craigie)[17] or gratuitous caveats on how legalism was a latent possibility in Deuteronomy's regard for the law (so R. E. Clements[18]). More appropriately, James Sanders has pointed out how there is a twofold aspect to Torah: it is both *mythos* (story) and *ethos* (ethics), gospel and law, good news as well as code of regulations.[19] The distinction is as important as it is helpful. Yet even in Sanders's analysis there is a dichotomy, an opposition, implied in the distinction. The notion is not appropriate to the authors of Deuteronomy because for them the statutes and ordinances are themselves a part of the good news of Yahweh's presence. In Deuteronomy the law itself is a gracious source of guidance and direction for Israel on how she might enter into

---

16. Terrien, *Elusive Presence*, 201.
17. Peter C. Craigie, *The Book of Deuteronomy*, (New International Commentary on the Old Testament [Grand Rapids: Wm. B. Eerdmans, 1976]), 43–45.
18. R. E. Clements, *God's Chosen People* (London: SCM Press, 1968), 61.
19. James A. Sanders, "Torah and Christ," *Interpretation* 29 (1975): 372–75.

fullness of life. The Protestant reformers spoke of the three uses of the law: the *usus civilis* (or *politicus*), the *usus theologicus*, and the *usus didacticus*, that is, the uses for governance and discipline in the body politic, for bringing souls to repentance, and for guidance.[20] Interpreters of the Book of Deuteronomy have abundant examples of how the law may be a source of guidance for theology and ethics. J. A. Thompson is already moving in this direction when he says:

> But even these [covenant stipulations] were part of a total movement of grace, a fact that made law neither a burden nor a means of achieving merit before God. His laws were rather His gracious gift of guidance for a peaceful life in the new land. They thus provided guidelines for a happy life and a means by which Israel might demonstrate her loyalty to the God who had redeemed her.[21]

THE DEUTERONOMISTIC HISTORY AS PARADIGMATIC HISTORY

The successors to the authors of the central chapters in Deuteronomy (Deuteronomy 4—30) were responsible for the creation of two great works: a reedited version of the Book of Jeremiah and the Deuteronomistic History (Deuteronomy — 2 Kings).[22]

20. See Emil Brunner, *The Divine Imperative*, trans. Olive Wyon (Philadelphia: Westminster Press, 1947; first published 1932), 150–51. See also the discussion by Gerhard Ebeling, *Word and Faith*, trans. James W. Leitch (London: SCM Press, 1963), 62–78.

21. J. A. Thompson, *Deuteronomy*, Tyndale Old Testament Commentaries (London: Inter-Varsity Press, 1974), 13. For a similar positive assessment, see also Clements, *God's Chosen People*, 58–61.

22. For critical background, see Martin Noth, *Überlieferungsgeschichtliche Studien* I, 3d ed (Halle [Saale]: M. Niemeyer, 1967; first published 1943); now available in English, *The Deuteronomistic History*, JSOT Supplement 18 (Sheffield, JSOT Press, 1981); Frank Moore Cross, "The Themes of the Book of Kings and the Structure of the Deuteronomistic History," in *Canaanite Myth and Hebrew Epic: Essays in the History of the Religion of Israel* (Cambridge: Harvard University Press, 1973), 275–89; Rudolph Smend, "Das Gesetz und die Völker. Ein Beitrag zur deuteronomistischen Redaktionsgeschichte," in *Probleme biblischer Theologie*; ed. H. W. Wolff (Munich: Chr. Kaiser, 1971), 494–509; Walter Dietrich, *Prophetie und Geschichte*; FRLANT 108 (Göttingen: Vandenhoeck & Ruprecht, 1972); and Ernst Würthwein, *Das erste Buch der Könige, Kapitel 1-16*, ATD 11/1 (Göttingen: Vandenhoeck & Ruprecht, 1977); and Anthony F. Campbell, S.J., *Of Prophets and Kings: A Late Ninth-Century Document (1 Samuel 1—2 Kings 10)*, CBQMS 17 (Washington, D.C.: Catholic Biblical Association, 1986).

Ralph W. Klein and Terence E. Fretheim, among others, have emphasized the element of grace to be seen through, in, and behind the element of judgment in the Deuteronomistic History.[23] Fretheim put it succinctly in the following terms:

> All of God's actions are directed to one goal: "That you might know that the Lord is God; there is no other besides him" (Deut. 4:35, 39; 30:6). It is finally this picture of God that is the interpretative key to the whole history of Israel.[24]

In other words, the theological key to the Deuteronomistic History is to be found already in the Book of Deuteronomy. To what extent this is true also of the theology of holiness in the Deuteronomistic History will be the subject of the next section.

A sensible and honorable solution to recent squabbles in which the heirs of the biblical theology movement have found themselves with respect to the meaning of "history" is, I submit, at hand.[25] In 1956 Eric Voegelin suggested in his now famous *Order and History* that a clear distinction should be made between "pragmatic history" (academic, scientific historical writing) and "paradigmatic history."[26] Authors of the latter, as the term suggests, write history in order to teach, to hold up models (paradigms) of action, attitude, and conduct. The biblical historical writing, without question, belongs to this category. It is simply anachronistic to call the biblical writing scientific, objective historiography. Voegelin made an exceedingly useful suggestion, which, surprisingly, to date few biblical scholars have picked up.

23. See Terence E. Fretheim, *Deuteronomic History*; Interpreting Biblical Texts, ed. Lloyd R. Bailey, Sr. and Victor P. Furnish (Nashville: Abingdon Press, 1983), 26; and Ralph W. Klein, *Israel in Exile: A Theological Interpretation*, OBT, ed. Walter Brueggemann and John R. Donahue, S.J. (Philadelphia: Fortress Press, 1979), 23–43.

24. Fretheim, *Deuteronomic History*, 26.

25. For background on the debate, see Brevard Childs, *Biblical Theology in Crisis* (Philadelphia: Westminster Press, 1970), 13–27; and James Barr, "Revelation Through History in the Old Testament and Modern Theology," *Princeton Seminary Bulletin* 56 (1963): 4–14; also in *Interpretation* 17 (1963): 193–205.

26. Eric Voegelin, *Order and History*, 5 vols. (Baton Rouge, La.: Louisiana State University Press, 1956–1987), see esp. vol. 1, *Israel and Revelation*, 122–24.

In a fine article several years ago John J. Collins[27] approached the idea of Voegelin; and others have done so,[28] but without the crispness and clarity that Voegelin's categorization carries.

THE THEOLOGY OF HOLINESS IN THE DEUTERONOMISTIC HISTORY

In several respects the understanding of holiness in the Deuteronomistic history is similar to that found in Deuteronomy 4—30. (1) The ark continues to be called the "ark of the covenant" in the material that we believe the Deuteronomistic Historian(s) assembled (Deut. 31:9, 25; cf. Jos. 3:6, 8; 4:7, 18; etc.). Far more explicitly than in the Book of Deuteronomy, however, in the Deuteronomistic History the ark is given prominence as a potent sacral force in war (Joshua 6). The Deuteronomistic Historians also reintroduce the older concept of the *mal'ak yahweh* ("angel of the LORD," 2 Kings 19:35; cf. Josh. 5:13–15), which the Deuteronomic authors had chosen to bypass. (2) The stress upon separation from idolatry and the importance of radical iconoclasm continues in force (see esp. Joshua 7, Judges 6, 2 Kings 22—23). (3) Some of the numinous aspects of the holiness of God are reaffirmed by the Deuteronomists—especially in the older material which they have preserved. Thus the stress on the fire of the Lord (Deut. 32:22) and on the cloud ('*ānān*, Deut. 31:15).[29] The Deuteronomists' references, however, are not as profuse as the references in Deut. 5:22, and the notion of the "pillar of cloud" resting over the door of the tent is closer to the old traditions of the Yahwistic and Elohistic sources (cf. Num. 12:5, etc.) than to the authors of Deuteronomy 4—30. (4) The

27. John J. Collins, "The 'Historical Character' of the Old Testament in Recent Biblical Theology," *CBQ* 41 (1979): 185–204.

28. See, e.g., Fretheim's careful discussion in *Deuteronomic History*, 27–48; and James Barr's suggestion (following Hans Frei) that "narrative is 'history-like'" ("Story and History in Biblical Theology," *The Journal of Religion* 56 [1976]: 1–17; reprinted in idem, *The Scope and Authority of the Bible*, Explorations in Theology 7 [London: SCM Press, 1980], 1–17). The reference is to Hans Frei, *The Eclipse of Biblical Narrative* (New Haven: Yale University Press, 1974), chap. 1.

29. George Mendenhall has argued—and it seems to me with some persuasion—that the '*ānān* should be seen as the mask of Yahweh, very nearly equivalent to the Akkadian *melammū*, the awe-inspiring splendor of Ashur (*Tenth Generation* [Baltimore: Johns Hopkins University Press, 1973], 48–59).

older notion of God as (holy) warrior continues in effect in the narrative (Deut. 31:8) as well as in some of the poetry from an older period (Deut. 32:29–43). The last-mentioned passage from the Song of Moses also contains a notion not found in Deuteronomy 4—30, namely, that of the vengeance of God.[30] Thus, similarities in the theology of holiness between Deuteronomy and his successors are also shot through with significant differences. Three of the more interesting dissimilarities not mentioned above may now be examined in greater detail.

(1) *Whereas the name "holy God" is entirely absent from Deuteronomy 4—30, it is found to a fairly limited extent in the work of the Deuteronomists and in the older materials preserved by them.* Too much should not be made of this fact, but it is of interest for it provides something of a model of how allusions to the Almighty will vary from generation to generation even among those who belong to the same circle or school of tradition. In the speech of Joshua to the Israelites at Shechem, he says, "You cannot serve the LORD, for he is a holy God; he is a jealous God; he will not forgive your transgressions or your sins" (Josh. 24:19). The issue of whether or not this speech is from the Deuteronomist or is of a pre-Deuteronomic origin need not concern us here. The point remains that holiness is directly attributed to God within the Deuteronomistic History, and—perhaps a point of equal importance—the attribution is on the lips of a northern leader at a northern shrine. Elsewhere in the Deuteronomistic History the holiness of God is given greatest explicit mention in the Song of Hannah (1 Sam. 2:1–10): "There is none holy like the LORD,/ there is none besides thee; there is no rock like our God" (1 Sam. 2:2). Shiloh, where the psalm is reported to have been delivered, is, of course, a northern shrine. In view of the last verse of the psalm ("The LORD will judge the ends of the earth;/ he will give strength to his king,/ and exalt the power of his anointed" 1 Sam. 2:10), scholars have suggested that this may be classified as a royal psalm. Again, the critical question is of no great moment inasmuch as the presence of the psalm within the Deuterono-

---

30. Mendenhall has suggested, and it seems to me correctly, that biblical use of *nāqām* stresses Yahweh's sovereignty over the state and is exercised either as the divine *imperium* or as a punitive vindication (*Tenth Generation*, 92–96).

mistic History is not at issue. Less significant from the perspective of the use of the term "holy" in relation to God—but not less significant insofar as the potency of the ark is concerned—is the fact that the deuteronomistic historians do record that the men of Bethshemesh say, after a number of them have been slain for looking into the ark, "Who is able to stand before the LORD, this holy God?" (1 Sam. 6:20). Similarly, it is not surprising that the name "Holy One of Israel" is found on the lips of Isaiah of Jerusalem (2 Kings 19:22) inasmuch as we saw above in the third chapter of this work how frequently that very name for God is used by the prophet. What is surprising is not that the term "holy" is used of God in the course of the Deuteronomistic History, but that it is used so seldom.

(2) *Whereas the term "holy people" occurs with some frequency in Deuteronomy, the term is missing altogether from the other parts of the Deuteronomistic History.* Perhaps the closeness of the fall of Jerusalem made the deuteronomists hesitate to use the term "holy people." The authors of Deuteronomy 4—30, writing—as seems to me probable—in the wake of the fall of Samaria did not hesitate to use the expression "holy people" (Deut. 7:6; 14:2, 21; 26:19; 28:9), but the Deuteronomists did. The closest these authors-editors came to the term is in Deuteronomy 33, in the introduction to the Song of Moses—which, in any event, is probably predeuteronomic: "Yea, he loves his peoples (*'amîm*), and all those holy to him (*qĕdōšāyw*) are in his hand" (Deut. 33:3a, au. trans.). The context, a blessing of the several tribes, makes it plain that the term *'amîm* is viewing each tribe as an *'am* (people). Here again, the nonuse by the deuteronomists of the term "holy people" should not, in my judgment, be given too great a theological significance. The shift, however, is instructive. In the Holiness Code (Leviticus 17—26), which in all probability comes from the same period as the Deuteronomistic History—that is, from the period of the Judean exile to Babylonia—a branch of deuteronomists very definitely did find the explicit attribution of holiness to the Lord as well as to the Lord's people not only to be acceptable, but to be a notion around which to organize their theological reflections.[31]

31. In contemporary liturgical usage, it is accurate to observe, I believe, that

(3) *Somewhat paradoxically, the deuteronomists, on the one hand, relativize the importance of the temple when they acknowledge that God has an even more exalted place in the universe than is acknowledged in the Book of Deuteronomy, but on the other hand, the deuteronomists place a greater stress on the human initiative and less on the divine election than do the authors of Deuteronomy.* It is widely acknowledged that the prayer of Solomon at the dedication of the temple in 1 Kings 8 is the product of the deuteronomistic editor. It is of interest that in this long prayer no term for holy or holiness is attributed to God even though reference is made to "holy vessels" (v. 4), "the holy of holies" (v. 6), and "holy place" (vv. 8, 10). It is asserted, however, several times that heaven is the dwelling place (vv. 30, 39, 43, 49) of God and that even the highest heaven cannot contain God, "how much less this house which I have built" (v. 27). God is thus in the mind of the deuteronomist exceedingly highly exalted, and the temple is made to be of limited and relative importance because it is emphasized that the earthly temple cannot contain the LORD, God of Israel. Two features make these affirmations especially interesting: (1) in three out of the four verses where reference is made to the heavenly dwelling place of God, the reference is accompanied in the same verse or in the following verse by a petition for forgiveness (vv. 20, 39, 50); and (2) these references stand side by side with palpably anthropocentric affirmations with respect to the temple. The temple is not referred to—as it is in the Book of Deuteronomy—as the place where the Lord will cause his name to dwell (see Deut. 12:5, 11, etc); rather, the temple is spoken of *by Solomon* in these terms: "*I have built thee an exalted house,/* a place for thee to dwell in for ever" (v. 13); "*I have built* the house for the name of the LORD, the God of Israel" (v. 20); "that they [namely, all the peoples of the earth] may know that this house which *I have built* is called by thy

explicit petitions that the people may be made "holy" are to be found in greater frequency in Roman Catholic worship than in (what used to be called) the mainline Protestant denominations. Thus Roman Catholic worship is closer to the theology of the deuteronomist wing of the priestly party who produced the Holiness Code whereas the so-called mainline Protestants are closer to the deuteronomists who produced the Deuteronomistic History. Both practices, of course, have good biblical precedent.

name" (v. 43); "the city which thou hast chosen and the house which *I have built* for thy name" (vv. 44, 48). As for the city of Jerusalem, it is acknowledged that God has chosen it; but as for the temple, it is the place Solomon asserts he has built. Paradoxical though it may be, an intensified expression of the divine transcendence and an appeal for the divine forgiveness is also accompanied by an increased stress upon human accomplishment for the divine (namely, the building of the temple). This paradox must be noted as one of the distinctive hallmarks of the deuteronomists' theology of holiness.

First Kings 8 also emphasizes the numinous element, most aspects of which have already been noted above: for example, its stress on the "cloud" ('*ānān*, v. 11), on God's dwelling in darkness (v. 12) and on God's glory (*kābôd*, v. 11; cf. Deut. 5:24). And, very much in concert with the monotheistic thrust of the *Shema'* and with the deuteronomist's characteristic anthropocentricity, is the final prayer of this chapter (vv. 56–61): "And may he [i.e., the LORD our God] maintain the cause of his servant, and the cause of his people Israel, as each day requires; that all the peoples of the earth may know that the LORD is God; there is no other" (vv. 59–60, RSV).

In another passage widely accepted to have come from the deuteronomists, namely, the peroration after the fall of Samaria (2 Kings 17:7–20), are also to be found some of the deuteronomist's general characteristics: the unmistakable conviction that idolatry is punished by God, explicit reference to the sin of having erected molten images of calves; a keen awareness of the two entities, Israel and Judah, the censure of divination (see also 1 Sam. 15:23), and, in short, the articulation of a fairly anthropocentric notion of retribution such as is found in the programmatic statement of the Deuteronomistic History in Judges 2:6—3:6. In this peroration, however, none of the particularly distinctive aspects of the deuteronomists' theology of holiness are developed.

SUMMARY

In none of the variations on the prophetic understanding of holiness examined in this chapter have we encountered as clear an expression of the normative prophetic theology of holiness as we did in the previous chapter. That is to say, in no one of the prophetic traditionists considered (Jeremiah, psalms on the kingship of Yahweh, Psalm 51, Deuteronomy, the Deuteronomistic History) did we find passages that unmistakably articulated that precisely the holiness of God requires the cleanness of social justice. The chief reason for this attenuation rests most likely in the fact that, with the exception of the psalms considered, none of the prophetic traditionists particularly favored or stressed the use of *terms* of holiness in connection with the deity. The attenuation referred to above was thus largely in vocabulary rather than in substance, for each one of the prophetic traditionists we have considered had clear and strong teaching on the numinous, awesome, mysterious aspects of God. Each one of the prophetic traditionists considered in this chapter also taught that ritual was of relative and proximate importance and that justice remained a foremost requirement of God. Psalm 51 constitutes something of an exception to the last point on justice; and with respect to its stress on the cleanness of *individual* integrity Psalm 51 is closer to the teaching of Israel's sages than it is to the prophets.

Other aspects of the holiness of God considered in this chapter may be summarized as follows. (1) In Jeremiah we saw a powerful, *implicit* prophetic doctrine of holiness, which stressed at once the divine judgment and wrath, mysteriousness and transcendence. The fuller ethical demands of the divine holiness in Jeremiah for justice (cf., e.g., Jer. 5:1–6) and separation from idolatry (cf., e.g., Jer. 2:1–13) were, however, in our survey left unexplored. (2) In the kingship of Yahweh psalms we observed a reappropriation of older hymns in explicit praise of God's holiness, righteousness, justice, and coming for judgment. (3) In Deuteronomy 4—30, by paying particular attention to the ancillary vocabulary of holiness we sought to expound its doctrine of the numinous presence of God in seven headings including an emphasis on the separation of Israel as a people. The latter, it was suggested, derived from a high monotheism and doctrine of election. In sum, we underlined the central role of the law in the Deuteronomic theology of holiness in numinous presence. (4) In the Deuteronomistic History we noted a reversal of usage from the Book of Deuteronomy with respect to "holy name" and "holy people," and a greater universalism and emphasis on human initiative. (5) In passing, we made a plea for the adoption of the notion of "paradigmatic history" as put forward by Eric Voegelin. We submitted that this notion will prove to be highly useful and that it is worthy of wider consideration than it has received.

We turn now to an examination of the third major portion of our thesis, that there developed among the sages of ancient Israel a view of the divine holiness and its requirements that, even though it stood in some continuity with that of the priests and prophets, at the same time had a discernibly distinctive emphasis.

CHAPTER 5

The Understanding of
Holiness among the Sages

*(Proverbs, Wisdom Psalms,
and Job)*

In several regards the writers of Israelite wisdom showed a greater consistency in their understanding of holiness than did the writers in the prophetic tradition. Throughout their long history not only did the sages of Israel teach that the holiness of God called for the cleanness of individual morality, they also shared two other foundational attitudes toward holiness from the beginning to the close of the biblical period. In this chapter and the next, we will explore this remarkably persistent emphasis on the three constants in ancient Israelite wisdom traditions. Focus in this chapter will be upon the monarchic and the Persian eras.

It is appropriate at this juncture also to say a word about the Israelite wisdom literature as a whole. It is widely agreed that the oldest Israelite sentences or proverbs are to be found in Prov. 10:1—22:16. Some of the 375 Hebrew sentences in the aforementioned section may well predate Solomon. The latest work of Israelite wisdom, the Wisdom of Solomon, was written in Greek some time between 100 B.C.E. and 38 C.E.; it constitutes a blending of the elements of Hebraic and Hellenistic philosophy. It can hardly be expected, therefore, in view of the longevity of Israelite wisdom, that either the one designated "sage" or his teachings should maintain the same contours throughout.

The author of the Wisdom of Solomon is more clearly a philosopher and theologian. Jesus ben Sira, the author of the second youngest work in Israelite wisdom, has recently been designated with some (yet not unambiguous) justification a "legal scholar."[1] The author of Ecclesiastes (Qoheleth) is hardly an orthodox sage but rather represents one disenchanted with traditional wisdom. Similarly, neither the authors of Job nor of the Wisdom Psalms[2] fit the mold of the typical preexilic sages who, even before the emergence of the Torah, were so deeply impressed by the order and regularity they saw in creation. Job challenges the preexilic orthodoxy and the Wisdom Psalms (esp. Psalms 1, 19, 119) represent its "Torahization." We are left then with the conclusion that the only typical sage is to be found in the Book of Proverbs. But even here, and even within the oldest section of Proverbs, it is by no means plain whether the sage[3] is instructor of the young (Proverbs 1—9), educator of courtiers (Proverbs 25—29), or secular, practical philosopher (approximately 325 out of the 375 sentences in Proverbs 10:1—22:16 do not mention the name of God). We may thus be alerted that the likelihood is high that a diversity of attitudes toward holiness will be found during the millenium in which Israel's wisdom literature came into being.

THE HOLINESS OF GOD IN THE OLD WISDOM TRADITIONS

Three foundational attitudes toward the divine holiness are set forth in the old wisdom traditions of Prov. 10:1—22:16. (1) There is a fascination and sense of mystery with respect to the divine omniscience (*mysterium et fascinans*). (2) There is a strong conviction that the fear of the Lord (*tremendum*) leads to life. (3) It is also affirmed that the all-knowing divine majesty (*majestas*) requires purity of heart and inner integrity. Despite

---

1. Joseph Blenkinsopp, *Wisdom and Law in the Old Testament* (New York and Oxford: Oxford University Press, 1983), 10. This designation is also in one sense exceedingly misleading because Sirach virtually ignores the pentateuchal food laws and laws having to do with purity.

2. The literature on the category "Wisdom Psalms" is fairly extensive. See below, pp. 129–33.

3. See the anthology *The Sage in Israel and the Ancient Near East*, ed. John G. Gammie and Leo G. Perdue (Winona Lake, Ind.: Eisenbrauns, 1990) wherein the identity of the sage in the various periods of Israel's history is examined in detail.

the anticipated diversity mentioned above, each one of these three attitudes or convictions remains, as noted above, a constant throughout the history of the wisdom movement even though the validity of the second is severely challenged by the authors of Job and Qoheleth.

(1) The sages of the early monarchic period were deeply convinced of the *divine omniscience*. Realms that were hidden from the sight of mortal beings and beyond human ken were open to God: "Sheol and the place of perishing (*'ăbaddôn*) lie open before the LORD,/ how much more the hearts (*libbôt*) of human offspring" (Prov. 15:11, au. trans.). In contrast to human limits in space, "The eyes of the LORD are in every place, keeping watch on the evil and the good" (Prov. 15:3). Not only does God see into the mental faculties of human beings, he tests and refines them—one presumes through calamities and trials: "The crucible is for silver, and the furnace for gold,/ so the LORD tests human hearts" (Prov. 17:3, au. trans.). This wondrous ability of the divine to know—which includes also a knowledge of the perverse in mind (Prov. 11:20), lying lips (Prov. 12:22), the one of devious ways (Prov. 14:2), and the inmost human spirit (Prov. 16:2; 21:2)—thus unmistakably belongs to the sapiential understanding of what constitutes the divine uniqueness and holiness.

(2) That *God is to be feared* is not so much taught by the old wisdom traditions as it is presupposed. From the fear of the Lord come many good things: long life (Prov. 10:27; 14:27; 19:23), honor (Prov. 15:33; 22:4), avoidance of evil (Prov. 16:6), humility (*'ănāwâ*: Prov. 15:33), and riches (Prov. 22:4).

(3) The distinctive relationship between *holiness and purity* which runs throughout the wisdom movement is also present in the old wisdom traditions. No one can be without defilement: "Who can say, 'I have made my heart pure (*zikkîtî*),/ I am clean (*ṭahartî*) from my sin'?" (Prov. 20:9).[4] Human standards of marking purity, however, are deficient: "All the ways of a person are pure (*zak*) in one's own eyes,/ but the LORD weighs the heart" (Prov. 16:2, au. trans.; cf. Prov. 21:2). Like the fear of the

---

4. This verse already anticipates the earlier positions of Eliphaz and Job. See below, pp. 140–48.

Lord, purity of heart may lead to favor: "The one who loves
purity of heart and whose speech is gracious,/ will have the king
as his friend" (Prov. 22:11). And despite its rarity, at least for
some of the sentence makers purity in conduct was a possibility:
"The mores (*derek*) of a foreigner (*'iš wāzār*) may be convoluted,/
but his deed may be pure and upright" (*wĕzak yāšār*, Prov. 21:8,
au. trans.).[5] Similarly, purity in speech before God was evidently
not understood to be an impossible attainment: "The thoughts of
an evil person are an abomination to the LORD,/ but the words
of someone pleasing may be clean" (Prov. 15:26, au. trans.). In
this proverb, it may be noted, there is a close link between the
divine omniscience and discernment of cleanness or its absence.
That the sapiential thrust is toward requirement of inner purity
is also apparent in the following: "Blows that wound cleanse
away evil; strokes make clean the innermost parts" (Prov. 20:30).

The same three convictions with respect to holiness that
emerge in Prov. 10:1—22:16 are to be found in the other collections from the monarchic period: Proverbs 25—29, which came
from "Hezekiah's men" (Prov. 25:1), and Prov. 22:17—24:22,
which parallels the Egyptian "Instruction of Amenemope"[6] (1)
on the divine omniscience (Prov. 24:12, 17–18); (2) on the notion
that the one who fears the Lord will be blessed (Prov. 28:14); and
(3) on the requirement of inner integrity (Prov. 28:6; cf. Prov.
16:8; 19:1).

There is a question whether all four artistically arranged[7] col-
lections that conclude the book, Sayings of Agur (30:1–14),
Numerical Sayings (30:15–33), Sayings of Lemuel (31:1–9),
Acrostic Poem (31:10–31), are from the monarchic period.[8]
Nonetheless, these concluding chapters also underline the same

---

5. Less radical emendation is required by this rendition than that found in the
RSV ("The way of the guilty is crooked, but the conduct of the pure is right").
Under either rendering, however, purity does not seem to be beyond human
reach as it clearly is for the author of Prov. 20:9.

6. For a survey of scholarly opinion on the relation of this section to the
"Instruction of Amenemope," see William McKane, *Proverbs: A New Approach*,
OTL; (Philadelphia: Westminster Press, 1970), 369–73.

7. On which see Blenkinsopp, *Wisdom and Law*, 21.

8. Blenkinsopp, e.g., is inclined to date the Sayings of Agur to the late Persian
or early Hellenistic period (ibid., 48).

three convictions on holiness mentioned above. The omni-science of God is implied in the emphasis on the limitations of human knowledge (Prov. 30:1–4); the fear of God is one of the characteristic points of honor of the ideal woman (Prov. 31:30); self-declared purity is insufficient (Prov. 30:12). The basic convictions of the wisdom writers found in the pre-exilic period are deepened and developed in the postexilic per-iod.

WISDOM PSALMS

The classification of wisdom psalms has been the object of particular scrutiny in recent times.[9] By a process that combines an observation of stylistic elements favored among the wise (the alphabetic acrostic; the 'ašrê-formula ["Happy is the person who . . . "]; the "better" [tôb min]-formula; contrast of the righteous and the wicked) and of typical ideas popular in wisdom circles (fear of God; control of tongue; ethical dualism; teaching of retri-bution [or challenging it!]; promise of long life or reward of offspring), scholars have come up with lists of wisdom psalms that vary in number from seven (Murphy) to nineteen (Castel-lino).[10] The present context is not the place to enter into a de-tailed discussion of this question. Three observations, however, may be made: (1) even among those who argue for form-critically tight criteria of the category "Wisdom Psalms" (i.e., Murphy and Kuntz), it is acknowledged that there are quite a few other psalms

9. See esp. Gunkel, *Einleitung in die Psalmen*, 381–97; Sigmund Mowinckel, "Psalms and Wisdom," in *Wisdom in Israel and in the Ancient Near East*, ed. M. Noth and D. W. Thomas, VTSup 3 (Leiden: E. J. Brill, 1955), 205–24; Roland E. Murphy, "A Consideration of the Classification 'Wisdom Psalms,'" in *Congress Volume, Bonn 1962*, VTSup 9 (Leiden: E. J. Brill, 1962), 156–67; reprinted in James L. Crenshaw, ed. *Studies in Ancient Israelite Wisdom* (New York: Ktav, 1976), 456–67; J. Kenneth Kuntz, "The Canonical Wisdom Psalms of Ancient Israel—Their Rhetorical, Thematic and Formal Dimen-sions, in *Rhetorical Criticism: Essays in Honor of James Muilenburg*, Pitts-burgh Theological Monograph Series 1; ed. Jared J. Jackson and Martin Hessler (Pittsburgh: Pickwick Press, 1974), 186–222.

10. For the reference see Roland E. Murphy, "A Consideration of the Classification 'Wisdom Psalms,'" 161, n. 4. Murphy's short list includes Psalms 1, 32, 34, 37, 49, 112, 128; his long list includes seven others that have "wisdom elements": Psalms 25, 31, 39, 40, 62, 92, 94. Castellino's list includes in addition to Psalms 1, 37, 49, 112, 128 Psalms 9, 10, 12, 14, 15, 17, 36, 52, 73, 91, 94, 119, 127, 139.

that contain wisdom elements; (2) in order better to track the impact of the sages on the psalms it seems advisable to include in consideration these other psalms, which contain a *cluster* of both form-critical elements acknowledged to be sapiential *and* ideational elements acknowledged to be sapiential; and (3) it is useful to consider also *types* of wisdom psalms. Keeping the above observations in mind, I submit that the following twenty-four psalms may rightly be classified as wisdom psalms under the subcategories indicated. (Psalms marked with an asterisk are alphabetic acrostics.)

1. Psalms of *juridical wisdom*, which emphasize the Torah (Psalms 1, 19, 119*).

2. Psalms of *natural wisdom*, which focus on the created order, offspring, life, abundance, or fruitfulness (Psalms 45, 91, 104, 127, 128, 133, 139, 147).

3. Psalms of *theological wisdom*, which probe matters of right conduct, theodicy, and retribution (Psalms 14, 15, 37*, 49, 53 [= 14], 73, 94).

4. Psalms of thanksgiving, which emphasize *practical wisdom* (Psalms 32, 34*).

5. *Hymns of praise*, which utilize traditional wisdom themes (Psalms 78, 111*, 112*, 145*).

In defense of this list a few comments may be made. (1) Not every acrostic psalm has been included; Psalms 9, 10, and 25, for example, have not been classified because they lack a sufficient number of typically sapiential-ideational elements. (2) Other scholars have already noted wisdom elements in these psalms, for example, in Psalms 92 and 94 (Murphy); in Psalms 78, 91, 111, 119, 127, 133 (Gunkel)[11] or have classified them as Wisdom Psalms, for example, Psalms 15, 73, 127, 133 (Dahood).[12]

---

11. Gunkel, *Einleitung in die Psalmen*, 381-97.

12. Mitchell Dahood, *Psalms 1-50*, Anchor Bible 16; *Psalms 51-100*, Anchor Bible 17; *Psalms 101-150*, Anchor Bible 17A (New York: Doubleday & Co., 1966-70). Dahood also classifies Psalm 78 as a "didactic psalm" (*Psalms 51-100*, 238). Dahood holds that Psalm 53 is a northern Elohistic edition of Psalm 14. Of Psalm 14 he writes: "Though commonly classified as a lament, this psalm (XIV) has many points of contact with wisdom literature and could, with equal validity, be put in the category of Wisdom Psalms" (*Psalms 51-100*, 19).

In these wisdom psalms the three fundamental convictions pertaining to the divine holiness noted above are also to be found. A sense of mystery and fascination is seen in Psalm 145 with respect to the divine king whose name is holy (v. 21), whose greatness is unsearchable (v. 3), whose kingdom is glorious (v. 12), and whose works are wondrous (v. 5). A similar awareness of mystery in the divine greatness, creation, governance, understanding, and law is seen in Psalms 19, 104, 139, and 147. Already in the opening psalm is expressed a clear belief in the divine omniscience ("for the Lord knows the way of the righteous," Ps. 1:6a). This sentiment is echoed in Psalm 37 ("The Lord knows the days of the blameless," Ps. 37:18) and in Psalm 73 where proud and arrogant scoffers say, "How can God know? Is there knowledge in 'the Most High'?" (Ps. 73:11). In Psalm 139, the psalmist's wonder at the divine omniscience is given classic expression:

> O LORD, thou has searched me and known me!
> Thou knowest when I sit down and when I rise up;
>   thou discernest my thoughts from afar.
> Thou searchest out my path and my lying down,
>   and art acquainted with all my ways.
> Even before a word is on my tongue, lo, O LORD,
>   thou knowest it altogether.
>
> Such knowledge is too wonderful for me;
>   it is high, I cannot attain it.
>   (Ps. 139:1–4, 6, RSV)

A sense of *tremendum* and of the awefulness of God also emerges in the wisdom psalms. In Psalm 139 the sense of wonder embraces both the divine omniscience and omnipotence: "I praise thee for thou art fearful and wonderful./ Wonderful are thy works!/ Thou knowest me right well" (Ps. 139:14). As in Proverbs, so here too blessings and life are closely linked: Pss. 34:10 (Engl., 34:9); 111:5; 112:1; 138:1, 4; 145:19. The Lord takes pleasure in those who fear him (Ps. 147:11) and bestows honor upon them (Ps. 15:4b). Similarly, in the wisdom psalms there is also to be seen a clear link between the divine omniscience and holiness, on the one hand, and an awareness of the need of *personal* purity, on the other. In virtually one breath the psalmist expresses doubt of God's knowledge (Ps. 73:11) and doubt about the wisdom of his having maintained a cleanness in mind and morality ("All in vain have I kept my heart clean and washed my hands in innocence," Ps. 73:13).

Especially in Psalm 15 the requirements of holiness are identified as residing in acts of individual morality. This wisdom psalm has also been identified as an "entrance ritual and liturgy"[13] or "liturgical act"[14] setting forth the "conditions for entrance into the temple." It makes more sense, in my judgment, to see in this psalm one that may have been latterly, secondarily, or derivatively pressed into service as an entrance liturgy. Its language indicates not one who is setting down external conditions to be applied to prospective worshipers, but rather the profound awareness on the part of its author of the individual conduct and attitude the divine holiness required of him if he would abide in its presence. For the proper interpretation and appropriation of the profound teaching of this psalm, it is imperative to heed the perceptive words of Jon Levenson that "thy holy hill" should not be associated exclusively with the geographical location of Mt. Zion.[15] Rather, Zion is a symbol of "a different kind of existence, marked by closeness to God."[16]

The concern in Psalm 15 with speaking the truth (v. 2c), proper control of the tongue and refraining from gossip (v. 3a), abiding

13. See John H. Hayes, *Understanding the Psalms* (Valley Forge, Pa.: Judson Press, 1976), 44.
14. See H.-J. Kraus, *Psalmen*, 2 vols., Biblischer Kommentar 15 (Neukirchen-Vluyn: Neukirchener Verlag, 1960), 1:111.
15. Jon D. Levenson, *Sinai and Zion*, New Voices in Biblical Studies, ed. Adela Yarbro Collins and John J. Collins (Minneapolis: Winston Press, 1985): "Jerusalem and . . . especially Mount Zion, are a sign that beneath and beyond the pain and the chaos of the realm we call history, there is another realm, upheld by the indefectible promise of God" (p. 101).
16. Ibid., 175. Levenson does not see the symbolic and physical ascent as distinct: "The ascent of the Temple mount was considered to be something more than simply a change of locale. It was, in fact, a way of entering a different kind of existence, marked by closeness to God, a life at the very center of the cosmos, the point on which the world is balanced, a true paradise. . . . One who would ascend the mountain must start at the bottom. The point is that the ascent into the Temple and participation in the liturgy that took place there were thought to endow the worshipper with a higher self, as it were. The ascent of the sacred mountain thus involved self-transcendence."

by promises (v. 4d), shunning evil (v. 4b), and fear of the Lord (v. 4c) are common wisdom themes. The sage has set down a decalogue of requirements for *individual* integrity and morality for the one who would continue to abide before the divine holiness.[17]

> 1   O LORD, who will sojourn in thy tent
>   who will dwell on thy holy hill?
> 2(1) The one who walks with integrity
> (2)   and does justly.
> (3)   The one who speaks the truth of the mind
> 3(4)   yet does not spy out faults with the tongue.
> (5)   Who does no harm to a neighbor
> 4(6)   and does not magnify the shame of the one
>   nearby.
> (7)   An evil deed is despised in his sight
> (8)   but he honors those who fear the LORD.
> (9)   When he makes a promise he does not break it
>   even if he suffers harm.
> 5(10) For his money he does not charge interest
>   and he does not take a bribe against the
>   innocent.
>   The one who does these things
>   will never be dislodged.
>   (Psalm 15, au. trans.)

The author of Psalm 24, which is closely related to Psalm 15 although itself not a "wisdom psalm," has summarized very well the requirements of holiness according to the sages in these words: "Who shall ascend the hill of the LORD?/ And who shall stand in his holy place?/ The one who has clean hands and a pure heart, who does not lift up his soul to what is false, and does not swear deceitfully" (Ps. 24:4). The holiness of God requires of would-be worshipers the purity of individual integrity and truthfulness.

PROVERBS 1—9

In Proverbs 1—9 the theme that reverence for the Lord leads to life is reiterated many times over. The route is not direct,

---

17. For a recent and full discussion on the moral, cultic, and sapiential dimensions of this psalm, see Walter Beyerlin, *Weisheitlich-Kultische Heilsordhung: Studien zum 15. Psalm*, Biblisch-Theologische Studien 9 (Neukirchen-Vluyn: Neukirchener Verlag, 1985).

however; fear of the Lord is rather an early product of knowledge, and, in turn, an entry into wisdom.

> The first fruits of knowledge (*rē'šît dā'at*) is
> reverence to the LORD.
> > (Prov. 1:7, au. trans.)
>
> The beginning of wisdom (*tĕhillat hokmâ*) is
> reverence to the LORD;
> and insight (*bînâ*) is constituted of knowledge
> of holy things (*qĕdōšîm*).
> > (Prov. 9:10 au. trans.)

The author or authors of Proverbs 1—9 do not elaborate on what might constitute the "holy things." Indeed, because of the parallelism, the word *qĕdōšîm* may be a synonym for the LORD, and thus perhaps should be translated "Holy One." The Lord is the source of wisdom (Prov. 2:6). And the one who finds wisdom is blessed (Prov. 3:13). For in her hands are length of days, wealth, and honor (Prov. 3:16).

> She is a tree of life to those who have taken
> hold of her,
> and the ones who have grasped her may be
> accounted blessed.
> > (Prov. 3:18, au. trans.)

On the contrary, those who do not choose reverence for the Lord will not find him (Prov. 1:28–29). Reverence for the Lord involves a high morality: both a turning away from (Prov. 3:7) and a hatred of (Prov. 8:13) evil. But God loves those who hate evil (Prov. 8:14–17), and healing and refreshment will be the lot of those who turn away from it (Prov. 3:8). The seemingly easy and apparently unquestioning assurance of the author(s) of Proverbs 1—9 in the operation of the principle of retribution is not shared by the authors of Job.

JOB

A fresh perspective on the achievements of the author of the Book of Job can be gained when one seeks to track the fate of the three foundational convictions on holiness inherited from previous generations of the sages. (1) Fascination and sense of mystery with respect to the divine omniscience remain strong. In-

deed, it may be argued that one of the most powerful induce-
ments to Job's final repentance rests precisely in the divine
reminder that there are severe limits to the areas of Job's knowledge whereas knowledge of the operations of the heavens and
seas (Job 38:1–41) as well as of the habits and ways of lion, raven,
mountain goat, wild ass, ostrich, war horse, falcon, and eagle (Job
38:39–41; 39:1–30) are thoroughly known by God. (2) The Joban
author accepts the appropriateness of the orthodox-sapiential
teaching of the fear of God. He calls attention to another and
unhealthy kind of fear and especially challenges the notion that
reverence for God necessarily leads either to prosperity or long
life (see esp. Job 21). (3) Despite this challenge to the traditional
formulation of how the divine will reward the righteous, the
author of Job reaffirms and even deepens the older sapiential
insight that the divine holiness requires purity of the individual
heart and mind (see esp. Job 31).

CAN YOU SEARCH OUT THE DEEP THINGS OF GOD?

Job is the only one of the five interlocutors in the Book of Job
who calls God holy (Job 6:10b: "I have not denied the work of the
Holy One"). He is not, however, alone in acknowledging the
limits of human knowledge. Thus Zophar asks:

> Can you find the mystery of Eloah?
> Can you find the limit of Shaddai?
> It is higher than heaven—what can you do?
> It is deeper than Sheol—what can you know?
>   (Job 11:7–8, Habel trans.)

In the very next speech, Job similarly acknowledges that God is
the one who "uncovers the deeps out of darkness" (Job 12:22)
and indeed that the knowledge of deceased human beings is
simply unable to penetrate the barrier of death (Job 14:21).

Job's conviction of the divine omniscience lends force to his
protests in the third cycle: Job is certain that God knows his way
(Job 23:10a) but he chides the Almighty for not holding times of
judgment on the unjust who thrust the poor off the road (Job
24:1–4); and he again chides God for not caring that the poor
seek food, lie all night naked, are wet with rain, and are both
hungry and thirsty even though they labor in the fields and vine-

yards of the wicked (Job 24:5-12). Thus what he has affirmed (Job 12:22; 23:10a) he does not deny, but he says, in effect, that the Almighty might just as well *not* know for he has failed to enter into judgment or to demonstrate care when the poor seek food in the wilderness (Job 24:5b). Conversely, Job is appalled that the same God who sees the ways of the wicked (Job 24:23b) in effect gives them support and security by doing nothing (Job 24:23a). God permits the murderer and adulterer to commit their crimes under cover of darkness (Job 24:13-17). The latter mockingly says, "No eye will see me" (Job 24:15b). The poem of chapter 24 thus flings the charge in the face of God that his omniscience is insensitive, vain, cruel, and ineffectual.[18]

The theme of divine knowledge also features in the second speech of Job in the third cycle (Job 26) and is reiterated in the ode to wisdom (Job 28:20-27).

In the first and third cycles of speeches, the poet has thus raised the divine omniscience to a level of prime theological importance. Contrary to the charge frequently made by scholars that the final speeches of God fail to deal directly with the specific protests raised by Job, the poet does give considerable prominence to the theme of the divine omniscience in the closing chapters of the book: (1) God directly answers the charges of absurd and ineffectual omniscience: (*a*) Job does not see how at dawn God shakes the wicked (or chieftains) out of the skirts of the earth (Job 38:13); (*b*) since Job has so mocked God's apparent callous disregard of the murderer and adulterer in darkness, God asks Job if he knows "the way to where the light is distributed" (Job 38:24); (*c*) since Job has implied that in the wilderness and beyond the reaches of ordinary human discernment the poor search for food as animals, God takes Job precisely to those same wilderness reaches and shows him how he not only knows but has furnished lions (Job 38:39), ravens (Job 38:41), mountain goats (Job 39:4), the wild ass (Job 39:8), the wild ox (Job 39:9-12), the

---

18. Norman Habel (*The Book of Job*, OTL [Philadelphia: Westminster Press, 1985], 351-63) is persuasive in his arguments for the unity of chap. 24. His argument that the chapter belongs to a friend, however, is unconvincing. Verses 1-17 and 21-23 are very much representative of Job's position and in vv. 18-20 and 24-25 he quotes his friends.

horse (Job 39:19–25), and the eagle (Job 39:26–30) with full provision so that they prosper.

(2) The divine also directly answers Job's charge of ineffectual omniscience through the example of the ostrich. The female ostrich is held up to Job as a parody of the severity of human limits of knowledge—and of Job's in particular. "Since God has made her forget wisdom,/ and has not allotted to her understanding,// for a time she acted defiantly and laughed at both horse and rider" (Job 39:17–18, au. trans.).[19]

(3) The poet underlines the remarkable centrality he wished to give to the themes of the limits of human knowledge and of the surpassing divine omniscience by the refrains with which the divine speeches begin and end: "Who is this that darkens counsel by words without knowledge" (Job 38:2; 42:3a), "I will question you and you (shall) declare to me" (Job 38:3b; 42:4b).

(4) That the aforementioned refrains do not simply furnish peripheral coloration to the final speeches of God is apparent also from Job's final response (Job 42:1–6). The mighty chief acknowledges that he has lost his case because his charge of ineffectual omniscience has been shown to be unestablished. The aspect of the divine holiness that he had thought to be most vulnerable has now become the object of praise. Neither is omniscience linked with ineffectuality nor can human discernment be given the laurel of triumph.

> I know that thou canst do all things,
> and that no purpose of thine can be thwarted . . .
> Therefore I have uttered what I did not understand,
> things too wonderful for me, which I did not know.
> (Job 42:2, 3bc, RSV)

"Things too wonderful for me": the mystery of the divine intention (mězimmâ) fascinates the poet and brings him to his final and deepest confession of his own limitations of knowledge.

19. I am indebted to Norman Habel for this observation. See ibid., 546–47.

For the notion that the divine instructs Job through the two beasts held up as examples in the second speech, see my "Behemoth and Leviathan: On the Didactic and Theological Significance of Job 40:15—41:26," in *Israelite Wisdom: Theological and Literary Essays in Honor of Samuel Terrien*, ed. John G. Gammie, Walter A. Brueggemann, W. Lee Humphreys, and James M. Ward (Missoula, Mont.: Scholars Press, 1978), 217–31.

TRIAL AND TERROR

The second foundational conviction with respect to the divine holiness that the Joban poet reflects upon and expands is that of the fear of God.

That the majesty and holiness of God call forth reverence and fear runs throughout the book as a minor theme. In the prose prologue, which the Joban poet used as the setting for the dialogues, one of the qualities in Job in which the divine takes pleasure is his reverence (Job 1:8; 2:3). Eliphaz explicitly accuses Job of doing away with reverence (Job 15:4) and sarcastically asks whether it is because of Job's reverence that God was chastening him (Job 22:4). Job, on the other hand, swears, in the midst of his oath of innocence, to his fear of destruction from God: "I was afraid of a divinely sent calamity (lit. "destruction of God"), lest I not be able to withstand his majesty" (*šĕ'ētô*: Job 31:23, au. trans.). There is a dynamic quality to the divine "majesty" as we see in an earlier speech of Job: "Will not his majesty (*śe'ētô*) terrify you, and the dread of him fall upon you?" (Job 13:11, RSV). The word for "his majesty" in this passage (as shown) is the same as in the one previously cited. Both are derived from the verb *nś'* and the connotation in both instances is that of an "exaltedness" for judgment as is plain from both contexts. Job's fear of holiness thus derives from the divine potential for judgment. Understandably, then, Job most laments God's failure to stipulate the terms of his indictment (Job 9:14–23, 27–35; 23:3–7; 31:35–37).

There is some disarray, as is well known, in the third cycle of the Book of Job.[20] Notwithstanding, five themes give to this cycle

20. I assign the speeches in this much-contested cycle as follows: Eliphaz (chap. 22); Job (chaps. 23–24); Bildad (chap. 25); Job (chap. 26); Zophar (Job 27:7–23); Job (Job 27:1–6; 28:1—31:40). Reasons for assigning chap. 24 to Job are given in n. 18 above. In the various scholarly schemes with respect to the third cycle, it is common to assign Job 27:13–23 to Zophar (so, e.g., Dhorme, Gordis, Terrien, Habel, et al.). This, however, leaves the speech without any introduction. Hence, I submit that vv. 7–12 should also be assigned to Zophar. This is not the place for a full discussion, but note the play on words in Hebrew in v. 7 which highly commends assignment to Zophar: *'ōyĕbî* ("my enemy") = *'iyyôb* (Job). In this reading in v. 12 Zophar berates the other friends for wavering and hesitating to draw the inevitable conclusion that Job is both wicked and unrighteous (and not simply deficient as are all human beings). For a demonstration that not only Eliphaz and Bildad change their

a remarkable unity and cohesiveness: the fear of God, contest as
at a court of law, divine omniscience, divine creation, and precious metals. The relation of the latter theme to cleanness will be
reserved until the next division on "Purity of Heart."

In the third cycle the Joban poet brings to a climax the teaching
of the appropriateness of the fear of God. The poet distinguishes
between types of fear. Reverence for God (*yir'â*) is in order and
commended either by the narrator (Job 1:1), God (Job 1:8; 2:3),
or Job (Job 6:14; 28:28), but Job makes it plain that some kinds
of excessive fear of God are neither especially to be desired nor
wholesome if sustained (see Job 13:21; 31:23). The latter fear
came in particular when Job felt his calamities were accompanied by terrors sent by God (Job 6:4; 7:14; 9:17, 34–35; 13:11,
21, 25; cf. 10:17). Each of the friends holds that terrors can be
expected to come upon the wicked (Job 15:21, 24 [Eliphaz];
18:10–11 [Bildad]; 27:20–21 [Zophar]). Job challenges the validity of the friends' claim:

> Why do the wicked live, reach old age,
>   and grow mightily in power?
> Their children are established in their presence,
>   and their offspring before their eyes.
> Their houses are safe from dread [*pahad*]
>   and no rod of God is upon them.
>   (Job 21:7–9, RSV adapted)

In this challenge Job too acknowledges that an excessive fear may
be God-sent by way of divine judgment. Despite this acknowledgement, Job does not abandon his affirmation of the crucial
importance of reverence (Job 28:28). Eliphaz comes closest to
Job in realizing the difference between reverence or fear (*yir'â*)
and excessive fear or dread (*pahad*) because Eliphaz alone of the
friends acknowledges that a dread (*pahad*) had come upon him
(Job 4:14). In the course of the visitation of dread upon Eliphaz,
he heard a voice, which asked whether both righteousness and
purity were attainable before God (Job 4:17). This revelation
contains an exceedingly important theological question, which
we shall explore further in the next section. It is sufficient to

estimates with respect to Job's relative purity, see below under "Purity of
Heart."

underline at this juncture that the Joban poet clearly distinguishes between the two types of fear: one is appropriate at all times; the other may be excessive, and may be difficult to endure for long but by no means always and necessarily constituted a cloud without a silver lining.

PURITY OF HEART

1. Of the three foundational, sapiential convictions under review in the Book of Job with respect to the requirements of holiness, the one most thoroughly explored is the conviction that holiness requires cleanness. This notion constitutes a leitmotif in the speeches of both the friends and Job. Examination of this theme at the same time furnishes us with fresh insights into dramatic movement within the dialogues.[21]

In the first cycle of speeches (Job 4—14), Eliphaz through his rhetorical question, Can a man be pure before his Maker? (Job 4:17b), in effect declares that *purity before God is unattainable.* Conversely, Bildad in his first speech presupposes the opposite: "If you are pure (*zak*) and upright, surely he [God] will rouse himself for you" (Job 8:6). For Bildad at the outset *purity* **is** humanly attainable and within Job's reach. Zophar neither takes Eliphaz's tack (that purity is beyond the reach of angels—how much more so of humans!) nor the tack of Bildad but bluntly asserts (deliberately misquoting Job) that Job's chief offense is to have claimed cleanness: "For you say my doctrine is pure (*zak*) and I am clean (*bar*) in thy [i.e., God's] sight" (Job 11:4; cf. 9:30; 10:14). Job in the first cycle claims no such thing. He acknowledges he sins, but refuses to acknowledge that he is willfully evil and so charges God with a failure to forgive (Job 10:14–15). He acknowledges that God requires cleanness, but charges God with

---

21. There is considerable diversity among scholars as to the extent to which the dialogues constitute a genuine back-and-forth discussion as over against a juxtaposition of monologues. Of recent commentators, J. Gerald Janzen in *Job*, Interpretation: A Bible Commentary for Teaching and Preaching (Atlanta: John Knox Press, 1985) seeks to draw out the dialogic aspects. A typical view is that expressed by Gerhard von Rad on the interchange: "In their own train of thought they do not adhere closely to that of the other. . . . The speeches are repetitive and, to a certain extent, move forward only in a circular fashion" (*Wisdom in Israel*, trans. James D. Martin [Nashville: Abingdon Press, 1972], 210). See also n. 25 below.

plunging him into an abhorrent pit (10:30–31). He acknowledges, in obvious agreement with Eliphaz, that the human lot is
unclean, but he charges God with unfairness in judgment in
expecting that the clean can be extracted from the unclean (Job
14:3–4). Despite these charges, Job also has confessed in this first
cycle—in anticipation of the final soliloquy—that the divine
requirement of ethical purity is profound: "He who withholds
kindness from a friend forsakes the fear of the Almighty" (Job
6:14).[22]

In the second cycle Eliphaz reiterates his conviction that cleanness is impossible for humans when even "the heavens are not
clean in his sight" (Job 15:15). Job, however, is beginning to
discriminate and to disassociate himself from this broad anthropological generalization. He asserts now that his prayer is pure
(*zakkâ*) and that his hands have been free of violence (Job 16:17).
As if in marked rejection of an uncritical affirmation of the a
fortiori refrain of which Eliphaz is enamored, Job asserts rather
that "he that has clean hands grows stronger and stronger" (Job
17:9b).

In the third cycle come surprising reversals. Eliphaz comes
round volte-face as if repentant for the overzealousness of his
prior rhetoric and concludes, "He will deliver an innocent man
and such a one will be delivered by the purity (*bor*) of your
hands" (Job 22:30, au. trans.).[23] Even though the Hebrew of this
verse is difficult and it constitutes a *crux interpretum*, and even
though it is possible that this verse, if taken alone, could be
interpreted as having been meant sarcastically, the context of vv.
20–30 rule out the possibility of so reading it. The rather convoluted way in which it is expressed suggests that Eliphaz is fully
aware and uncomfortable about expressing altogether forth-
rightly his clear reversal of judgment with respect to the unattain-
ability of human cleanness.

A second reversal takes place in the third cycle with respect to
the possibility or impossibility of the human attainment of pur-

22. For further discussion on the profundity of the purity required by the
divine holiness, see section 4 below.
23. For justification for this rendering, see E. Dhorme, *A Commentary on the
Book of Job* (Leiden: Brill, 1967), 342.

ity. Bildad, who had previously taken it for granted that Job could in fact be both pure and upright now denies it—taking the a fortiori argument out of Eliphaz's notebook and giving it his own twist: "Behold even the moon is not bright and the stars are not clean (*lō'zakkû*) in his sight; how much less man" (Job 25:5–6a).[24]

Even the position of Zophar does not remain static[25]—and this is so especially with respect to whether or not Job should be classified as wicked. In the first cycle, Zophar is altogether ambivalent on this point: on the one hand he—more harshly than the other friends in the first cycle—bluntly states his judgment that God is exacting from Job less than his guilt deserves (Job 11:6b). On the other hand, he urges that if Job puts away his iniquity he could then lift up his face "without blemish" (*mimmûm*: Job 11:15a). Zophar's position on the possibility of attaining cleanness in his opening speech is very close to the one that Job comes to, namely, that sinlessness may be unattainable but for the repentant a cleanness is.[26] Zophar, in any event, contrasts the wicked (Job 11:20a) with his imaginings of a repentant Job who has resolved to "let not wickedness dwell in [his] tents" (Job 11:14b). Where Zophar's overall position shifts more markedly, however, is with respect to whether or not Job should be classified as wicked. In chapter 11 he rejects that classification, as we have just noted. In the second cycle he shows his fixation on the issue of the fate of the wicked but makes no explicit mention of

24. Habel calls these verses "a subtle shift from the versions of this tradition found in Eliphaz's earlier speeches" (*Book of Job*, 369). Habel does not, however, call attention to the fact that these verses constitute a reversal of Bildad's own previous position.

25. In a recent article David J. A. Clines has curiously argued: "Even in their style of argumentation, the friends provide a static stylized background against which the tortured but adventurous hero of the book excites our imagination and sympathy" ("The Argument of Job's Three Friends," in David J. A. Clines, David M. Gunn, and Alan J. Hauser, eds., *Art and Meaning: Rhetoric in Biblical Literature*, JSOT Supplement Series 19 [Sheffield, JSOT Press, 1982], 213). Clines is, in my judgment, quite correct with respect to the more stilted, stereotypical *style* of the friends. As shown above, however, *positions* taken in their arguments can hardly be classified as static and constant. The judgment of the Lord pronounced in the Epilogue on the inadequacy of the friends' words (Job 42:8) is thus quite demonstrable on the grounds of inconsistency alone.

26. This point is explored more fully in section 2 below.

Job (Job 20). By the time of the third cycle, if our reconstruction is correct, he has come to reject the possibility he once entertained (that Job could become free from iniquity and stand in contrast to the wicked). Zophar concludes that Job must be classified as wicked (Job 27:7–12) and therefore outlines again the fate of such (Job 27:13–23). Eliphaz also berates Job for his shortcomings (see esp. Job 15:1–6) and thinks his particular deficiency rests with respect to the fear of God (Job 4:6; 15:4; 22:4), but Eliphaz and Zophar come in the end to opposite conclusions on their formerly wealthy friend: one, that he is clean (Eliphaz: Job 22:30); the other, that he is wicked (Zophar: Job 27:7).

Thus we have demonstrated how the question of the attainability of cleanness constitutes a leitmotif and also enables us to trace with remarkable clarity a hitherto undervalued movement and themal unity within the three cycles of speeches.

2. In the same way that the figure of Job in the Book of Job is the one who distinguishes between healthy fear of God (reverence) and unhealthy (dread), so Job's words furnish the reader with clarity on the vexed issue of the attainment of cleanness by making another important distinction. Job claims that cleanness and integrity are both required and attainable but he does not claim sinlessness. Thus Job maintains his integrity (Job 9:21; 27:5). He denies that he has committed violence (*ḥāmās*, Job 16:17); he tells God that God knows Job has not been willfully wicked (*lō' 'eršā'*, Job 10:7). He charges that even if he has erred (Job 19:4), such error is altogether disproportionate to the violence (*ḥāmās*, Job 19:7) which God has brought on him. In his final summation and plea of innocence, Job makes it plain that his case does not rest on a claim of sinlessness; rather, the culpable offense would have been such a claim—"If I had concealed my transgressions (*pěšā'āy*) like Adam, so that I had hidden my iniquity (*'ěwônî*) in my bosom" (Job 31:33, au. trans.).[27] What our hero maintains, then, is that his friends have been wrong in

27. In Job 7:21 Job queries why God does not pardon the same two offenses. He does not, however, claim innocence of these offenses. The same point is made by Anthony R. Ceresko in his fine study, *Job 29–31 in the Light of the Northwest Semitic. A Translation and Philological Commentary*, Biblica et Orientalia 86 (Rome: Pontifical Biblical Institute, 1980), 172.

labeling him as wicked, that is, as a willful sinner, and that God has been proportionate in judgment; for these reasons he vows to hold fast to the righteousness of his case (Job 27:5–6). The phrase the RSV translates as "I hold fast my righteousness" (*běsidqātî hehězaqtî*, Job 27:6) does not constitute a claim to sinlessness.

3. In a discussion above on the third cycle of speeches, it was argued that the interweaving of five themes give this cycle a remarkable unity. Particular attention may be called now to the theme of precious metals and its bearing on the theme of cleanness. The name Eliphaz, it will be recalled, means "my God is pure gold." As we have seen in part, the Joban poet playfully, yet seriously, examines this theme in the third cycle (Job 22—31). Eliphaz introduces it by suggesting that if Job were but to lay his gold or precious metals (*beṣer*) in the dust and make the Almighty his precious metal and silver (Job 22:24–25), then he would experience a turn of events "and light will shine upon your ways" (Job 22:28). Job picks up on this theme in response: "When he has tried me (*behānanî*), I shall come forth as gold" (Job 23:10). The verb used means to test, examine thoroughly, and hence to "try" in the sense of determining what the true nature of the metal is. Zophar, in his description of the fate of the wicked, reiterates the charge of Eliphaz but envisions quite a different end for the wicked than Eliphaz has envisioned for Job: "Though he [the wicked] heap up silver like dust, and pile up clothing like clay; he may pile it up but the just will wear it, and the innocent will divide the silver" (Job 27:16–17).

In the reconstruction of cycle three proffered above, Job responds to Zophar in Job 27:1–6; 28—31. In Job 27:1–6 the embattled hero reasserts his integrity and then, commencing with Job 28:1, picks up the precious metal motif and gives it a new twist: "Surely there is a mine for silver and a place for gold which they refine (*yāzōqqû*)." The notion that even gold must have its impurities burned away in the refining process is alluded to but certainly not developed. Rather, the fresh development is put on the idea that human beings know how to mine and refine precious metals from the depths of the earth, but do not know where "wisdom" resides. Eliphaz has told Job to lay his "gold of Ophir among the stones of the torrent bed" (Job 22:24), and Job responds that wisdom cannot be compared to the "gold of Ophir" (Job 28:16), it cannot be gotten for gold (v. 15), gold and glass cannot equal it (v. 17a), "nor can it be exchanged for vessels of fine gold" (*kĕlî paz*: v. 17b). The play on the name of Job's friend from Teman is apparent. The poet, however, has not chosen to dwell on the theme of precious metals as they pertain either to Job or Eliphaz. Rather, he uses it to emphasize the surpassing greatness of the treasure, wisdom, which is beyond the price of gold. Only the Creator God knows where it is to be found; he searched out its way when he gave the wind its weight (vv. 23–27). Chapter 28 then brings the third cycle to its first climax by turning the theme of gold and treasure in a way Eliphaz hardly could have expected. In the second climax of the cycle, Job's final speech and oath declaring innocence (Job 31), the poet returns briefly to the advice given by Eliphaz when Job acknowledges culpability, "If I had made gold my trust, or had called fine gold my confidence" (v. 24), but what even more significantly brings this cycle to a climax is that the entire chapter eloquently demonstrates from many different perspectives that Job indeed has made God his treasure.

The theme of refinement, of purging away impurities, does not constitute the climax or chief emphasis of the precious-metal theme in cycle three. The idea is alluded to but not pursued by means of the metaphor of gold and silver. Rather, in the fourth round of speeches by Elihu (Job 32—37) the *idea* is developed: out of trials there comes refinement, out of suffering learning, out of severe chastisement an ultimate benefit for the chastised (Job 33:12–25; 34:10–15, 31–37; 36:13–23). The idea of the pedagogic view of suffering[28] is not new, of course: Eliphaz expresses it first (Job 5:17) and Job acknowledges that even the beasts may teach humans a lesson (Job 12:7–14), but the Joban poet nowhere *explicitly* develops the idea of learning (and purgation) in relation to the metaphor of the refinement of metals. It is rather Isaiah of Babylon who eloquently and specifically draws out what remains only implicit in Job: "See how I refined you, not as silver

---

28. The notion of a "pedagogical explanation of suffering" is from O. S. Rankin, *Israel's Wisdom Literature* (Edinburgh: T. & T. Clark, 1936; reprinted 1964), 19–22.

is refined, but in the furnace of affliction; there I purified you"
(Isa. 48:10, NEB adapted).

4. In perhaps the most moving chapter of the book, the Joban
poet demonstrates that what the Almighty requires of humans
above all is purity of heart. Chapter 31 constitutes a high-water
mark in Old Testament ethics. It merits a prominent position in
any discussion of biblical ethics,[29] for here, in brief compass, is
expressed the depth of the purity required in the heart and mind
of one who in the limit situation of suffering has walked in the
presence of holiness. Job 31 contains the summation and epi-
tome of the requirements of the holy God whose wondrous omniscience and omnipotence have been intuited and already apprehended in the inner consciousness—even before the fuller instruction of the divine speeches of Job 38—41. Indeed, it may be
argued that chapter 31 describes Job's entry into the first chamber of the presence of the divine holiness; that chapters 38–39
describe the second chamber, and chapters 40–41 the third.

In no fewer than seven passages prior to Job's final oath of
innocence, he affirms that his conduct has not been deficient: he
has not bribed his friends (Job 6:22–23), nor spoken an ill thing
with his tongue (Job 6:30); he has maintained his integrity (Job
9:21), avoided violence, and kept his prayer pure (Job 16:17); he
has not transgressed with his feet (Job 23:11); he swears in God's
name that his case is sound (Job 27:1–6); and in his description
of the brightness of days past, he recounts his noble deeds in
behalf of the poor and defenseless (Job 29:12–17). A climax to
these pleas of innocence is reached, however, in chapter 31. It
constitutes a climax not simply by virtue of the sheer number of
disclaimers that are made. As Robert Gordis has observed: "Job
lists fourteen possible transgressions from which he has kept
himself free."[30] Nor does the climax consist in the distinctiveness
of all the claims, for some of them had been made before: guard-

29. Alongside Job 31 as meriting special attention in a study of the ethics of
the Old Testament, I would also include Leviticus 19, Deuteronomy 5, Psalms
15, 24, 50, 51, Amos 5, Jeremiah 10, Ezekiel 18, and Sirach 2.
30. Robert Gordis, *The Book of Job* (New York: Jewish Theological Seminary
of America, 1978), 339.

ing his feet (Job 31:5, 7; cf. 23:11), holding to his integrity (Job 31:6; cf. 27:5); having defended widow and orphan (Job 31:16–19; cf. 29:12–17). What is distinctive about the final plea of innocence is its *interiority*. Hard pressed as he has been, having just reviewed his former weal (Job 29) and present woe (Job 30), the protagonist now is brought to a new awareness of the extent to which he has already apprehended that the all-seeing God (Job 31:4) requires purity of motive and not simply outward compliance with a norm. The oath is an oath as in a law-court, as if Job were already standing within the chamber of the divine tribunal. But as J. Gerald Janzen has profoundly observed in his comments specifically on Job 31: "The prominence of courtroom language in Job (e.g., Job 9) attests the appropriateness, in some measure, of the tribunal as a metaphor for conscience."[31] Not simply pressing his case any more outwardly to his friends, in his final plea of innocence it is as if reflection on the past and his present "limit situation"[32] have brought him to a deeper awareness of the depth of his own past striving to live appropriately before holiness. Holiness lays claim to conscience. Deep suffering and a recollection of it together with reflection on the persistent divine omniscience have brought him to this high point of Old Testament ethics. God knows even if an individual has made a pact within to seduce one innocent of sexual experience (Job 31:1). God knows whether one's thoughts of wrongdoing have followed after one's mental calculation of the possibility of doing it (Job 31:7). God knows in what humans place their inner trust (Job 31:24). God knows whether one has taken inner delight in wealth (Job 31:25) or gloated over the demise of another (Job 31:29). God knows whether the mind has been secretly enticed to render to some object in the heavens a veneration due only to the creator (Job 31:26–28). In each of these instances the poet affirms that holiness requires not simply outward purity but purity in the

31. Gerald Janzen, *Job*, 211.
32. For profound and helpful discussion on the effect of "limit situations" on the human quest for meaning, see esp. Peter L. Berger, *The Sacred Canopy* (Garden City, N.Y.: Doubleday & Co., 1967), 23–24; and David Tracy, *The Analogical Imagination: Christian Theology and the Culture of Pluralism* (New York: Crossroad, 1981), 160–61, 163, 165, 193, 380.

inner recesses of thought and conscience. Thus the Joban poet also probes, affirms, and deepens the traditional sapiential teaching on the moral requirements of the Holy God.[33]

The oath of Job 27:1–6 is flawed by both anger and bitterness (cf. esp. 27:2b). It culminates in the angry and bitter protests of Job's injured sense of justice. Job 27:1–6, therefore, is best seen as the suffering plantiff's next but last step into an awareness of the divine holiness before Job has been purged of bitterness. By the time of the oath of chapter 31, Job's bitterness has been left behind. And that is the difference. Through the process of reflection on the place of wisdom (chap. 28), recollection of the past (chap. 29), and facing the present (chap. 30), Job crosses the threshold and enters into the first of the three chambers of the divine presence and holiness. The first, as if he had already entered into the chamber of the divine tribunal, is within his own conscience (Job 31). Holiness has beckoned and succeeded in calling forth the deepest self-examination and inner honesty. The second of the three chambers of the divine presence is in the regions beyond normal human habitation (in the heavens above and in the world of nature: Job 38—39). The third is before the royal throne for counsel rather than judgment and again within the protagonist's own heart and spirit. In the third chamber, the comfort of the divine sage reaches the humbled suppliant through a parabolic allusion to two wondrous beasts (Job 40—41).[34] Thus a significant message of the Book of Job with respect to holiness pertains not only to the more obvious omnipotence, but also to the immanence and pervasiveness of the divine omniscience which requires purity within and begins to bring it to pass even before the two more dramatic and final theophanies.[35]

33. Gustavo Gutierrez in his *On Job: God-Talk and the Suffering of the Innocent* (Maryknoll, N.Y.: Orbis Books, 1987) is, I think, correct in pointing out the extent to which Job in this chapter shows himself to be a father of the poor because of his identity with them (see pp. 40–42).

34. On the sense in which the second divine speech should be taken as providing comfort to Job, see my "Behemoth and Leviathan," 217–31; and Habel, *Book of Job,* 564–74.

35. The reader familiar with Rudolph Otto's magnificent treatment of the numinous in the Book of Job will be aware that quite a different tack is taken here. Otto understandably focuses on the theophany but even then fails to see the extent to which the speeches of Yahweh (not of Elohim as Otto curiously

SUMMARY

We have shown that Israel's sages responsible for Proverbs, the Wisdom Psalms, and Job placed a distinctive emphasis on the requirement of the cleanness of individual morality and integrity before God. That this requirement issued from the sages' awareness of the divine holiness is perhaps most apparent in Psalm 15 where the psalmist lists the acts a human should strive to perform in order to stand before holiness.

In the case of Job we showed that debate on whether or not cleanness is attainable constitutes a leitmotif in the first three cycles of the book (chaps. 3–31) and, further, we showed that the numinous sense of the presence of God in the inner recesses of Job's conscience (Job 31) also constitutes a moving demonstration of the validity of our thesis that for the sages the holiness of God issues a profound summons to individual cleanness, inner integrity, and purity of heart.

Along with the theme of individual morality required for holiness, we observed how the theme of fascination with the divine omniscience and the theme that the fear of God leads to life were also distinctive and persistent aspects in the sages' understanding of holiness. How the three basic themes of the wisdom tradition on holiness are treated in the wisdom books of the Hellenistic era will be the subject of the next chapter.

and mistakenly thinks) have a very definite rational content in that they stress the divine omniscience and thus directly respond to Job's charges that the divine omniscience is ineffectual. See our development of this point above, pp. 135–37; see also Rudolph Otto, *The Idea of the Holy*, 76–83. In his treatment Otto argues that the fullest sense of "the holy" is reached in the Prophets and the Gospels. He explicitly refers to Isaiah and Deutero-Isaiah (pp. 77–78). In the treatment above we have sought to show that the deepest sense of morality—a sense penetrating even to the innermost being and thoughts—is present also in the Book of Job, especially in Job 31. Wherever holiness is present, there humans sense the deep call to nobility and purity of heart.

CHAPTER 6

Variations on the Understanding of Holiness in the Wisdom Traditions

(Qoheleth, Sirach, and The Wisdom of Solomon)

In the previous chapter we set forth and defended the thesis that Israel's sages have a distinctive doctrine of holiness: holiness summons human beings to a cleanness of individual morality and to a purity of inner integrity. The reader will have noticed some points of overlap between the priestly and sapiential teaching on the requirements of holiness, for the priestly tradition also stressed individual morality (cf., e.g., "Walk before me and be blameless," Gen. 17:1). In the interests of accuracy, therefore, it must be acknowledged that the normative sapiential teaching on the requirements of holiness is relatively, rather than absolutely, distinctive. Inquiry, however, was not confined to the above thesis alone for added to it were, we noted, two other characteristic and persistent apprehensions of God's holiness among the sages of the earlier period: one that remained fascinated at the divine omniscience and kept alive the sense of the divine mystery; and another stressing the awesomeness of the divine creator, and therefore reverence and fear before the Lord. These *three* characteristic and relatively distinctive apprehensions of holiness among the sages included the first mentioned above, that holiness calls for, and forth, a cleanness within the individual which would be expressed in speech and conduct.

In the present chapter we will examine the development of these themes in the works of wisdom composed in the Hellenistic era or—in the case of the Wisdom of Solomon—shortly after its close. Particular attention will be given to the nature and extent of the pessimism in Ecclesiastes (Qoheleth), the relationship of the twin themes of omniscience and reverence to the development of ethics in Ecclesiasticus (Sirach), and the developments in the doctrine of retribution in the Book of Wisdom (Wisdom of Solomon).[1]

PESSIMISM AND HOLINESS IN QOHELETH

In two recent studies, James Crenshaw has concluded that there is a deep pessimism in the Book of Qoheleth.[2] Pessimism for Crenshaw includes a loss of hope of achieving a better world; pessimists "lack both a surge for transcendence and faith in human potential," "pessimists can muster no base upon which to stand and from which to criticize God and the world."[3] He concludes, "The inevitable result is a sense of being overwhelmed by an oppressive reality."[4] If Crenshaw is correct, it would seem that there would be little room in the Book of Qoheleth for anything other than a very bleak doctrine of holiness. Accordingly, it will be appropriate to probe the validity of Crenshaw's conclusions.

A convenient starting point will be a comparison with the Book of Job. Qoheleth and Job share the same genre. Both belong to what J. Coert Rylaarsdam called "reflective essays." In contrast to the other main division of the wisdom literature, "prudential admonitions," stand the "reflective essays on the meaning and significance of life, often in a pessimistic vein."[5] Yet the

1. To avoid confusion, we will refer to Ecclesiastes as Qoheleth, Ecclesiasticus as Sirach, and the Book of Wisdom as Wisdom of Solomon.
2. See James L. Crenshaw, *Old Testament Wisdom: An Introduction* (Atlanta: John Knox Press, 1981), 126–48, 190–211; and idem, *A Whirlpool of Torment: Israelite Traditions of God as an Oppressive Presence*, OBT (Philadelphia: Fortress Press, 1984), 77–92. He puts it this way: "Two canonical texts, the teachings of Agur and Qoheleth, belong to the category of pessimism. From this observation it follows that I concur in John Priest's judgment that 'The skepticism of Koheleth ends, however much some commentators cry to the contrary, as pessimism pure and simple'" (cf. Priest, "Humanism, Skepticsm, and Pessimism in Israel," *JAAR* 36 [1968]: 323–24 and Crenshaw, *Old Testament Wisdom*, 259 n. 5).
3. Crenshaw, *Old Testament Wisdom*, 191.
4. Ibid., 190–91.
5. Coert Rylaarsdam, *Revelation in Jewish Wisdom Literature* (Chicago: Uni-

profound sense of the immediacy of the divine presence which obtains in Job 31, as expounded above, is hardly shared by Qoheleth. For Qoheleth the deity (*hā'ĕlōhîm*) is remote. Far from addressing the protagonist and expounding his work, as is the case in Job 38—41, the deity for Qoheleth "has given humans a sense of time past and future (*hā'ōlām*), but no comprehension of God's work from beginning to end" (Qoh. 3:11b, NEB adapted). Remoteness, distance, aloofness would seem to be more accurate summations of Qoheleth's doctrine of God than presence and accessibility.

Qoheleth also seems to be less confident in his assessment of the divine omniscience. So remote is the deity for this author that emphasis no longer falls, as it does with Proverbs and Job, on the divine knowing but rather on the eternity and unchangeableness of the divine work: "I know that whatever God does lasts for ever; to add to it or subtract from it is impossible" (Qoh. 3:14, NEB). There even resides in this author a profound faith in the "work" of the divine, that is, in the divine sovereignty: "Consider the deity's handiwork (*ma'ăśēh*); who can straighten what he has made crooked? When all things go well, be glad; but when things go ill, consider this: the deity has set the one alongside the other in such a way that no one can find out what is to happen next" (Qoh. 7:13–14, NEB adapted). Though Qoheleth obviously has virtually no confidence in human ability either to probe the divine mind (Qoh. 3:11) or to alter the divine "work" (Qoh. 7:13–14), he nonetheless affirms the divine power and action.

Indeed, life itself and the power to enjoy it are gifts from the divine: "It is a gift of the deity that every person to whom he has granted wealth and riches and the power to enjoy them should accept his lot and rejoice in his labour" (Qoh. 5:19, NEB adapted). The author counts the gift of enjoying life as supreme. Even in the midst of this pessimism, he affirms that the deity

versity of Chicago Press, 1946), 4. These two subdivisions of the wisdom literature may more properly be called paraenetic literature and the reflective essays; in turn, the latter may be divided into two parts: disputations, e.g., the Book of Job and reflections, e.g., the Book of Qoheleth; see my essay, "Paraenetic Literature: Toward the Morphology of a Secondary Genre," in the forthcoming volume in *Semeia: Paraenesis: Act and Form*, ed. Leo G. Perdue and John G. Gammie (Atlanta: Scholars Press, n.d.).

grants the power (*yašlîṭenû*) to enjoy the goods he has received (Qoh. 6:2). The author thus counsels enjoyment as something both possible and attainable because enjoyment itself is a gift from the hand of the sovereign God (Qoh. 5:17-18; 9:4-10; 11:7-8). Death and a long darkness await, says the author (Qoh. 3:19-22; 11:8), but even in the face of death and old age, this author nonetheless proffers a remarkably positive affirmation of life as a precious and treasured gift. This is so not only in the famous verse where he says, "The one who is attached to all the living still has hope, for surely a live dog is better than a dead lion!" (Qoh. 9:4, Gordis trans. adapted).

At the conclusion of the famous ode on old age (Qoh. 12:1-8), the author employs four metaphors of life. He has enjoined the reader: "Remember your creator . . . before the *silver cord* is snapped, the *golden bowl* is broken, the *pitcher* is shattered *at the spring* and the *wheel* is drawn down to the pit" (Qoh. 12:1a, 6, au. trans.). In each of the four metaphors for life underlined in the preceding translation, one finds an immensely positive affirmation of life: it is likened to the two most precious of metals; it is likened to that which holds refreshing and revivifying waters; it is compared to the mechanism at the well that permits the drawing of sustaining waters from below. The final metaphor employed by our author is symptomatic, in my judgment, of his accomplishment. The "pit" (*habbôr*) is obviously also a symbol for death and the grave. Thus the final metaphor speaks of drawing waters from "the pit." So the author—in the face of a most realistic acknowledgment of the limits of death—has extracted a theology of the affirmation of life as a precious gift and treasure. In sum, a final verdict of "pessimist" cannot justly be declared of this author. To shift the metaphor, Qoheleth has interwoven many dark hues into the tapestry of his reflections. The author has triumphed over despair. He has clearly done so by overlooking neither life's anomalies nor the final anomaly of death (Qoh. 7:2-3).[6]

---

6. For further discussion on the author's theology of death, the date of his writing and possible entering into dialogue with a contemporary school of philosophy, see my "Stoicism and Anti-Stoicism in Qoheleth," *Hebrew Annual Review* 9 (1985): 169-87.

Having thus briefly reflected on the extent of Qoheleth's overall pessimism, we are now in a better position to consider the relation of the author to the three traditional sapiential stances on holiness.

First, Qoheleth shares with his predecessors the notion of the extreme limits of the human capacity for knowing: "You do not know how a pregnant woman comes to have a body and a living spirit in her womb" (Qoh. 11:5a, NEB). Whereas for the psalmist the formation and growth of the fetus was considered a "wonder" (Ps. 139:13–16), Qoheleth refrains from such language. Instead, for him, the cause for comment is the "beauty" of the divine work: "Everything which he [the divine] has done is beautiful (*yāpeh*) in its season" (Qoh. 3:11a, au. trans.). The element of fascination thus does not focus, as it does with Qoheleth's predecessors, upon the divine omniscience, but rather upon the pattern of appropriateness and beauty in the divine handiwork. Similarly, the divine handiwork is a particular object of reverence: "And the deity has acted (*wĕhā'ĕlōhîm 'āśā*) so that humans should fear him" (*šeyyir'û millepānāyw*, Qoh. 3:14c, au. trans.).[7] With respect to the third persistent element in the sapiential doctrine of holiness, namely, noting a contrast between holiness and the impure, Qoheleth is a traditionalist who scarcely carries the doctrine further than his predecessors:

> Everything transpires for all according to one fate: for the righteous and the ungodly, for the upright, for the clean and unclean, for the one who sacrifices and the one who does not; the sinner is like the upright and the one who swears an oath like the one who fears to do so. (Qoh. 9:2, au. trans.)

In this verse Qoheleth is similar to the Book of Job in its challenge of the dogma of retribution, but he accepts the categories of clean and unclean as a matter of course. Earlier we had occasion to note the expression "the deity has tested them" (*lĕbārām hā'ĕlōhîm*, (Qoh. 3:18). Literally, this phrase means, "the deity

7. For further explication of the fear of God in Qoheleth in the sense of awe before the numinous, see Roland E. Murphy, "Qohelet's 'Quarrel' with the Fathers," in *From Faith to Faith*; D. G. Miller Festschrift; ed. D. Y. Hadidian, Pittsburgh Theological Seminary Monograph Series 31 (Pittsburgh: Pickwick Press, 1979), 235–45.

has purged them" (cf. Heb. *bar*, "pure"). Thus it would seem that on the face of it Qoheleth, like Isaiah of Jerusalem, possesses a doctrine of purgation. Inasmuch as this thought is scarcely hinted at outside of the present passage, however, it would be hazardous to press for such a conclusion. We may now turn to the doctrine of holiness in Sirach.

MARVELOUS ARE THE WORKS OF GOD

The Book of Sirach was composed in Hebrew, in Jerusalem, within a generation after the composition of Qoheleth. It resembles somewhat its immediate predecessor, but chiefly differs, for in its author, ben Sira, we see a return to orthodoxy. The Book of Sirach is an anthology belonging to Israel's paraenetic literature.[8] In the same way that the reflections of Qoheleth are arranged in a rather loose and sometimes thematic fashion, so are the longer units (clusters of sentences, poems, and hymns) of the Book of Sirach.

Studies that identify the units of the Book of Sirach may be extremely helpful. In the course of a section in Sirach which Thomas H. Weber has identified as "True Glory" (Sir. 10:19–11:6),[9] ben Sira asserts:

> For wondrous are the works of the Lord (*thaumasta*) and hidden from humans are his works. (Sir. 11:4, au. trans.)[10]

In this middle portion of the verse cited, ben Sira shows at once his agreement, yet disagreement, with Qoheleth. The same is so in the opening verses of a hymn that commences in chap. 18:

> [1]The One who lives forever has created all things in common;
> [2]the Lord alone can be declared just.
> [4]He has permitted no one to declare his works....
> [6]It is impossible to take away from them and to add to them,
> nor can anyone trace out the marvelous deeds of the Lord.
> (Sir. 18:1, 2, 4a, 6, au. trans.)[11]

8. The Paraenetic Literature is a major subdivision of the Wisdom Literature along with Reflections. For a recent discussion, see my essay "Paraenetic Literature."

9. *Jerome Biblical Commentary*, (ed. Raymond E. Brown, Joseph A. Fitzmyer, and Roland E. Murphy [Englewood Cliffs, N.J.; Prentice-Hall, 1968]), 542, 545.

10. Unless otherwise noted, translations from Sirach are based upon the Greek text.

The opening portion of v. 6 seems to be a direct citation of Qoh. 3:14, but the second portion again stresses that aspect of ben Sira's teaching on holiness in which he departs from his predecessor, namely, in his explicit praise of the "wondrous, marvelous" works of God.

Three other hymns may be cited in which there is both a point of contact with, a diverging from, or an affirmation of a teaching found also in Qoheleth.

1. The hymn in Sir. 16:24—17:14 celebrates the creative works of God in the heavens and contrasts with them the divine creation of humans. That scholars may differ in their discernment of the beginning and ending of the sections in Sirach is illustrated by the fact that the New American Bible and the *Jerome Biblical Commentary* identify it as extending from 16:22—17:18, Sigmund Mowinckel sets its limits at Sir. 16:26-17:24,[12] and Luis Alonso-Schökel at Sir. 16:24—17:14.[13] We follow Alonso-Schökel. The opening portion of the poem celebrates God's creation in nature (16:24–30); the next focuses on the divine creation of humankind (17:1–9); and the last on the gift of law and covenant to Israel (17:11–14). To humans God has given intelligence, eyes, ears, and speech for the purpose of describing the divine wonders and reciting praise of "his holy name" (vv. 6–9). Thus in this hymn ben Sira differentiates himself from Qoheleth in two regards: (a) in his unabashed lack of hesitation to declare the purposiveness of creation, and (b) in his recognition of covenant and law as preeminent gifts.

2. In another hymn, Sir. 39:12–35, ben Sira also displays a similarity and dissimilarity with the teachings of Qoheleth on holiness. This psalm is in many ways a restatement of the theme

---

11. As is occasionally the case in the Book of Sirach, skipping a verse number may mean that the majority of texts omit the material contained in the verse. In the above citation we have omitted vv. 4b, 5. The shorter v. 2 and the absence of v. 3 go back to the majority textual tradition.

12. Sigmund Mowinckel, "Psalms and Wisdom," in *Wisdom in Israel and in the Ancient Near East*, VTSup 3, H. H. Rowley Festschrift (Leiden: E.J. Brill, 1955), 218.

13. See Luis Alonso-Schökel, "The Vision of Man in Sirach," in *Israelite Wisdom: Literary and Theological Essays in Honor of Samuel Terrien*, ed. John G. Gammie, Walter A. Brueggemann, W. Lee Humphreys, and James M. Ward (Missoula, Mont.: Scholars Press, 1978), 235–45.

of Psalm 103, only with a theologically reflective emphasis on the divine retribution. Verses 32–35 read in the Greek:

> [32] Therefore, from the beginning I have been confirmed,
>   I have pondered it and have committed it to writing.
> [33] All the works of the Lord are good,
>   every need he will supply in season.
> [34] There is no one who can say, "This is more evil than that,"
>   for all things at the right time will be appropriately esteemed.
> [35] And now with full heart and voice
>   sing praises and bless the name of the Lord. (au. trans.)

The Hebrew for the middle verses is stronger:

> [33] The work[s] of God,
>   all of them are good.
> [34] For every one of your adversities
>   he will be sufficient in season. (au. trans.)

No matter which translation is preferred, we see in this hymn the reiteration of the observation so common to the sapiential tradition—including Qoheleth—on the seasonableness of the Lord's works. In contrast to Qoheleth, ben Sira here stresses the divine purpose, the divine retribution and capacity for exercise of judgment.

3. Sirach 42:15—43:35 is a third hymn on creation illustrating ben Sira's distinctive doctrine of the wondrous aspect of divine holiness. It is last in his anthology before the famous "Praise of the Fathers," Sirach 44—50.

The points of contact in this magnificent hymn on creation are much closer to the Joban poet of the speeches of God (Job 38–41; cf. 26:14) than to Qoheleth. In this hymn also are intermingled the focal themes of the Book of Sirach. The Hebrew in the older texts is defective in the last verse. The Greek reads, "The Lord has made all things and upon those who show true piety (*eusebesin*) he bestows wisdom" (Sir. 43:33, au. trans.).

Two further comments may be made about this hymn. First, in the conclusion of the penultimate strophe (Sir. 43:13–27) and at the beginning of the last, we see a remarkable movement to an abstract theological statement and the author's summation of his recital of the wonders of God in nature:

> The final word (is this): *hû' hakkôl*: he is the all.
> Let us continue to glorify him
>   for we cannot search him out.
> Since he is greater than everything he has made.
>   (Sir. 43:27b–28, au. trans.)

The very abstraction invites thought, but ben Sira does not tarry long on the abstract. He is more comfortable dealing with the words inherited from the sages. Verse 27b is all the more remarkable for its relative isolation.

Second, in this final hymn words for wondrous and wonder occur five times in the Greek (Sir. 42:17; 43:2, 8, 25, 29) and elsewhere in the book eleven times. This focus upon the wonders of the creation is characteristic of ben Sira. In him we continue to have a pragmatic prudentialism, but one tempered by a sense of the divine wonders and that which is beyond human ken to fathom. Precisely this *mysterium et fascinans*, this sense of mystery and wonder at the divine holiness, is a major factor in delivering the prudentialism of ben Sira from banality.

A God Wondrous, Holy, Wise, and Great

In a second regard ben Sira emphasizes the element of fascination to an extent that differentiates him from Qoheleth. Not only are the works of God wondrous and glorious for this author, so is the godhead itself. To Moses God showed his glory (Sir. 45:3d); Ezekiel had a vision of it (Sir. 49:8), and everything (Gk. *to pan*) was established firmly by it (Sir. 42:17d). In the final (and acrostic) poem of the book, the author pledges to render glory to the one who has given wisdom to him (Sir. 51:17). In the next to last portion of the book, "The Praise of the Fathers" (chaps. 44–50), the author gives praise, of course, to the men of renown, but even their greatness he saw as being derivative: "The Lord has created great glory, namely, his magnificence from of old. For they ruled in their kingdoms and were distinguished men in power" (Sir. 44:2–3a, au. trans.).

Ben Sira addresses God as "the Holy One" (Sir. 4:14; 23:9; 43:10; 48:20) whose name, as we saw earlier, the creator intended to be praised as holy whenever humans were shown the majesty of his works (Sir. 17:8–9).

In the opening line of the book, the Lord is acknowledged to be the source of all wisdom (Sir. 1:1). Indeed, "There is but one who is wise, exceedingly fearsome, seated upon his throne" (Sir. 1:8, au. trans.).

The holiness of God for ben Sira includes not only the elements of wonder, glory, wisdom, and judgment. "For lovingkindness and wrath are with him; he is mighty in pardon and in pouring out wrath. His great reproving is commensurate with his great kindness" (Sir. 16:11c–12a, au. trans.). "Who can count the power of his greatness? And who can add to the declaration of his kindnesses?" (Sir. 18:5, au. trans.). The holiness of God for ben Sira meant a surpassing greatness in the very being of the divine as well as in his wondrous works.

OMNISCIENCE AND ETHICS

Of the divine attributes that elicited ben Sira's admiration and praise, a place of considerable prominence must be given to the omniscience of God.

> He searches out the great deep and the human mind,
> And he understands their designs;
> For the Most High possesses all knowledge,
> And looks upon the portent (*sēmeion*) of eternity.
> (Sir. 42:18, Goodspeed trans.)

In words that approach the sentiments of Psalm 139, ben Sira similarly is caught up in wonder at the extensiveness of the divine knowing: "No thought escapes him,/ Not one word is hidden from him" (Sir. 42:20, Goodspeed trans.). In yet another regard, then, ben Sira shows agreement with traditional wisdom in contradistinction to Qoheleth.

As with the traditional sages, ben Sira also posits the closest of relationships between the divine omniscience and human conduct. "He knows a human's every deed" (Sir. 15:19b, au. trans.). "The works of all flesh are open to him (*enōpion autou*),/ and nothing is hidden from his eyes" (Sir. 39:19, au. trans.; see also 16:18; 17:15, 19). There is not the same interiority in these passages as is found in Job 31, but the line nonetheless between morality and the divine knowing is exceedingly plain and direct. The Most High not only sees and observes, he possesses the resources to catch and punish the evildoer when the latter least expects it (Sir. 23:18–21). It will be recalled, as noted above, that ben Sira has an unambiguous doctrine of divine retribution, unlike Qoheleth.

THE ETHICS OF REVERENCE

Of all those things that the Most High sees, there can be little doubt that for ben Sira one of the most pleasing of human attitudes and conduct was reverence: "Those who fear the Lord are honored in his eyes" (Sir. 10:20b, Goodspeed trans.). The centrality of the theme of the fear of God in the Book of Sirach was demonstrated some twenty years ago in a thoroughgoing study by Josef Haspecker.[14] Even though Gerhard von Rad challenged the main thesis of Haspecker, that the fear of God constituted the "fundamental theme" of the book, von Rad does acknowledge that the fear of God remains a central concept.[15] As Haspecker argues, the themes of wisdom and the fear of God are interwoven.[16] It seems to me that both Haspecker and von Rad are right! The goal is wisdom but the essential ingredient of wisdom is the fear of God.[17] Logically, the fear of God is primary for ben Sira, but topically—and also in terms of both his interest and desire to ponder—wisdom is primary. Some of the major aspects in the ethics of the Book of Sirach may be summarized under five headings.

1. *Sirach's is an ethics of prudentialism grounded in the fear of God.* Much of the advice ben Sira has to give is of the most practical sort: how to seek out proper counsel (Sir. 37:7–15); on proper speech (Sir. 4:20–28; 6:32–37; 8:19; 9:17–18; 19:5–12; 20:1–8, 24–26; 27:4–7; 33:4–6); on acquiring and keeping friends (Sir. 6:5–17; 7:18; 9:10; 19:13–17; 22:19–26; 27:16–21; 28:8–12; 37:1–6). Some of his advice is so narrowly focused on

---

14. Joseph Haspecker, *Gottesfurcht bei Jesus Sirach*, Analecta Biblica 30 (Rome: Pontifical Biblical Institute, 1967).

15. Gerhard von Rad, *Wisdom in Israel*, trans. James D. Martin (London: SCM/Nashville and New York: Abingdon Press, 1972), 242, 259 n. 26.

16. Haspecker, *Gottesfurcht bei Jesus Sirach*, 95.

17. Haspecker makes the second point (ibid., 96); whereas von Rad makes the first (*Wisdom in Israel*, 242).

proper individual conduct that it may rightfully be called "instructions in etiquette" (Sir. 31:1–31; 32:1–12). His reflections on women seem misogynous and unenlightened (Sir. 25:16–18) but withal, like the author of the concluding acrostic poem in Proverbs, he appreciates the value (Sir. 26:1; 36:23–24), as well as its stabilizing effect (Sir. 36:25–26), of marriage for a man. In addition to the traditional themes already mentioned, three ethical themes are prominent in the Book of Sirach: his stress on retribution, almsgiving, and generosity. As for retribution, in some instances he seems to be rather traditional (Sir. 27:8, 25–30), but, on the other hand, he makes a tremendous advance in the history of this central, sapiential idea. In Sir. 14:3–10 ben Sira profoundly analyzes how the niggardly and stingy person receives a judgment in his very niggardliness; he suffers from the inability to enjoy whatever possessions he may have accrued: "Evil injustice shrivels up the soul" (Sir. 14:9b, au. trans.).[18] Almsgiving, ben Sira taught, would be rewarded (Sir. 17:22–23). Further, he links it with his strong doctrine of retribution and the emerging doctrine of the treasury of merits (Sir. 29:11–13). That almsgiving is in the theology of ben Sira already vying with the sacrificial cultus for a place of importance is especially apparent in the following: "As water will quench a blazing fire, so almsgiving will propitiate for sin" (Sir. 3:30, au. trans.; see also 3:1–16; 17:22–23). Nurturing a spirit of generosity in ben Sira is perhaps best exemplified by his encouragement of the practice of lending, which is quite contrary to the familiar advice given by Polonius to his son in *Hamlet* (Sir. 39:1–7).

Two convenient summaries of the ethics of ben Sira are to be

---

18. James L. Crenshaw suggests that ben Sira developed "two wholly new responses to the problem of theodicy"—one of them on the basis of psychology and the other on the basis of metaphysics (*Old Testament Wisdom*, 172). The above-cited passage, Sir. 14:3–10, may surely be included among those that illustrate the development in Sirach on the basis of psychology. (Note, however, in the sketch of what happens to the niggardly man, Sirach may, in my judgment, be dependent upon the sketch of the stingy man by Theophrastus [c. 371–287 B.C.E.]; see Warren Anderson, *Theophrastus: The Character Sketches* [Kent, Ohio: Kent State University Press, 1970], 92–95.) Crenshaw is correct in asserting that ben Sira makes occasional forays into the metaphysical when it comes to explaining the opposition of the good to the evil (cf. Sir. 33:14–15), but these endeavors are so tentative that it does not seem to me to be altogether convincing to consider them to be a development.

found in chapter 2 (on "The Ethics of Reverence") and in Sir. 41:14—42:8 (on "True and False Shame" [Thomas H. Weber's designation]). The first summary emphasizes God's mercy (Sir. 2:7, 9, 11, 18) and how from the fear of God there will follow faith, joy, obedience, adherence to his ways, search for divine favor, a satiation with the law, and humbleness of mind (Sir. 2:7–9, 15–17).

2. *In the ethics of Sirach there is a high valuation placed on the priesthood, temple, and cult.* Of all the fathers praised, Aaron receives the fullest treatment (Sir. 45:6–22). At the conclusion of the Praise of the Fathers, Simon the high priest is extolled in grandiose terms—and the very first of his accomplishments extolled is his building and beautification program with respect to the temple (Sir. 50:1–21). Although ben Sira in some regards seems to have accepted the prophetic critique of an overreliance on sacrifices (Sir. 34:18–26), he nonetheless enjoins the presentation of a variety of offerings for which the donor can count on a sevenfold repayment from God (Sir. 35:1–11).[19] He expected that the *tāmîd* offerings at the temple would be continued in perpetuity (Sir. 45:14).

3. *The ethics of Sirach, however, takes quite a different tack than the priestly ethics of the Pentateuch with respect to food laws, sexuality, and distancing one's self from other peoples.* Because ben Sira values both priesthood and law, his divergence from the priestly traditions of the Pentateuch is frequently overlooked. The fact remains, however, that *nowhere in the entire Book of Sirach does the author even suggest that adherence to the dietary laws of the Pentateuch is of any importance!* To the contrary, in a long section on the proper conduct at banquets, he enjoins instead: "Eat as a man the things set before you" (Sir. 31:16a au. trans.). One can imagine the horror with which the priestly writers of Leviticus would have read this injunction. Ben Sira was interested in music (Sir. 32:3–6; 40:20–21), in travel (Sir. 39:4; 51:13), and in the sumptuous aspects of the temple and priestly finery (Sir. 45:7–13; 50:11–15). Ben Sira may have been con-

19. For further treatment on temple and cult, see Leo G. Perdue, *Wisdom and Cult*, SBLDS 30 (Missoula, Mont.: Scholars Press, 1977), 189–211.

servative in many regards, but one of them was certainly not with respect to the dietary laws. Similarly, in the course of his many ruminations on women one never encounters a reiteration of the kind of sexual morality such as is enjoined in Leviticus 18 and 20. Ben Sira simply does not share with either the writers of the Priestly or the Holiness Code the same strictures with respect to whom one should not marry, homosexuality, and menstrual blood. If he does share the same strictures, he does not articulate them—and the burden of proof thus shifts to those who would argue that he does.

4. *History and law are given a prominence in Sirach beyond that found in most other sapiential writings.* In comparison to both Job and Qoheleth, Sirach gives extraordinary room to Israel's history. The final portion of the book is devoted to a type of historical survey that still enjoys popularity today.[20] If one fears the Lord, one will keep the law (Sir. 19:24). Wisdom that found a resting place in Jerusalem is equated with "the book of the covenant of the Most High" (Sir. 24:23). "The fear of the Lord is the sum of wisdom,/ and the doing of the law is included in the sum of wisdom" (Sir. 19:20, au. trans.)

5. *The law, however, does not enjoy for Sirach a position of unambiguous centrality as it does, for example, for the sapiential authors of Psalms 1, 19, and 119.* As argued at the outset of this section, wisdom and reverence are the central themes of Sirach. The law is clearly given a place of importance, as acknowledged above. The law, however, is subsidiary throughout to wisdom. Happiness is not said to come to the one who makes the law the object of his meditation and recitation—as is the case for the author of Psalm 1—rather, "Happy is the man who meditates *on*

---

20. See esp. Martin E. Marty (*Pilgrims in Their Own Land: 500 Years of Religion in America* [Boston/Toronto: Little, Brown and Co., 1984]), who relates American religious history through focusing on its protagonists. This portion of Sirach (chaps. 44–50) has been the object of two exceedingly fine and illuminating studies: Burton L. Mack, *Wisdom and the Hebrew Epic: Ben Sira's Hymn in Praise of the Fathers*, ed. Jacob Neusner, Chicago Studies in the History of Judaism (Chicago/London: University of Chicago Press, 1985); and Thomas R. Lee, *Studies in the Form of Sirach 44–50*, SBLDS 75 (Atlanta: Scholars Press, 1986). This portion of Sirach with its emphasis on praise undoubtedly manifests the impact on ben Sira of the Greek epideictic (display) oratory. For an exploration of this thesis, see the above works.

wisdom,/ Who reasons with his understanding;/ Who considers her ways in his mind,/ And reflects on her secrets" (Sir. 14:20–21, Goodspeed trans.). Mastery of the law is not conceived to be an end in itself, but rather a means to acquire wisdom (Sir. 15:1). Similarly, in chapter 24, where the law is seemingly equated with wisdom, the law is seen to be "that which fills [humans] with wisdom" (v. 25). A Hebrew text for chapter 24 is not extant, but if ben Sira's grandson has been faithful to the Hebrew, ben Sira did not extol the unsearchability and counsel of the law, but rather the unsearchability and counsel of wisdom (vv. 28–29). The rhetorical centrality given to the law in Psalms 1, 19, and 119 is given to wisdom in Sirach (Sirach 1, 24, 51).

WISDOM IN A NEW KEY

The Wisdom of Solomon, or Book of Wisdom, as it is commonly called in Roman Catholic circles, is one of the most remarkable of the proto-canonical and deutero-canonical books. It is the only biblical, sapiential book to have been written in Greek; it is remarkably prophetic in character; and it carries the traditional, sapiential concern for retribution to a new settlement—in a doctrine of immortality. Before proceeding to a consideration of the unique development of the doctrine of holiness in the Wisdom of Solomon, we may take a brief look at the setting of this book and some of the ways in which it differs from its sapiential predecessors.

Recent students of the Wisdom of Solomon are by no means agreed as to its date or provenance. Dieter Georgi puts it between 130 and 100 B.C.E., in a setting outside of Alexandria in Syria.[21] David Winston puts it at about 38 C.E. in Alexandria.[22] James M. Reese puts it some time before 28 B.C.E. also in Alexandria.[23]

---

21. Dieter Georgi, *Weisheit Salomos*, ed. Georg Kümmel et al., Jüdische Schriften aus hellenistisch-römischer Zeit 3 (Gütersloh: Gerd Mohn, 1980), 395–97.

22. David Winston, *The Wisdom of Solomon*, Anchor Bible 43 (Garden City, N.Y.: Doubleday & Co., 1975), 20–25.

23. James M. Reese, *Hellenistic Influence on the Book of Wisdom and Its Consequences*, Analecta Biblica 41 (Rome: Pontifical Biblical Institute, 1970), 153–62; and idem, *The Book of Wisdom/Song of Songs*, Old Testament Message 20 (Wilmington, Del.: Michael Glazier, 1983), 17.

Because the book is so sharply critical of the kind of idolatry and syncretistic religion practiced in Ptolemaic Egypt (see esp. 14:15–26), the arguments for a setting in Alexandria, the capital of Ptolemaic Egypt, are not at all persuasive. From the Letter of Aristeas, a Jewish sapiential work written in Greek in Alexandria in the middle of the second century B.C.E., we know that at least a portion of the Greek-speaking Jewish community in Alexandria was very interested in reaching out to find points of contact with the religion of the Ptolemies.[24] The Wisdom of Solomon, however, shows no such concerns or sensibilities. In my reading, the author distances himself too much from the idolaters he condemns to have been a resident Alexandrian.

The author of the Book of Wisdom (Wisdom of Solomon) makes two significant contributions to Israel's sapiential traditions. (1) He develops the doctrine of retribution on three fronts. (2) He shows a deep affinity with the prophetic traditions of Israel in his sharp polemics against idolatry. Both of these developments contain an implicit doctrine of holiness which will be drawn out after each has been considered in turn.

(1) *Developments of the doctrine of retribution: eschatological, definitional, and wondrously contrasting.* The doctrine of retribution is given its classic statement in the Book of Proverbs, it is challenged vigorously in the Books of Job and Qoheleth, reaffirmed and advanced in a psychological fashion by ben Sira, but only in the Book of Wisdom is it eschatologized and redefined in Platonic terms. The basic argument of the first five chapters of the book may be simply put: death is not the end; following the physical death of every righteous soul there awaits an immortality—and for the ungodly, annihilation. The basic structure of these chapters is derived from Psalm 1, namely, the contrast between the righteous and the ungodly. They constitute, as it were, a neo-Platonic midrash on the sacred text that the righteous will stand (Wis. 5:1), but the hope of the ungodly will be

---

24. For the arguments for this date and concern of the Letter of Aristeas, see my essay, "The Hellenization of Jewish Wisdom in the Letter of Aristeas," in *Proceedings of the Ninth World Congress of Jewish Studies*, Division A, The Period of the Bible (Jerusalem: World Congress of Jewish Studies, 1986), 207–14.

like the chaff which is driven away (Wis. 5:14). As for the righteous,

> The souls of the upright are in the hand of God,
> And no torment can reach them.
> In the eyes of foolish people they seemed to die, . . .
> But they are at peace.
> For though in the sight of men they are punished,
> Their hope is full of immortality (*athanasia*),
> And after being disciplined a little, they will be shown
>   great kindness.
> For God has tried them,
> And found them worthy of himself.
>   (Wis. 3:1–5, Goodspeed trans.)

The future judgment on the impious which the Sage[25] describes in Wis. 5:20–23 also draws liberally on the imagery of Psalm 1 in that it multiplies the notion of a winnowing wind, tempest, and storm. Upon the wicked, however, the divine judgment does not entirely await for the eschaton; rather, in a moment of insight the Sage allows the wicked to acknowledge the truth of the neo-Platonic doctrine that the punishment of evil is nonexistence: "So we also, as soon as we were born, ceased to be,/ And had no sign of virtue to show,/ But were consumed in our wickedness" (Wis. 5:13, Goodspeed trans.).

The Sage solved the problem of the early death of the righteous through an ingenious rereckoning of what constitutes old age (Wis. 4:8–11). In the Sage's scheme of things the seemingly premature death of an upright person would not have been considered untimely because, by definition, a blameless life is declared to be the equivalent of old age! And better an early death than a confrontation with the future terrors of the divine tempest or the virtual nonexistence of the wicked from birth.

The third development of the doctrine of retribution in the Book of Wisdom has already been anticipated in the proto-canonical books—most clearly in the Book of Psalms (see esp. Ps. 18:26–28; Engl. 25–27). The anticipation, however, is inexact. For the Sage develops the notion of retribution-in-kind

---

25. This is the name for the author suggested by Reese, *Book of Wisdom/Song of Songs*, 13.

into a principle and at the same time he is thunderstruck by another principle of retribution—the very substance that may bring punishment to the idolatrous may be the source of divine blessing to the people of God. In the first (Wis. 11:1–16) of seven contrasts in which the Sage shows how at the Exodus the means of deliverance for the Israelites served also to punish the idolatrous Egyptians, the author of the Book of Wisdom also unfolds his principle of retribution-in-kind:

> In response to the senseless reasonings of their injustice—by which reasonings they were misled—they venerated serpents incapable of speech and common beasts, Thou didst send a multitude of speechless creatures in retribution so that they might know that *one is punished by the very means with which one sins.* (Wis. 11:15–16, au. trans.)

The Sage develops the principle of contrasts and of retribution-in-kind in chapters 16–19. The combined principles are neatly summed up: "For by the same means by which thou didst punish our enemies thou didst call us to thyself and glorify us" (Wis. 18:8, RSV). Thus the Sage carried three steps further the teaching of retribution which he inherited from the sages before.

(2) *The prophetic and anti-idolatrous stance of the Sage.* In another regard the author of the Wisdom of Solomon advances beyond his predecessors: he is an uncompromising iconoclast who elevates to the level of a principle the notion that folly of idolatry is the root of evil. The central portion of the book (chaps. 13–15) is devoted to a diatribe against idolatry.[26] The linkage between idolatry and sexual infidelity, which the Israelite prophet Hosea demonstrated with such pathos, is put into a pithy one-liner in the Book of Wisdom: "For the idea of making idols was the beginning of fornication,/ and the invention of them was the corruption of life" (Wis. 14:12, RSV). The Sage's avowal in this verse has had a tremendous impact on Western thinking. The very same linkage between sexual immorality and idolatry is

---

26. It is interesting to note that in Gerhard von Rad's magisterial work, *Wisdom in Israel*, he does not devote a separate chapter to the Wisdom of Solomon, but he does do so for the topic "The Polemic Against Idols" (pp. 176–85) in which the Wisdom of Solomon 13—15 is given a place of prominence.

made by St. Paul (Rom. 1:18–32) and it becomes a major chord in St. Augustine's *City of God* (Books I–IV). In none of the other sapiential writings of Israel does the prophetic stricture against idolatry burn as fiercely as it does in the Book of Wisdom. He shows himself to be a synthesizer of Israel's sapiential and prophetic traditions with Hellenism. Once again, he has accomplished his end—very much in keeping with the sapiential tradition—in a maxim: "For the worship of idols not to be named/ is the beginning and cause and end of every evil" (Wis. 14:27, RSV).

New Dimensions in the Doctrine of Holiness

In view of these developments in the Book of Wisdom, it is not surprising that we can observe decided advances with respect to the author's teachings on holiness. First, with respect to the element of *mysterium et fascinans*, the author is struck, as we found in examining his doctrine of retribution, by the wondrous management of the world. The sevenfold illustration of this divine working in the Exodus story furnishes eloquent testimony to this fascination. It is already given expression in the following: "You are ever ruling the world with holiness and righteousness,/ and with fair-mindedness you pass judgment" (Wis. 9:3, au. trans.). The holiness of God for the Sage is thus not in question. His greatest development of the doctrine, however, is not found with respect to the godhead itself, but with respect to Wisdom and Spirit. "Wisdom is a holy spirit kindly disposed toward humankind" (Wis. 1:6a, au. trans.). This Spirit of Wisdom is not only holy, but all-powerful, all-seeing, pure, undefiled, "a spotless mirror of the activities of God" (Wis. 7:22–26). Those who acquire the great treasure of Wisdom are made friends of God (Wis. 7:14, 27). Wisdom is a search of the works of God (Wis. 8:4b), she conducts everything well (8:1b); evil cannot overpower her (7:30a); she is the one who teaches the virtues of temperance, prudence, justice, and courage—the very virtues the Stoic philosophers had stressed. Rapturous words in description of Wisdom suffuse chapters 7 and 8; little wonder that in the moving prayer in chapter 9 the author sets forth Solomon's prayer for Wisdom and in chapters 10–11 he describes Wisdom's saving power. In these two chapters sacred history is related not so much as *magnalia Dei*, but rather as *magnalia sapientis*. In Qoheleth the fascination with the holiness of God focuses on the divine works and the beauty of the seasons, and in ben Sira it focuses on the divine creation and omniscience. In the author of the Wisdom of Solomon this fascination focuses on Wisdom with whom Solomon sought kinship that he might know immortality in the life beyond, and in this life the pure delight of friendship with her (Wis. 8:13).

The second element in the holiness of God, which the Sage held in common with his predecessors in the sapiential tradition and yet developed, is the element of *tremendum*, of fear before the divine majesty, of awe in face of the divine power. This element has already been alluded to in part in the discussion above. The eschatological judgment on the ungodly is described in frightening terms (Wis. 5:17–23); similarly, the Sage's descriptions of the past judgment on the idolatrous at the Exodus carry to a new height of intensity and detail the numinous and frightful aspect of the divine retribution noted by Eliphaz in the Book of Job (Wis. 17:2–21; 18:5–20). What impresses the Sage is the power of God. This power in the Sage's mind was intimately linked with the divine capability of judgment and justice (cf. Wis. 16:18c). Wisdom, to be sure, is extolled by the Sage in terms of fascination and endearment that carry us beyond those found in Proverbs and Sirach, but the Sage remains a monotheist. In a verse that seems to second the Sage's assertion that the source of all evil is found in idolatry, he says: "For to know you is perfect righteousness,/ and to know your power is the root of immortality" (Wis. 15:3, au. trans.).

In a third respect also, namely, in the extent to which the Sage is conscious of the polarity between holiness and cleanness, he demonstrates an advancement beyond his immediate, sapiential predecessors. Ben Sira, to be sure, maintains the polarity. In his final acrostic poem on wisdom he affirms, "Through purification I found her (namely, wisdom)" (Sir. 51:20b), but the consciousness of ben Sira is not suffused with the notion that he here articulates. It is quite the contrary for the author of the Wisdom of Solomon. The Spirit of Wisdom he so extols is not only cited as holy, but also in the language of purity: as "unpolluted" (*amolunton*), "a pure (*eilikrinēs*) emanation of his glory"; "nothing defiled (*memiammenon*) can enter her"; "a spotless (*akēlidōton*) mirror of the workings of God" (Wis. 7:22, 25, 26). Similarly, in an autobiographical rehearsal Solomon (speaking as if he were Wisdom) relates, "I entered an undefiled (*amianton*) body" (Wis. 8:20). The author uses in a synonymous parallelism the phrases "holy people" (*laon hosion*) with "blameless seed" (*sperma amempton*, Wis. 10:15). Thus with respect to the doctrine of holiness not only does the Sage utilize the vocabulary of the holy to an equal if not greater extent than ben Sira—"holy mountain" (Wis. 9:8); "holy tent" (Wis. 9:8); "holy heavens" (Wis. 9:10); "holy persons" (Wis. 10:17; 18:1, 5); "Thy holy name" (Wis. 10:20); "holy prophet" (Wis. 11:1); "holy land (Wis. 12:3); "holy nation" (Wis. 17:2); and "holy children" (Wis. 18:9)—he carries within his thinking a far deeper sense that purity of individuals is the counterpart and requirement of holiness. This difference is illustrated perhaps most clearly in the course of the Sage's deliberations on the contrast between the righteous and ungodly in chapters 1–5. In deliberate contradiction to the sapiential tradition which sees the gift of children as a blessing from God (see, e.g., Ps. 127:3–5), the Sage declares that offspring of the ungodly are no blessing (Wis. 3:12); instead:

> For happy is the barren women who is undefiled (*amiantos*),
> Who has not known a sinful union;
> For she will have fruit when God examines human souls.
> (Wis. 3:13, au. trans.)

If with ben Sira we find an ethics of reverence, with the Sage, it is *an ethics of holiness.* "For those who observe holy things in a holy fashion will be declared holy,/ and those who have been taught them will find a sure defense" (Wis. 6:10, au. trans.). Indeed, holiness (*hosiotēs*) is an invincible shield" (Wis. 5:19). It should be noted, however, that the difference—clear though it is—is one of nuance rather than in kind. Both the author of the Wisdom of Solomon and ben Sira saw piety to be the foundation stone of ethical behavior.[27]

27. Of recent writers in the realm of religious ethics, James M. Gustafson has

SUMMARY

In this second inquiry into the wisdom traditions, we have again found basic confirmation of the thesis that for the sages in ancient Israel the holiness of God required the cleanness of individual morality. The vocabulary of holiness with respect to the deity, persons, places, and things is most explicit in the Wisdom of Solomon and least explicit in Qoheleth. In Sirach and also in the Wisdom of Solomon the holiness of God is expressed in a number of indirect ways. Both Sirach and the Sage lay stress on the wonder of the divine omniscience (and thus on the elements of *mysterium* and *fascinans*, which Otto so closely associated with holiness) and both emphasize the fear of God (and thus the element of *tremendum*, another element in Otto's schema on holiness). Sirach's largely individual ethics, we saw, grows out of his piety and sense of reverence for the omniscient, wondrous, and fearsome God. Sirach is not as explicit in his use of the vocabulary of cleanness and purity in the development of his ethical teaching, but in the acrostic poem in his book he is (Sir. 51:20b). The Wisdom of Solomon, in contrast, employs a more explicit vocabulary of cleanness as the counterpart and requirement of holiness. We suggested that the ethics of the latter may properly be called an ethics of holiness. As for the requirements of holiness of cleanness in Qoheleth, the author appears to accept the traditional categorization of clean and unclean, but does not expand upon the meaning of the clean.

In the above chapters we considered the doctrine of holiness in Israel's historical writing in the priestly vein (in chapter 2, following our treatment of the priests), in the prophetic vein (in chapter 4, following our treatment of the prophets), and in the sapiential vein (in the present chapter, following our treatment of the earlier sages). In the present chapter, however, the barest attention was given to inquiry into the treatment of holiness in the specifically historical sections of Sirach and the Wisdom of

most emphatically argued that piety must be the starting point of every religious ethical system. In this assertion, of course, he shows himself to be not only in the Protestant reformed, but also in the biblical-sapiential tradition. See his *Ethics from a Theocentric Perspective*, 2 vols. (Chicago: University of Chicago Press, 1981–84); 1:87–113, 201–4.

Solomon. We simply noted that Sirach's emphasis was on the achievements of great persons and the Sage's upon Wisdom's role in history and on the folly and horrendous aspects of idolatry from which Israel, at all costs, was enjoined to remain separate. In this latter regard we submitted that the author showed himself to be a synthesizer in particular of Israel's prophetic and sapiential traditions.

Other features of this chapter included an examination of the extent of the pessimism in Qoheleth and an exposition of Sirach's prudential ethics of reverence under five headings (its grounding; its high valuation of priesthood, temple, and cultus; its disregard of Israel's food laws; its stress on history and law; and its valuation of wisdom above law). We also briefly discussed two remarkable advances in the Wisdom of Solomon over his predecessors with respect to the doctrine of retribution and his extremely strong teaching against idolatry. Each of these inquiries throws light, we argued, on the respective sage's doctrine of holiness.

We turn now to the final stage in our inquiry, in which the priestly, prophetic, and sapiential are combined. One of the particular points of interest in the apocalyptic literature will be the extent to which the normative responses to holiness outlined in the above chapters continued to be operative when the three strands became interwoven.

CHAPTER 7

The Understanding of
Holiness among
the Apocalyptic Writers

(Isaiah 24—27; Zechariah 9—14,
Joel, Ezekiel 38—39, Daniel)

The last writings from ancient Israel and the diaspora to be
considered in this thematic investigation of the theology of holiness come from those portions of the Hebrew Scriptures/Old
Testament called "apocalyptic." The term itself is contested and,
as will be noted below, some would not confine the apocalyptic
literature in the Old Testament to the above-mentioned parts of
the prophetic books, and some would not include all of Daniel.
The reader will find below some of my own judgments with
respect to the present state of the study of apocalyptic, but the
chief endeavor in this chapter will be to describe what Old Testament apocalyptic—as others and I understand that term—has to
say about holiness.

Significant problems affecting the assessment of the Old Testament apocalyptic literature are: (1) the matter of dating—this
seems to me to be especially critical with respect to Zechariah
9—14, Isaiah 24—27, and Ezekiel 38—39; (2) the growth of the
prophetic books (Is the process of accretion, supplementation,
and redaction such as is outlined for Ezekiel by Gese, Zimmerli,
Hossfeld, Fishbane, and Talmon[1] or by Vermeylen for Isaiah[2] the

1. See chap. 2, n. 10.
2. J. Vermeylen, *Du prophète Isaïe à l'apocalylptique Isaïe, I–XXXV, miroir*
d'un demi-millenaire d'experience religieuse en Israël, 2 vols. (Paris: J.
Gabalda, 1978–79).

most likely process by which the prophetic books took shape?);
(3) the relationship of the oracles against the foreign nations
(Amos 1—2; Isaiah 13—23, 34—35, 47; Jeremiah 46—51; Ezekiel 25—32) to the development of apocalyptic,[3] and (4) the relationship of the prophets to the cultus.[4] It seems to me that more
light will be cast on the development of apocalyptic out of prophecy as these problems are carefully pursued.[5] Limits of space do
not permit their pursuit here. A recent survey touching on some
of these matters with which I find myself in considerable sympathy is to be found in the Peter Ackroyd Festschrift.[6]

THE DOCTRINES OF HOLINESS IN APOCALYPTIC

In an influential study of apocalyptic, Klaus Koch identified
eight motifs.[7] These motifs, he averred, are "distributed more or

3. It seems to me that this problem has received insufficient attention. Even though scholars such as Paul D. Hanson have noted in passing the points of contact between the cultic hymns in praise of God as divine warrior and the oracles against the foreign nations (*The Dawn of Apocalyptic* [Philadelphia: Fortress Press, 1975], 312–20). Few scholars, to my knowledge, have picked up on the observation made by Hans-Peter Müller, *Ursprung und Strukturen alttestamentlicher Eschatologie*, Beihefte zur Zeitschrift für die alttestamentliche Wissenschaft 109, ed. Georg Fohrer (Berlin: Alfred Töpelmann, 1969): "In the oracles of woe against all the nations as well as in the proclamations to Israel of a salvation, which will take place in the sight of all the nations, *prophecy opens out into apocalyptic.* From the perspective of the history of traditions we have evidence, very nearly throughout, of the impact of the Zion-tradition, and indeed in its mythic sense" (p. 123, italics added). For a helpful discussion on their probable usage in the cultus, see John H. Hayes, "The Usage of Oracles Against Foreign Nations in Ancient Israel," *JBL* 87 (1968): 81–92. This suggestion is especially important in view of the next and fourth area I have suggested above as one that merits further probing.

4. Richard Coggins has raised the question anew with respect to Joel, Habakkuk, and Nahum, "An Alternative Prophetic Tradition?" in *Israel's Prophetic Tradition: Essays in Honour of Peter Ackroyd*, ed. Richard Coggins, Anthony Phillips, and Michael Knibb (Cambridge: Cambridge University Press, 1982), 77–94. In the same volume, see John Eaton, "The Isaiah Tradition," 58–76; and Robert Murray, "Prophecy and Cult," 200–16.

5. Not that the pursuit has not been undertaken! See, e.g., the fine essay by Robert North, "Prophecy to Apocalyptic via Zechariah," in *Congress Volume, Uppsala, 1971*, VTSup 22 (Leiden: E.J. Brill, 1972), 47–71; and esp. Joseph Blenkinsopp, "The Transformation of Prophecy," chap. 6 in *Prophecy and Canon: A Contribution to the Study of Jewish Origins* (Notre Dame/London: University of Notre Dame Press, 1977), 124–38.

6. See Michael A. Knibb, "Prophecy and the Emergence of the Jewish Apocalypses," in *Israel's Prophetic Tradition*, 155–99.

7. Klaus Koch, *The Rediscovery of Apocalyptic*, trans. Margaret Kohl, SBT 22

less equally throughout the various apocalypses":[8] (1) closeness of the coming reversal of events; (2) the coming end will be accompanied by a cosmic catastrophe, hence there is a prevailing pessimism; (3) periodization of the present age, belief in a determinism for nations, and numerology; (4) belief in angels and demons—in the coming age the faithful will shine as the stars; (5) paradisal character of the salvation beyond the catastrophe—hence there is a correspondence between descriptions of the last days in accordance with those of the primeval days (the so-called *Endzeit-Urzeit* schema); (6) salvation will come from a heavenly throne and the kingdom of God will become visible on earth—frequently there is a dualism of This Age and an Age-to-come; (7) the end time will be ushered in by a mediator (Messiah, Son of Man, or Elect One)—possibly an angelic being; and (8) because of the transformation of communal structures, the catchword of the end time will be Glory—in their notions of radical transformations of human relations and in the manner of judgment the apocalypticists differ from the prophets. It will be noted that Koch numbers only eight items, but, cleverly, under each number he often includes several other related features. In our treatment of the doctrines of holiness in the apocalyptic portions of the Old Testament we will focus upon two items found in Koch's list: (1) Glory and (2) Kingdom. Consideration of two other items (not found on Koch's list) will round out our study: (3) Sacred Mountain and (4) the Ethical Requirements of Holiness.

(1) *The Glory of God.* In a classic study on the Glory of God written at the turn of the century, Freiherrn von Gall observed that the Hebrew *kābôd* carries with it the connotation of "wealth,

---

(Naperville, Ill.: Alec R. Allenson, n.d.; first published in German in 1970), 28–33. In my article "The Classification, Stages of Growth, and Changing Intentions in the Book of Daniel," *JBL* 95 (1976):191–204, building upon Koch, I have endeavored to bring even greater precision to the determination of what constitutes a work of "apocalyptic literature." An important work in this regard is John J. Collins, *Apocalypse: The Morphology of a Genre*, Semeia 14 (Missoula, Mont.: Scholars Press, 1979). My chief criticism of Collins's fine study is his failure to take sufficiently into account that the apocalyptic literature is a composite genre and that some of the works in this genre are not apocalypses.

8. Collins, *Apocalypse*, 33.

might, well-being and power."[9] In the piel form (*kibbed*) the verb means "to ascribe weight" (lit. "to make heavy"), hence, "to honor." In the apocalyptic literature Glory is more than a catchword.

Everywhere the apocalypticists saw the Glory of God and in turn expressed it in doxologies. In the Book of Daniel even kings recognize the Glory of God and ascribe it to him: "Truly your god is indeed God of gods and Lord over kings, a revealer of secrets" (Nebuchadnezzar, Dan. 2:47, NEB); "There is no other god who can save men in this way" (Nebuchadnezzar, Dan. 3:29, NEB); "How great are his signs, and his marvels overwhelming!" (Nebuchadnezzar, Dan. 3:33a; Engl. 4:3a, NEB); "He is the living God, the everlasting . . . a saviour, a deliverer, a worker of signs and wonders in heaven and on earth, who has delivered Daniel from the power of the lions" (Darius, Dan. 6:26–27, NEB). These doxologies—so important a feature of the stories of Daniel 1—6, as Sibley Towner demonstrated[10]—constitute a liturgical feature of apocalyptic that remains fairly constant throughout, and in the Christian tradition reaches a climax, as it were, in the doxologies of the Book of Revelation, where angels, elders, and the four living creatures around the heavenly throne burst forth: "Amen. Blessing and glory and wisdom, thanksgiving, honor, power, and strength be ascribed to our God for ever and ever. Amen" (Rev. 7:12, au. trans.). The fact that the doxologies just cited from the Book of Daniel are in the mouths of foreign kings probably shows that the author of the stories was imbued with a sense that prophecies telling of the praise of foreigners and kings such as were found in Isaiah of Babylon were being fulfilled: "Surely God is among you and there is no other, no other god" (Isa. 45:14c, NEB).[11]

Curiously, in the visions of Daniel 7—12 it is not the wisdom

9. Freiherrn von Gall, *Die Herrlichkeit Gottes* (Giessen: J. Ricker [Alfred Töpelmann], 1900).

10. W. Sibley Towner, "The Poetic Passages of Daniel 1–6," *CBQ* 31(1969): 317–26.

11. For a further exploration of this topic, see my "On the Intention and Sources of Daniel I–VI," *Vetus Testamentum* 31 (1981): 282–92. What I did not see as clearly as I do now is the probable impact of the paradigm of prophecy and fulfillment in the Deuteronomistic History on the author-editor of the Danielic stories.

and revealing of secrets that are the objects of attention and praise, but rather the Glory of the heavenly throne (Dan. 7:9–10) and the working of the divine will in history (Daniel 8, 11).

> Flames of fire were his throne and its wheels blazing fire;
> a flowing river of fire streamed out before him.
> Thousands upon thousands served him
> and myriads upon myriads attended his presence.
> The court sat, and the books were opened.
>   (Dan. 7:9–10, NEB)

Energy (*energicum*), brilliance (*maiestas*), and fear (*tremendum*) are the aspects of the divine holiness that impress themselves on the seer in this apocalyptic vision of impending judgment as the Ancient in Years makes ready to hand over to One Like a Son of Man "sovereignty and glory (**yĕqār*) and kingly power" (Dan. 7:11–14).[12]

In other passages of the Old Testament apocalyptic, amazement before the divine glory is equally apparent. In the Little Apocalypse of Isaiah we read:

> On that day the LORD will punish
>   the host of heaven, in heaven,
>   and the kings of the earth, on the earth.
> They will be gathered together
>   as prisoners in a pit;
> they will be shut up in a prison,
>   and after many days they will be punished.
> Then the moon will be confounded,
>   and the sun ashamed;
> for the LORD of hosts will reign
>   on Mount Zion and in Jerusalem
> and before his elders he will manifest his glory.
>   (Isa. 24:21–23, RSV)[13]

---

12. The debate, of course, over the identity of the One Like a Son of Man (Aram. *kĕbar 'ĕnāš*) is extensive. In the original vision—but certainly not in later Christian interpretation—it seems to me that this figure must be a leader among the heavenly host and therefore most likely Michael, inasmuch as this figure's receipt of the kingdom in heaven constitutes at the same time a reception of the kingdom for the faithful in Israel on earth (Dan. 7:27). In the spatial (heaven-earth) dualism of apocalyptic it is a regular and recurring feature that earthly events are but reflections of heavenly actions. For further discussion and a tracing of this idea, see my "Spatial and Ethical Dualism in Jewish Wisdom and Apocalyptic Literature," *JBL* 93 (1974): 356–85.

13. It seems to me to be terribly difficult to date Isaiah 24—27. It is very plain,

A similar association of glory and judgment on kings and nations is seen in the apocalypse of Ezekiel, when the mysterious Gog shall come down from the north and suffer defeat: "And I will reveal (lit. give) my glory among the nations, and all the nations shall see my judgment which I perform and my hand which I place on them" (Ezek. 39:21, au. trans.).[14] That the holiness and glory of God were synonymous to the author and editor of the Ezekielian apocalypse is plain when one compares the verse cited above with the concluding verses in chapter 38.

Similar manifestations of the divine glory are found elsewhere in passages clearly apocalyptic or proto-apocalyptic. In Trito-Zechariah, at the time when "the LORD my God will come with all his holy ones" (Zech. 14:5), nature will be transformed with the creation of a new east-west valley, the elimination of cold and heat, and the elimination of the distinction between night and day: "At eventide there shall be light" (Zech. 14:4–7). In this same passage, though there is neither explicit use of the term "judgment" nor reference to a heavenly court, there is described God's striking down all the nations who warred against Jerusalem (Zech. 14:1–3, 12). Thus the association between divine glory/brightness and judgment on the nations seems to obtain here also.[15] The same is so in the Book of Joel wherein the prophet pronounces judgment on the wickedness of the nations and God will dwell on his fruitful and flourishing holy mountain (Joel 4:13–21; Engl. 3:13–21).

however, that it qualifies for the classification as "apocalyptic literature." By my count there are in Isaiah 24—27 no fewer than fourteen typically apocalyptic ideological and thematic elements.

14. Because of passages such as this and the previous ones from Daniel 7 and Isaiah 24, it seems to me that James P. M. Walsh, S.J., in his lively book, is entirely justified when he says of apocalyptic: "It unmasks the pretensions of the oppressor and pulls the veil of anguish and despair away from the minds of the oppressed" (*The Mighty From Their Thrones: Power in the Biblical Tradition*, OBT [Philadelphia: Fortress Press, 1987]), 143.

15. Scholars commonly divide these chapters as Deutero-Zechariah (chaps. 9–11) and Trito-Zechariah (chaps. 12–14). Hanson includes a handy survey of the criticism of these chapters in *Dawn of Apocalyptic*, 287–90. Though Hanson makes an attractive case for seeing chaps. 10–14 against the backdrop of a hierocratic struggle, he is not as convincing when it comes to the specification of dates. Hanson's thematic analysis of the poems of Zechariah 9—14 as Divine Warrior Hymns that contain the same themes as many psalms, however, is at once most compelling and interesting. See *Dawn of Apocalyptic*, 280–401.

In Isaiah 56—66, which Hanson has found to be "early apocalyptic," glory is celebrated in a homily (chap. 60), but not a glory
associated with judgment on the nations, but rather with *their*
witnessing the return of glory to Jerusalem (cf. also Isa. 62:2).[16]
Indeed, in Isaiah 62 the prophet reiterates this role of the nations
as witnesses of Jerusalem's glory: "All kings shall see your [fem.]
glory" (Isa. 62:2).

(2) *The Kingdom of God.* The English word "kingdom" is one
of four permissible translations of the Hebrew *malkût, mamlakâ,*
and the Aramaic *malkû*—the other three being: "kingship,"
"reign," and "realm." Thus the Scottish scholar John Gray has
chosen to write recently on *The Biblical Doctrine of the Reign of
God*[17] rather than on the kingdom or kingship of God. In an age
that seeks to be more inclusive in its language, there is much to be
commended in Gray's choice. Reign, however, focuses on the act
of ruling; kingship focuses on the one exercising the rule; realm
focuses on the area ruled; and kingdom focuses on the area ruled
as well as on the ruler, namely, the sovereign. Hence the choice
here of the "kingdom of God," despite its liabilities in terms of
the welcome recent thrust in religious communities toward to a
more inclusive language. In the apocalyptic writings the focus is
equally upon the sovereignty of the godhead and upon the realm
ruled. In the preceding section on the Glory of God, we have
already touched on some of the aspects of the majesty and mystery of the godhead. Attention may accordingly turn to the locus
or realm of the divine rule.

In the Book of Daniel the stories set the tone for our under-
standing what the reign of God will be. God is above the kings.
When Nebuchadnezzar learns this (Daniel 4), his rule is restored.
And after his restoration he utters the following doxology:

---

16. Hanson sees a particularly close relationship between Zechariah 14 and
Isaiah 60—62. The group that produced these passages, he avers, was at fierce
odds with the Zadokite responsible for the latest edition of Ezekiel 40—48.

17. John Gray, *The Biblical Doctrine of the Reign of God* (Edinburgh: T. & T.
Clark, 1979). For two recent excellent studies on this subject, see Benedict T.
Viviano, *The Kingdom of God in History*, Good News Studies 27, ed. Robert J.
Karris (Wilmington, Del.: Michael Glazier, 1988); and Wendell Willis, ed., *The
Kingdom of God in 20th-Century Interpretation* (Peabody, Mass.: Hendrickson,
1987).

> His [namely, the Most High's] rule (*šoltānēh*) is never-ending
> and his kingdom (*malkûtēh*) with generation after
>   generation;
> all dwellers upon earth count for nothing
> and he deals as he wishes with the host of heaven;
> no one may lay hand upon him
> and ask him what he does.
>   (Dan. 4:31–32; Engl. 4:34–35, NEB adapted)

In this passage there is a clue to the notion of how the kingdom of God operates: namely, what God has established in the heavens will have its counterpart on earth. This principle of correspondence is a very important element in the middle and later apocalyptic. In the Book of Revelation, for example, Michael's successful casting of the dragon down from heaven to earth is already a sign that the battle on earth will soon be won because it has already been won in heaven (Rev. 12:7–9).

Precisely the same principle of the correspondence between heavenly rule and earthly rule is operative in the very disputed passage in Daniel 7. "Sovereignty and glory and kingly power" are given to One Like a Son of Man (Dan. 7:14), which at the same time constitutes a bestowal of "kingly power, sovereignty and greatness" to "the people of the saints of the Most High" (Dan. 7:27). There is—and the text suggests that there will continue to be—a correspondence between the transmittal of power in heaven to the transmittal of power on earth. It is interesting that this notion of correspondence between things heavenly and things earthly, which become such a regular feature in apocalyptic, is exceedingly familiar: "Thy kingdom come, thy will be done, on *earth* as it is in *heaven*." André Lacocque has used an even more cogent term for this heaven-earth correspondence: "the dialectic of power." "Few of the other Israelite writings go as far as the Book of Daniel in the dialectic of power. Every reign, all grandeur, all glory, and all majesty [Daniel 5] (v. 18) can only be the echo of the lordship of God."[18]

If we have pointed to the dynamics of the kingdom, namely, that the coming of the kingdom on earth will correspond to the

---

18. André Lacocque, *The Book of Daniel*, trans. David Pellauer (Atlanta: John Knox Press, 1979; first published in French in 1976), 101.

establishment of the kingdom in heaven, what of the accompanying effects of the kingdom on earth? Here the apocalyptic writers are both quite explicit and yet vague.

> And the kingdom and the dominion
> and the greatness of the kingdoms under the whole heaven
> shall be given to the people of the saints of the Most High;
> their kingdom shall be an everlasting kingdom,
> and all dominions shall serve and obey them.
>
> (Dan. 7:27, RSV)

As noted above, judgment upon the nations is a recurring feature of the rule of God among the apocalyptic writers. This judgment may be characterized by either a courtly and legal act from the divine throne (as in Daniel 7) or by a military victory (as with Ezekiel 38—39, Joel, Zechariah 14, and Isaiah 24—27). Towner has suggested, and it seems to me rightly, that the implications of Daniel 7 and its notion of kingdom are not pessimism and failure of nerve; rather, this literature points toward the dynamic of an interim ethic of active waiting and faithfulness to God in all things.[19] The writers of the apocalyptic literature, he says, "presuppose God's goodness, God's power to create and recreate, God's triumph in the cosmic struggle, God's willingness and ability to achieve self-vindication before Israel and indeed before all the other nations."[20] The effect of this expectation, says Towner, is not surrender in a sense of powerlessness, but rather empowerment to act within the context of an ethics of fidelity. We may, however, press the matter a bit further.

For the apocalyptic writers the kingdom of God meant not only the affirmation of a future divine rule in which the faithful would be given to share on earth. There *is* another worldly aspect to their vision of the kingdom of God. What they foresaw would happen communally among the kingdoms of the nations on earth, they also foresaw would have a counterpart for them individually in heaven: "And many of those who sleep in the dust of the earth shall awake, some to everlasting life, and some to

---

19. W. Sibley Towner, *Daniel*, Interpretation: A Bible Commentary for Teaching and Preaching, ed. James Luther Mays (Atlanta: John Knox Press, 1984), 113-15.
20. Ibid., 114-15.

shame and everlasting contempt" (Dan. 12:2, RSV). Corresponding to the transmittal of the kingdom and rule on earth to
the people of the saints of the Most High, there would be a
resurrection from the dust to a heavenly glory: "And those who
are wise shall shine like the brightness of the firmament; and
those who turn many to righteousness, like the stars for ever and
ever" (Dan. 12:3, RSV). A similar notion is found in the "Little
Apocalypse" of Isaiah: "Thy dead shall live, their bodies shall
rise./ O dwellers in the dust, awake and sing for joy!//For thy dew
is a dew of light,/ and on the land of the shades thou wilt let it
fall" (Isa. 26:19, RSV). Herein lies the major accomplishment
and contribution of the apocalyptic writers: they took the prophetic and priestly notion of the kingdom of God, and pressed on to
affirm that after a future divine judgment the faithful would be
given to share in the heavenly majesty of God's kingdom.

The apocalyptic writers did not let drop the problem of retribution with which the sages wrestled so mightily. Rather, they
saw, as John Gray has pointed out in the conclusion of his study
"The Reign of God in Apocalyptic,"[21] that in the coming denouement of the final revelation of the power and purpose of God, one
of the great earthly mysteries—that of the suffering of the faithful
and apparent triumph of the ruthless and cruel—would be resolved. The dead among the ungodly of the nations will not rise
(Isa. 26:14), "and many . . . shall awake . . . some to shame and
everlasting contempt." (Dan. 12:2). For the apocalyptic writers
the holiness of God includes the justice of God. There will be for
the faithful, no matter how much they may have suffered on
earth, a sharing in the divine majesty.

Perhaps the most surprising of all the eschatological visions of
the kingdom of God among apocalyptic authors is that found in
Trito-Zechariah. Even though the Lord does battle against the
attacking nations (Zech. 14:1–3):

> All who survive of the nations which attacked Jerusalem shall come
> up year by year to worship the King, the LORD of Hosts, and to
> keep the pilgrim-feast of Tabernacles. If any of the families of the
> earth do not go up to Jerusalem to worship the King, the LORD of

21. Gray, *Biblical Doctrine of the Reign of God*, 272–73.

Hosts, no rain shall fall upon them. (Zech. 14:16-17, NEB; cf. vv. 18-19)

The kingdom of God in the end time will include a worshiping of the nations at Jerusalem and an implementation of a strict retribution for any nation that does not comply with the cultic requirement at Tabernacles! (See also Zech. 14:18-19.)

The focus of the apocalyptic writers, however, is not altogether beyond death or in an ideal future. As we saw in the psalms that proclaim the divine kingship, and in the prophets, the kingship of God includes also a judgment upon idolatry. The writers of apocalyptic stressed particularly a present need for purification of the land because of the defilement. Thus the authors of Daniel lamented how foreign forces had "profaned the sanctuary" (*wĕḥillĕlû hammiqdāš*), had caused the regular sacrifices (*hattāmîd*) to cease, and had set up an abomination that desolated (Dan. 11:31). So also the author(s) of the Little Apocalypse in Isaiah lamented: "The earth lies polluted (*ḥonpâ*) under its inhabitants;/ for they have transgressed the laws, violated the statutes, broken the everlasting covenant" (Isa. 24:5, RSV). For this distant disciple of Isaiah of Jerusalem the removal of the pollution is described in cultic terminology: "Therefore by this the guilt of Jacob will be purged (*yĕkûppar*),/ and this will be the full fruit of the removal of his sin: // when he makes all the stones of the altars/ like chalkstones crushed to pieces,/ no Asherim or incense altars will remain standing" (Isa. 27:9, RSV). So in Trito-Zechariah, the apocalypticist foresees how a fountain will open up for the house of David and the inhabitants of Jerusalem "to cleanse them from sin and uncleanness" (Zech. 13:1, RSV).[22] For Trito-Zechariah, priestly action will not obtain remission; rather, the sovereign himself will effect it: "On that day, says the LORD of Hosts, I will erase the names of the idols from the land, and

---

22. There is no verb in the Hebrew text corresponding to the RSV rendering "to cleanse." This example of translation by dynamic equivalence, however, is justified by the context. Wilhelm Rudolph suggests that the fountain here is reminiscent of the "waters of remission" (*mê ḥaṭṭā't*) and the "lustral waters" (*mê niddâ*) of the priestly traditions (Num. 8:7; 31:23; cf. 19:9); cf. W. Rudolph, *Haggai/Sacharja 1-8/Sacharja 9-14/Maleachi*, KAT 13/4 (Gütersloh: Gerd Mohn, 1976), 227-28. This comment is on target but perhaps not quite as much so as Rudolph suggests.

they shall be remembered no longer; I will also remove (*'a'ăbîr*) the prophets and the spirit of uncleanness from the land" (Zech. 13:2, NEB).

For the apocalyptic authors, not only the land but the people themselves had become defiled. Thus one of the authors of Daniel wrote: "Many shall purify themselves (*yitbārrû*), and make themselves white, and be refined; but the wicked shall do wickedly" (Dan. 12:10a). The concern in all of these passages for dealing with defilement reflects a profound conviction that human acts of defiance against the divine sovereign can pollute land as well as persons. They also profoundly believed that the holiness of the sovereign and the laws of his realm required that some action had to be taken to purge both land and people. In the apocalyptic or proto-apocalyptic work of Proto-Zechariah (Zechariah 1—8), purgations of both land and persons are also described (Zechariah 3, 5). Thus we have seen that the apocalyptic writers eloquently declare that the kingdom of God is resolutely intolerant of simply letting stand any obvious defilements of land and persons.

(3) *The Holy Mountain.* A third doctrine so prominent in the apocalyptic portions of the Hebrew Bible that it can hardly be omitted is that of the holy mount. At the denouement of the historical retrospectus of Daniel 11, where the writers look beyond the events of the past and recent past, the visionary predicts the attacking king from the north: "And he shall pitch his palatial tents between the sea and the glorious holy mountain; yet he shall come to his end, with none to help him" (Dan. 12:45, RSV). The apocalypticist proclaims at once a portion of the divine glory which was visible on earth, victory over a foreign oppressor, and the sanctity of the mountain. We will return to the latter theme in Daniel in a moment, but first some background will be helpful.

There is a rich history to the doctrine of the holy mount. Richard Clifford has traced its background in Canaan, in the Old Testament, and in the so-called Intertestamental Literature.[23] And more recently, Jon Levenson has sought to explore its theo-

---

23. Richard J. Clifford, *The Cosmic Mountain in Canaan and the Old Testament*, HSM 4 (Cambridge: Harvard University Press, 1972).

logical significance.[24] Allusion has already been made to both studies and justice can hardly be done them here. Levenson's citation of Clifford may serve to introduce our comments:

> In the case of the cosmic mountain, it should be noted at the outset that the term "cosmic" can be misleading. Clifford's point is not that the cosmos is envisioned in ancient Canaan as a mountain, but rather that a mountain is given characteristics and potencies of cosmic, that is, of an infinite and universal scope. Four characteristics of the cosmic mountain that Clifford delineates will prove essential to the present analysis of the traditions about Zion. First, one of the most important aspects of the cosmic mountain is that it is "the meeting place of the gods," like the Greek Olympus. Second, it is also "the battleground of conflicting natural forces." Third, and most significantly, the cosmic mountain is the "meeting place of heaven and earth," the tangent of celestial and mundane reality. And since it is the meeting place of heaven and earth, it follows that the mountain is also "the place where effective decrees are issued," in other words, the moral as well as the physical capital of the universe, a place "involved in the government and stability of the Cosmos." To these points of Clifford's it should be added that from the cosmic mountain there frequently is thought to issue a miraculous stream, whose waters teem with supernatural significance.[25]

Because of the supreme significance of the mountain in Israelite tradition—priestly, prophetic, sapiential as well as apocalyptic—it is perhaps superfluous to observe that the mount is, not infrequently, called holy. It is a place set apart, sanctified by the presence of God. Levenson's development of the notion that the mountain is a moral capital of the universe as well as a physical capital is a point well taken—a point briefly alluded to in our treatment at the outset of chapter 5 on the notion of the holy in the wisdom psalms. It may be recalled also that in the course of our treatment of Isaiah of Jerusalem's doctrine of holiness, we mentioned Levenson's expounding the universalistic, symbolic meaning of Zion.[26]

The sanctity of the mountain in one way or another constitutes

24. Jon D. Levenson, *Sinai & Zion: An Entry into the Jewish Bible*, New Voices in Biblical Studies, ed. Adela Yarbro Collins and John J. Collins (Minneapolis: Winston Press, 1985), 89–184.

25. Ibid., 111–12.

26. See above, p. 95.

an important element in each of the Old Testament apocalypticist's vision of God and the world, with the exception of the apocalypse in Ezekiel. In view of the prominence that the return of the divine glory to Jerusalem is given in the successors of Ezekiel, however, the Book of Ezekiel is hardly an exception: "The whole territory round about upon the top of the mountain shall be most holy" (Ezek. 43:12b, RSV).

Perhaps the best place to begin is with the Isaian Apocalypse. At the conclusion of the first chapter, in a verse already cited above, we see a conjoining of the three elements of the apocalyptic doctrine of holiness:

> Then the moon will be confounded,
>   and the sun ashamed;
> for the LORD of hosts will reign (*mālak*)
>   on Mount Zion and in Jerusalem
> and before his elders he will manifest his glory.
>   (Isa. 24:23, RSV)

The elements, of course, are: (1) the brightness of God's glory—hence the confounding of the moon and shame of the sun; (2) the exercise of God's kingdom; and (3) the sanctity of the mountain. In the concluding verse of the Apocalypse the apocalypticist does not leave the sanctity of mount and city implicit, but rather says, "And in that day a great trumpet will be blown, and those who were lost in the land of Assyria and those who were driven out to the land of Egypt will come and worship the LORD on the holy hill in Jerusalem" (Isa. 27:13, RSV adapted). Here we do not quite see the universalism of Isaiah of the Restoration where the kings are witnesses of the return of the divine glory (Isa. 62:2; cf. 60:14b) nor of Trito-Zechariah where the survivors from among the nations will go up to Jerusalem year after year to worship the king, the Lord of hosts, and to keep the Feast of Tabernacles (Zech. 14:16–19). Rather, the emphasis is upon the return of the faithful and gathering of the dispersed to worship.

In the apocalyptic or proto-apocalyptic Book of Joel, in both parts of the book, Jerusalem/Zion is seen to be holy (Joel 2:1; 3:17 [Engl. trans. 4:17]). In the first passage Zion, "my holy hill," is the place from which the trumpet is to be blown to sound the alarm of the coming day of the Lord; in the second there is an

allusion to the protectiveness of the holy city and of the divine
resolve to keep it a separate place:

> And the LORD roars from Zion,
>   and utters his voice from Jerusalem,
> But the LORD is a refuge to his people,
>   a stronghold to the people of Israel.
> So you shall know that I am the LORD your God
>   who dwells in Zion, my holy mountain (*har*).
> And Jerusalem shall be holy
>   and strangers (*zarîm*) shall never again pass through it.
>   (Joel 3:16–17; Engl. trans. 4:16–17, RSV)

Here, as in Isaiah 24—27, the sanctity of the holy mountain is
taken to imply separation from the nations and foreigners.

And we saw at the outset of this section on holy mountain, in
the final vision of Daniel 11, which pronounces judgment on the
attacking king from the south, it is plain that the apocalypticist
foresees a divine protection of the holy city. The extent to which
the authors understood God to be calling for complete separation
from strangers once the defilement of the abominating desolation
(Dan. 9:27; 11:31) had been removed is not as plain in Daniel.[27]

In the synagogal prayer of Daniel the petitioner asks, "O Lord,
by all the saving deeds we beg that thy wrath and anger may
depart from Jerusalem, thy city, thy holy hill through our own
sins and our fathers' guilty deeds" (Dan. 9:16, NEB). Jerusalem is
God's holy hill. The object of the petition is not simply the city,
but the sanctuary (*miqdāš*): "O Lord, make thy face shine upon
thy desolate sanctuary" (Dan. 9:17b, NEB). Not only in the
prayer, but in the narrator's explanations of the circumstances
surrounding the offering of the prayer, the author reiterates that
he has been praying "before the Lord my God on behalf of his
holy hill" (Dan. 9:20b, NEB). Since the narrator records that he
was praying "at the time of the evening sacrifice" (Dan. 9:21), the
narrator reinforces the association of the prayer between God's

---

27. It is widely agreed among commentators that this "abomination that makes
desolate" (Dan. 11:31, RSV) was a statue or idol of Zeus Olympios that
Antiochus IV Epiphanes, the Greco-Syrian king, had ordered to be erected in
the temple when he also ordered the cessation of the regular temple offerings
(*hattāmîd*) and the sacrificing of swine. See the commentaries and 1 Macc.
1:41–50.

holy city and the temple. In none of this, however, do the authors make a clear statement on the relation of the nations and kings either to the temple or the holy mount once the regular burnt offerings had been restored. Thus we have seen that *even though there is virtually unanimous agreement among the apocalyptic writers on the sanctity of Mount Zion, there was clearly also a divergence of judgment among them on the extent to which the holiness of the mount should and would exclude foreigners from observing the glory of the restored and holy mount.* It should be observed that this divergence in attitude on the degree of separation that holiness requires with respect to foreign peoples mirrors almost exactly the divergence found within the Chronistic Work of History. Among priestly historians as among apocalypticists there were in postexilic Israel on the one hand those more inclined toward a religious universalism and on the other hand those who were inclined to be more ethnocentric. Thus divergencies within the Scriptures provide religious communities today with a mirror of ourselves.

(4) *The Ethical Requirements of Holiness in Apocalyptic as a Recapitulation of Biblical Ethics.* As we shall see in this concluding section, the apocalyptic writers in Israel during the exilic, Persian, and Hellenistic periods appropriated sapiential, prophetic, and priestly traditions. In the apocalyptic writings therefore one finds a microcosm of biblical ethics. Because the apocalyptic writers appropriated traditions from sages, prophets, and priests, our survey of the response of the apocalyptic writers to the demands of holiness will to an extent also constitute a recapitulation of the demands the holiness of God impressed upon the sages, prophets, and priests.

The apocalyptic writers were *heirs of the sages.* In chapters 5 and 6 of this volume we outlined how there runs throughout Israel's long sapiential tradition a stress on the omniscience of God, the importance of reverence, and the requirement of inner integrity. In the apocalyptic traditions we see evidence throughout of these same emphases. God is the Knower; with the godhead rests supreme secrets hidden from most mortals, but revealed to his faithful (Daniel 2, 4, 5, 7). Reverence in the apocalyptic tradition remains a matter of individual piety (Daniel 6) but also expresses itself above all in concerns for the cultus. The apocalyptic authors of Daniel 7—12 are not so much concerned with the end of history as they are with when the regular offerings will be restored. The proto-apocalyptic writers of Zechariah 1—8 and Isaiah 56—66 were concerned not simply with fasting but with probing the nature of the requirements of the true fast on the inner attitude and individual acts of the one fasting (Zech. 7:1–10; 8:16–17; Isaiah 58). The proto-apocalyptic writer Joel summarizes this concern:

> "Yet even now," says the LORD, "return to me with all your heart, with fasting, with weeping, and with mourning; yet rend your hearts and not your garments." (Joel 2:12–13a, RSV adapted)

Thus the apocalyptic writers show themselves to be heirs also in the third sense of the sages. They are heirs in their concern for the maintenance of individual integrity, that is, purity within.

The apocalyptic writers were also *heirs of the prophets.* In our treatment above in chapter 3 on the prophetic understanding of holiness, it was stressed that the prophets—and Isaiah of Jerusalem and his successors in particular—held up not simply the cleanness of individual integrity but also social justice as the requirement of holiness. ("Wash yourselves; make yourselves clean . . . seek justice, correct oppression," Isa. 1:16–17). The concern for justice among the apocalyptic and proto-apocalyptic writers can be seen especially clearly in the passages alluded to above having to do with the requirements of fasting. The apocalyptic ethic—the interim ethic, as Towner calls it—is expressed especially forcefully and beautifully in the advice Daniel gives to the humbled king, Nebuchadnezzar:

> Break off your sins by practicing righteousness
> and your iniquities by showing mercy to the oppressed,
> that there may perhaps be a lengthening of your tranquility.
> (Dan. 4:24; Engl. 4:27, RSV)

In chapter 3 we noted how it was revealed to Isaiah of Jerusalem that the majesty and rulership of the Lord of hosts were global.[28] This global dimension of the apocalyptic writers is per-

---

28. See above, p. 95.

haps their most precious heritage from the prophets. As we saw in the section above on the Kingdom of God, the apocalyptic writers often associated the manifestation of the divine glory at the holy mount with the conception of war against or judgment upon the nations. It would be cynical as well as incorrect, in my judgment, to say that the apocalyptic writers' concern for the nations is more sadistic than gracious. There is, undeniably, a certain ethnocentricity among them (see e.g., Ezek. 39:17–27; Dan. 7:27). But, there is also a great universalism; for example, in Trito-Zechariah where all the nations will go up to Jerusalem to keep the Feast of Tabernacles (Zech. 14:16–19). Nonetheless, the concern of the apocalypticists—whether more or less universalistic—remains global. The interim ethics of the apocalypticists, as the ethics of the prophets, calls for justice within Israel and among the nations. An important bridge here between the prophets and the apocalypticists is to be found in that relatively neglected portion of the Old Testament, the oracles against the nations. For in the oracles against the nations the prophets and their successors declare not only the judgment of God upon the nations, but the causes (see Amos 1—2; Isaiah 13—23; 34—35; 47; Ezekiel 25—32; Jeremiah 46—51). In the prophetic eschatology, of course, the nations shall go up to Jerusalem to learn the *tôrâ* and the ways of peace (Isa. 2:1–4; Mic. 4:1–4).

To be sure, the apocalyptic world view is more decidedly future oriented; it is more eschatological—envisioning transformations in nature and among human communities. But the distance between the apocalyptic eschatology and the prophetic should not be exaggerated. In the messianic prophecies of Isaiah of Jerusalem the prophet also looked forward to a future with remarkable transformations in nature ("the wolf shall dwell with the lamb," Isa. 11:6) and in the relations of nations ("every boot of tramping warrior . . . will be burned," Isa. 9:4, Engl. trans. 9:5). As Paul Hanson has stressed in his several writings on apocalyptic eschatology, it is best to think in terms of a continuum of biblical eschatology.[29] In some prophetic eschatology—such as in

---

29. This idea of the continuum of biblical eschatologies is perhaps developed most completely by Hanson in his essay "Jewish Apocalyptic against Its Near Eastern Environment," *Revue Biblique* 78 (1971):31–58, where the interesting

the passages just alluded to—the prophet is already moving over into a more transcendental vision of transformations in nature and society. If apocalyptic eschatology is a whipping boy, we must whip too—if we are consistent—Isaiah, Ezekiel, and, I believe, Jeremiah as well.

The apocalyptic writers were also *heirs of the priestly traditions.* As we have seen above from their emphasis on holy mount, temple, and the glory of God, these writers saw the present, heavenly, and future worlds very much from the perspective of persons deeply involved in a community of worship. Their ready use of doxologies (on which a word more will be said at the conclusion of this chapter), their concern with defilement of the land and the restoration of worship, their debating who among the nations would participate at worship at Jerusalem are but a few of the many indicators at hand that caution us to give due weight to the fact that many of the concerns of the apocalyptic writers were cultic and priestly.

As we saw in the opening chapter of this volume, the priests stressed that the call of ritual purity was required among the people in order to approach for worship. Ritual purity included thinking through an ethics of separation, and extended to all areas of life: sexuality, diet, handling of bodily emissions, conduct on the sabbath, individual morality, the ordination of priests, and ways to handle individual and corporate guilt in the cultus. The defects and datedness of this system are all too apparent. Nonetheless, initial soundings were made in chapter 1 to discern what principles at work in the priestly doctrines of holiness might be of service and instruction for religious communities today. Among the apocalyptic writers, we can see very nearly the same concerns as were in evidence in the priestly traditions. The requirements of holiness were not compartmentalized according to our categories. Thus the prophetic or proto-apocalyptic writer, Isaiah of the Restoration, opens his collection with the words: "Thus says the Lord: 'Keep justice, and do righteousness, for soon my salvation will come, and my deliverance

comparison is made between the changing forms and styles of ancient Near Eastern pottery *and* biblical eschatology!

be revealed. Blessed is the one who does this, and the human offspring who holds it fast, who keeps the sabbath, not profaning it, and keeps his hand from doing any evil'" (Isa. 56:1-2, RSV adapted). Sabbath observance remains an item of importance with this prophetic or proto-apocalyptic writer. And if we may extrapolate from the stress on prayer in Daniel, it remained so for the authors of the latest apocalyptic writing in the Hebrew Bible (Daniel 6). Keeping the dietary laws of the Pentateuch seems already to have been a point at issue for the author of the opening chapter of Daniel—as it was not, we know, in the early second-century work, the Book of Sirach.[30] The stress on fasting in the apocalyptic writings would also seem to indicate that many of the writers may have been observers of the dietary laws of the Pentateuch.

The priestly principle of separation, however, becomes considerably attenuated in some of the apocalyptic writings. Thus, for Trito-Zechariah sacrality becomes democratized. That is, not only the plate hanging from the high priest's headdress would have inscribed on it "Holy to the LORD" (Exod. 28:36-37), but the very same inscription would be placed even on the bells of horses (Zech. 14:20). And, further, every pot in Jerusalem and Judah would be holy to the Lord at the time of the pilgrim festival of all nations (Zech. 14:20-21). One recent commentator has ingeniously suggested that this tradition serves to underline how numerous the hordes of peoples coming from all nations would be; every pot in Jerusalem will have to be pressed into service and declared holy for those who come to sacrifice.[31] No matter what the explanation, with Trito-Zechariah we see a democratization of sacrality. With this apocalypticist the circle of sanctity is writ large.

In conclusion, an element in the apocalypticists' priestly ethic alluded to above may be emphasized, namely, the prominence of doxologies and rendering praise to the glorious and holy God. In his book *The Elusive Presence,* Samuel Terrien points out how

30. For Sirach's views on the dietary laws, see the discussion above on pp. 162-63.
31. Karl Elliger, *Das Buch der zwölf Kleine Propheten*, ATD 25 (Göttingen: Vandenhoeck & Ruprecht, 1950), 2:174-75.

the cultus is the place where the memories of past appearances of God are kept alive. In apocalyptic the doxologies utter praises to God for *future* events hailed as if they were already *present* accomplishments. This is so not only in the famous Victory Song in the War Scroll from Qumran, but in the scriptural apocalyptic. In Deutero-Zechariah is found the more famous Song of Jubilation, celebrating the triumphant arrival in Jerusalem of the humble and peace-bringing king (Zech. 9:9–17). The Isaian Apocalypse is so strewn with songs of thanksgiving (Isa. 24:6–16a; 25:1–5; 26:1–14) and a song of jubilation (Isa. 27:2–11) that Johannes Lindblom suggested we have here a cantata written in celebration of the Persian victory over Babylon in 485 b.c.e.[32] Even though Otto Kaiser is quite right in asking what such an interpretation does to the Isaian Apocalypse as a piece of apocalyptic (i.e., eschatological) writing,[33] Lindblom's interpretation does point up the prominence of the doxological. The last chapters of Zechariah have visions of such a bright future that they too are suffused with a sense of proleptic thanksgiving (Zechariah 9—14). The same is so for the Ezekielian apocalypse (Ezekiel 38—39) and, of course, the conclusion of Daniel (Dan. 12:1–4). Thus the spirit, if not always the form, of doxology is hardly a peripheral part of the apocalyptic writings.

Both spirit and form betray an indebtedness of the apocalyptic writers to the cultus, to the holy place and congregation of worship where praises were uttered to the Most High. Because of the prominence of the doxological in apocalyptic it is difficult to accept the thesis of Sigmund Mowinckel that eschatological expectations in Israel began to grow strong with the collapse of the sense of immediacy experienced in the cultus.[34] If the analyses above are on the right track, it would seem that Mowinckel was quite correct in one regard—in positing a close connection between cultus and eschatology—but not so in another—in the

32. Johannes Lindblom, *Die Jesaja-Apokalypse: Jes. 24–27*, Lunds Universitets Årsskrift, 34, 3 (Lund: C. W. K. Gleerup, 1938).

33. Otto Kaiser, *Isaiah 13-39*, OTL, trans. R. A. Wilson (Philadelphia: Westminster Press, 1974; first published in German in 1973), 175.

34. Sigmund Mowinckel, *Psalmenstudien II: Das Thronbesteigungsfest Jahwäs und der Ursprung der Eschatologie*, Skrifter utgitt av Det Norske Videskaps-Akademi i Oslo (Oslo, 1921; reprinted in Amsterdam: P. Schippers, 1961).

suggestion that eschatology flourished when a sense of vitality had vanished from worship. The above analyses rather suggest that the cultus both nurtured the form of the apocalyptic doxologies—a point Hanson also has fully demonstrated[35]—and also the spirit of the doxologies. If the apocalypticists had given up on worship, it is passing strange that they continued to hold for it such a central place. In making this judgment we are also indirectly making the point that it may be necessary to reassess the extent to which the several biblical apocalyptic writers had given up on the sociopolitical order. In antiquity, as I suspect is still the case on both sides of the Iron and Bamboo Curtains, where and whether one worships may constitute a very definite statement and concern with respect to the present sociopolitical order.

35. For a convenient discussion, see Paul D. Hanson, "Old Testament Apocalyptic Reexamined," *Interpretation* 25 (1971): 454–79; see also his *Dawn of Apocalyptic*, 98, 118, 120–26, 203–4, 300, 315–16, etc.

Summary

1. Holiness in Israel was not first and foremost something for human beings to achieve, but rather that characteristic of ineffability possessed only by God, the Lord of Hosts, the Holy One of Israel. As we have seen in the above pages, holiness in Israel constituted a commanding, inviting, summoning presence. Holiness calls. The vocation of holiness to the successive generations of ancient Israelites did constitute a vocation to holiness in a second sense, holiness as spirituality, but this holiness was more than a self-contained, inward-turning spirituality. Holiness in Israel was a summons to Israel to aspire to the justice and compassion characteristic of her summoning God. In the majesty and glory of holiness—for glory, as we saw, is but holiness made manifest—the God of Israel extended to the sons and daughters of Israel an invitation to nobility of spirit and action.

2. Noblesse oblige. The nobility to which God summoned Israel obligated her to a social conduct and individual morality befitting the majesty and dignity of the Most High. Holiness encountered in Israel had the overpowering effect of impressing on heart and consciousness the need for inner cleansing and purity. Thus I have put forward the thesis that for the entire Old Testament/Hebrew Scriptures, holiness summoned Israel to cleanness. A unity of the Old Testament can be discerned in this unified response to holiness on the part of Israel: holiness requires purity.

3. Diversity within unity is to be discerned in the fact that for the different groups of religious persons within Israel—prophets,

priests, and sages—the kind of cleanness required by holiness varied. For the prophets it was a cleanness of social justice, for the priests a cleanness of proper ritual and maintenance of separation, for the sages it was a cleanness of inner integrity and individual moral acts. Each of these groups set forth its teaching in response to holiness and what holiness had impressed upon their hearts and minds. No claim of exclusive apprehension of holiness and the requirements of holiness is possible for any one of the three groups. The lessons for contemporary religious denominations that look to the Scripture for guidance are obvious.

4. In chapters 1, 3, and 5 in this study I have set forth the normative responses to holiness of the priests (chap. 1), the prophets (chap. 3), and the sages (chap. 5); in the other chapters I have sought to trace *variations* of the ideal types on holiness and its requirements. In each set of variations on the priests, prophets, and sages we observed a shifting, blending, and interpenetration of the ideal types. Thus in Ezekiel the concepts of holiness, glory, and holy name became central and organizing concepts integrating both typically priestly and prophetic utterances. In Deuteronomy the prophetic thrust toward justice and against idolatry became infused with a priestly emphasis on separation and with the humanitarianism of the sages. So also in the sapiential traditions the process of interpenetration of the more ideal types came to be expressed (e.g., in the Book of Sirach the author increasingly employs the literary genres of the cultus in the praise of the Most High). Similarly, among the apocalyptic writers, especially in the depiction of the requirements of holiness, the priestly remains of utmost importance (e.g., the maintenance of the *tāmîd*, the regular sacrifices in Daniel) along with the prophetic pursuit of social justice and of the typically sapiential individual morality.

5. In each of the chapters on variations on holiness we also observed in the *writing of history* an interpenetration of, and tension between, the normative priestly, prophetic, and sapiential views on holiness. Thus in the first part of the Chronistic Work of History there is less emphasis on the typically priestly insistence on separation from other peoples than in the Books of Ezra and Nehemiah—and this is so even though the Books of

Chronicles employ the term "holy people." So in the Deuter-onomistic History which uses the more typically priestly term "holy name," there is a prophetic relativization of the centrality of the temple and cultus (1 Kings 8). And in the sapiential, historical writing, Sirach shows himself to be in the line of the sages (with his accent on the achievements of *individual* persons: Sirach 44—50) but also of the priests; and the Wisdom of Solomon incorporates in his historical survey (chap. 10), in his dia-tribe (chaps. 13–15), and in his contrast between Egyptian and Israelite ways (11:1–14; chaps. 16–19) a strong priestly emphasis (on separation) together with the prophetic (against idolatry).

6. The works of the historians of Israel are best understood, I submitted, as "paradigmatic history," a concept put forward by the late Eric Voegelin. Paradigmatic history, I further suggested, should not be made to bear the requirements of modern, objec-tive historiography because it was told to instruct by the models (paradigms) it held up.

7. In the light of the overview of the preceding pages it cannot be claimed that holiness in Israel is the central, major, or unify-ing concept of the Old Testament/Hebrew Scriptures. It is fair to claim, however, that the concept of the holiness of God is *a* central concept in the Old Testament, which enables us to dis-cern at once an important unity and diversity. It is my hope to have demonstrated that the concept of the holiness of God is a major concept in the Hebrew Scriptures, contrary to the asser-tions of some recent writers.

8. Supplementary to the main thesis of this volume—that holi-ness calls for and forth cleanness—is an analysis of the themes of kingdom, glory, retribution, and praise. The majesty of the holi-ness of God is described in terms of the sovereign (King), espe-cially in the prophetic and apocalyptic literature. The glory of God—holiness unveiled—is a theme common to the priestly, prophetic, and apocalyptic literature. Glory is the aspect of the holiness that the divine manifests in some way to human eyes. Israel believed that the divine glory was present with her, but could and would depart if unaccompanied by the pursuit of justice and individual morality. Retribution is, as Friedrich Schleiermacher correctly observed a number of years ago, a

theme that can hardly be avoided in a study of the Old Testament—so pervasive is it. It concerns the question of how God deals with human wrongdoing. The priests taught that sacrifices were necessary for the attainment of atonement. The prophets taught that sacrifices could not be used as a substitute for the performance of justice. The traditional sages taught that individual morality was what God would bless. A consideration of holiness therefore inevitably involved, even if occasionally indirectly and in passing, a consideration of retribution: How does the holy God act in response to human sin, cruelty, and injustice? If God is holy and possessed of glory (Greek *doxa*), then words of praise (doxology) to God are an appropriate response along with the pursuit of the purity, nobility, and justice that the holy God requires.

9. In chapter 7 we argued that probing the themes of glory, kingdom, holy mount, and the ethical requirements of holiness constituted a viable entrée into the doctrine of holiness among the biblical apocalyptic writers. In particular, we argued that in the ethical responses to holiness the apocalyptic writers recapitulate biblical ethics in that they combine typically priestly, prophetic, and sapiential concerns.

10. Nowhere in this volume has the attempt been made to spell out how a sense of the holiness of God might be regained in our day. That is, I have not explicitly attempted to show how spirituality might be enhanced. However, many clues are to be found in the simple rehearsal of how holiness was discerned in Israel. Job 31 and Psalm 51 illustrate most profoundly that whenever a person has been led to honest self-examination, that person has already begun to enter into the presence of holiness. Insofar as a recovery of a sense of holiness may be affected by human initiative, I have suggested that there is no one, single way. Whatever the way, it will include an attempt to keep the sabbath holy, a wholehearted pursuit of justice, and some attention to individual moral attitudes and acts.

Index of
Modern Authors

199

Index of
Ancient Sources

OLD TESTAMENT

APOCRYPHA